IDEAS AND MUSIC

MARTIN COOPER

IDEAS AND MUSIC

CHILTON BOOKS
A DIVISION OF CHILTON COMPANY
Publishers
Philadelphia and New York

© 1965 BY MARTIN COOPER · FIRST PUBLISHED 1965 BY BARRIE AND ROCKLIFF (BARRIE BOOKS LTD) 2 CLEMENT'S INN, LONDON WC2 · PRINTED IN GREAT BRITAIN BY ROBERT CUNNINGHAM AND SONS LTD, ALVA, SCOTLAND

PUBLISHED IN THE UNITED STATES OF AMERICA, 1967, BY CHILTON BOOKS, A DIVISION OF CHILTON COMPANY, PUBLISHERS, PHILADELPHIA AND NEW YORK

Library of Congress Catalog Card Number 67-10572

Contents

FOR ANNA KALLIN
AND IN MEMORY OF
RICHARD CAPELL

Acknowledgments

All but one of the following essays have already been before the public, either as broadcast talks or as lectures, articles, etc. I owe permission to republish them here to the following: British Broadcasting Corporation and the *Listener*, the *Daily Telegraph*, *Music and Letters*, Oxford University Press, Royal Musical Association and the *Times Literary Supplement*, to all of whom I should like to express my thanks.

Part I

General Criticism

1 Moral and Emotional Elements
in Musical Taste

Music is the Janus of the arts, one whose backward-turning face is more strongly illuminated and better loved than that which faces the future. For all but a very small minority in every country music is still the romantic art *par excellence*, the art of a nineteenth century which may be said to have begun in the 1780's and ended in 1914. Until recently the little music written before 1780 or after 1914 familiar to the modern music-lover was understood in terms of the nineteenth century, for our ears and our sensibilities were trained and formed by the music of that period – the period of Germany's musical hegemony of Europe. This hegemony was assured by the Viennese masters, in whose music many eighteenth century elements persisted, giving it solid, bony structure and emotional stability; it covered the mixed romanticism and neo-classicism of Schumann, Mendelssohn and Brahms; and its fullest expression is to be found in the music of Wagner, radiating far beyond the borders of Germany and giving his name to a whole epoch of musical history. There were great figures in other countries, all through this period, and especially in the years after Wagner's death in 1883, when Russia and France were preparing movements and individuals destined eventually to replace the German pantheon and its mythology. But Berlioz, Mussorgsky and Verdi were lonely figures in a German ocean, greater for the solitariness that exaggerated their self-reliance and put them on their mettle. It was an era of great vitality, physical, emotional and intellectual; and since musical standards were taken from Germany, the Latin or Horatian qualities of economy, restraint – *aurea mediocritas* – were at a discount. But the 'excessive' character of much nineteenth century music was far from being simply a matter of national, German, taste. Only think of Berlioz. And it was a Frenchman, Alfred de Musset, who may be said to have unwittingly provided the motto, the clue to the problem of the taste of the period, when he wrote that 'the most despairing songs are the most beautiful' (*les plus désespérés sont les chants les plus beaux*). This instinctive favouring of the extreme emotional states, occasionally pleasurable but far more often painful, is a hall-mark of romantic taste in every age, including our own. The strong anti-intellectual bias which such a taste implies has implications which can perhaps best be understood by examining the historical situations in which this taste seems to recur.

If we cast our minds back, we find one feature common to all ages in which this taste for what we may call with Musset 'despair' has been most highly developed. Think only of Euripides, Virgil, the Elizabethan and Jacobean dramatists and the nineteenth century romantics (and I make no apology for choosing poets, music being either in her infancy or, for our purpose, non-existent). Each of these ages was the aftermath of a great upheaval of the human mind, a period of acute mental disturbance when the security of an old faith had been broken, a whole hitherto unquestioningly accepted way of life suddenly questioned and rudely rejected. Euripides and Virgil wrote in the ages that followed immediately on the dethronement of the old gods in Athens and Rome; the Elizabethan and Jacobean dramatists in the void left by the dissolution of the mediaeval order in that dramatic process whose first act was the Reformation; and the Romantics after the playing of the second act in the French Revolution. We ourselves are the actors in a less spectacular but equally real revolution – the third act of the same drama, if you will – in which the full implications and consequences of the first two acts are for the first time visible and sensible, not only to the student of history but to the humblest and most unthinking individual.

What have each of these upheavals meant to the men who lived through them or the generation following? Many different things, of course; but always, I believe, a sense of diminution. The intoxi-cation of what seemed like a new freedom and an enlarging of man's scope has in each case been followed by a cold, grey morning of anxiety and questioning. The progressive revelation of the immen-sity and complexity of the physical universe has been followed in each case by the apparent retreat of the Creator, from a daily contact with his creatures to a remote inaccessibility hard for the simple mind to distinguish from non-existence. Man, no longer able to think of himself as his Creator's darling, has been left with a sense of diminished importance, of inferior status. Everyday life, no longer shared with his Creator or illuminated by the supernatural, has come to seem colourless and uninteresting, only worth living in moments of unusual excess, tragic or sensual. Thus, for example, it was the 'romantic', the tragic and 'excessive', incident of Dido that caught the imagination of both Virgil and his first readers, and so enriched literature with one of the earliest examples of that luxuriant melancholy which we now recognise as a specific of the romantic pharmacopoeia in all ages.

In fact man's progressive deprivation of the supernatural, the progressive starving of an innate appetite, led to a gradual deprav-ing of that appetite, to cravings for strange foods and to attempts to satisfy by other means an instinct which finds itself denied natural satisfaction. In place of food and drink for his spirit man has looked in the arts for spices, stimulants or narcotics. Taught to expect neither help nor sympathy from outside or above himself, he takes to worshipping his own image and investing his own emo-tions with an absolute value, rating them simply by their intensity and no longer referring them to absolute standards of good and evil. Hence the taste for the macabre in the most critical periods of man's disillusion – in the Elizabethan and Jacobean dramatists, in France during the 1830's and afterwards, and again a hundred years later, when Berg's *Wozzeck* and Shostakovich's *Lady Macbeth of Mtsensk* were representative works. This cultivation of feeling for its own sake, in a vain attempt to achieve heightened significance in his own eyes, was not the only distinction between the new 'romantic' artist and his predecessor. Music, oddly neglected and despised by many romantic poets, became one of the chief vehicles not only of poetic, but even of moral aspiration. Both the immedi-

acy of its appeal and the ambiguity with which its utterances can
be interpreted fitted music for this role; and we find in Beethoven's
Missa Solemnis and ninth symphony the first rites -- we might
almost say, the first liturgical works – of a new religion, Camille
Mauclair's 'religion of music'. These works mark the appearance
of an emotion not only new to music but never expressed with such
force since the beginning of the Christian era. This emotion, which
has been called 'cosmic' and linked with the names of Prometheus
and the Titans, finds its completest expression in the first movement of the ninth symphony, just as Beethoven's humanitarian
aspirations are most clearly expressed in the last. In that first movement the frontiers of space have rolled back, we stand on Lucretius'
flammantia moenia mundi – the flaming battlements of the universe
– and in these vast spaces (which had inspired only fear in Pascal)
Beethoven-Prometheus hurls defiance and exults like a giant.

This was something new not only in art but in the experience of
humanity since the Christian era. Compare it with Milton, with the
grandest Bach or with the introduction to Haydn's *Creation*. Milton, Bach and Haydn are centred on something outside themselves,
they are consciously *creatures*, creature-like, dependent and humble.
Beethoven's centre lies in himself, he refuses to be dependent;
almost he persuades himself – and has persuaded others – that he
is creator, not creature. And so, in the words of a recent American
historian of literature, 'the so-called Romantic movement represents the turning-point of a Titanic assertion of human self-suffi-
ciency'. In fact Pride, the sin of Milton's Satan (a character significantly admired by the Romantics) received a new name and
became one of the corner-stones of the romantic artist's religion, a
religion of which even orthodox Christians, like Gounod, were
sometimes happy to call themselves priests. Liszt may have had an
inkling that cosmic emotion and this romantic religion of music
had their close obverse in Satanism – what in any case is Prometheus but a sentimentalised Satan? – and this may be the explanation of the mingling of all three elements in some of his greatest
works, the piano sonata and the Faust Symphony. In any case this
'endeavour to impart some sort of numinous sanction to the craving
for independent power' was at the root of all the aesthetic mysti-
cisms of the nineteenth century, from Wagner to Scriabin and

Mahler. Not perhaps for nothing was Wagner spoken of as a 'wizard' or 'magician' and compared with his own Klingsor.

The chief result for musical taste of this new interest in the emotions – an interest that had been growing since the 60's of the eighteenth century – was the demand that a work of art should be the communication of some definite *personality*. It is by their modes of feeling rather than their intellectual processes that human beings are sharply contrasted; the 'romance' reflects its author's temperament, whereas the text-book or the philosophical treatise is impersonal. The pattern-types elaborated by the eighteenth century – sonata form in particular – provided an abstract, impersonal framework whose satisfactory use by the composer and appreciation by his audience required considerable intellectual effort. Beethoven stretched these forms to their limit and such whole-hearted, younger romantics as Chopin and Schumann often rejected them in favour of short, poetic forms all of which aimed at giving the impression of impromptu – that is, directly and immediately *inspired* emotional creations. It would be hard to mention a single composer born between 1760 and 1860 whose overwhelming concern, whatever his style or nationality, was not with *emotional expressiveness*. The fact that this period coincided with a flowering of the art of music hitherto unparalleled in history, and quite out of proportion with that of the other arts during the same period, will be taken by some to show that this is indeed music's chief role: that music is primarily just that, the art of emotional expression in sound and that all other ideals – architectural or pictorial, sensual or intellectual – are secondary and incidental.

While among listeners these nineteenth century ideals have spread and penetrated further and deeper, composers, professional musicians and connoisseurs have for more than half a century been in violent reaction against them. After Wagner and his immediate successors the limits of emotional expression in music seemed to have been reached, the vein exhausted; and creative artists, not content simply to write interminable codas to the great nineteenth-century symphony, looked for wholly new approaches to music. Debussy was the first explicit rebel.

Without denying Wagner's genius [he wrote] we may say that he brought to perfection the music of his own day, rather as

Hugo summed up the poetry that preceded him. We must make our researches after Wagner not in accordance with him (*après Wagner et non d'après Wagner*).

'Researches' with Debussy began the period of experimentation in music, the prospecting for new veins of wealth. This search hardly interested the general public. While composers teased their brains and experimented with every kind of new technical device, the public remained content with the nineteenth-century music of emotional expression. The First War seemed to be a break with every kind of past. But in this moral and intellectual chaos the ordinary music-lover only turned with more ardour to the music in which he was still sure of moral exhilaration and emotional consolation and relief. Music, at least in England, came as a new discovery to thousands of new listeners, who found moral and emotional satisfaction in the music of the past, but were neither able nor willing to follow the intricate intellectual courses and experiments in pure sonority that characterised the new music. That music is now no longer new, but much of it has been gradually assimilated by the younger and the more intelligent members of the musical public. Stravinsky and Bartok are accepted as twentieth century classics by all intelligent music-lovers, and the New Viennese School is no longer spoken of as an undifferentiated unity. Berg has fallen into his place as the natural heir of Mahler's romanticism, Webern in perspective appears as the incorruptibly idealist master of *hai-kai* miniatures and Schoenberg alone remains enigmatic, still incomprehensible to the average music-lover and dividing musicians themselves into two camps – the one proclaiming him a towering creative genius and the other regarding him primarily as a musical thinker and inspirer of others. Almost imperceptibly the exclusively nineteenth-century musical ideals of the public have changed, and the increasing understanding of twentieth-century music is unmistakably part of a larger shift of interest that includes hitherto unfamiliar music of the past, from the lesser eighteenth-century masters back to the Middle Ages. What seemed an impasse has turned out to be a potential highway linking the newly discovered territories of the past with the still hardly imagined world of the future.

2 The Familiar in Music

Both the English and the French languages have a revealing phrase for sustained and intimate knowledge – whether it be of a list of telephone numbers, of the part of King Lear or the score of Wagner's *Ring*. We say that we have such things *by heart*; and in using this expression we pay tribute to a psychological fact. The German *auswendig können* stresses the exteriority, what we call the 'parrot-like' character, of such knowledge; and certainly this element is present. But though the parrot in us may memorise telephone numbers in general, it is very much the human being who remembers the number of a friend but forgets, or never manages to memorise, the number of a bore. Our whole personalities – our wills, our hearts, our emotions, call them what you will – must be engaged if we are really to *get to know* anything more complicated than a row of figures.

'Knowing' a work of art is very like 'knowing' a foreign language. Each form of knowledge has many different degrees. There are some who can read but cannot speak, others who speak fluently but badly; and probably a majority who have no idea that each language, and each art, connotes a slightly different mode of thinking and of feeling, an approach to reality from an angle slightly more acute or obtuse. The analogy can be extended to many details – the 'recognition vocabulary', for example. Travellers who hardly boast a smattering of German will still recognise *Ausgang* and *Eingang* though they could not tell you the German for 'exit' and 'entrance'.

IM B

And in the same way those who could not whistle the opening bars of, say, the scherzos in Beethoven's third and ninth symphonies would know at once if one were substituted for the other in performance. Few except professional performers know more than a handful of works 'by heart', but many concert-goers have a large 'recognition vocabulary' of music; and the problems connected with familiarity are of increasing interest when many of the most enthusiastic and discerning music-lovers derive their musical experiences not from the concert-hall but from broadcasting and from gramophone records, with the consequent possibilities of indefinite repetition and easily achieved familiarity.

That there is, in the case of almost every work, a point of satiety after which familiarity breeds, if not contempt, at least boredom, is I think undeniable. And it is not only the more brilliant and superficial works that exhaust the listener's interest. It is plain that no one could bear to hear Scriabin's *Poème de l'Extase* as often as he hears any Beethoven symphony. But many people have been brought up on an ill-proportioned musical diet, in which Beethoven's symphonies and piano sonatas formed so overwhelming a part of the menu, that even these great works must be first half-forgotten and then rediscovered before they can really live again in the individual consciousness of the listener. The case of Beethoven is illuminating, partly because his music is probably more familiar than that of any other composer and partly because it contains the most durable elements – intellectual power, strong and simple emotion and great variety of technical interest – often combined with a violence and excessiveness of temperament which is a quickly-palling characteristic; for drama, especially self-dramatisation, loses its power as it becomes familiar. Colour, the quality in which Beethoven's music is poorest, is one of the first to attract and the first to tire the listener. Beauty of line 'wears' far longer, so that we find the pure classical profile of, say, Bach or Chopin wearing very much better than the beauty of complexion – of surface and consistency – which distinguishes the music of Liszt or Puccini, all roses and snow at first but taking on, with years of familiarity, a somewhat raddled and haggard look, as of a great actress in decay.

The dramatic element is more susceptible than any other to

changes of fashion and taste, forming part as it does of the literary alliance which has proved so fatal to so much excellent music. Thus, without involving any judgments of absolute value and speaking very generally, we can say that the best Schubert song *wears* better than the best Hugo Wolf and Handel's *Messiah* bears more repetitions than Beethoven's *Missa Solemnis*.

The alliance of music with literature has its own splendours and miseries, both seen at their crudest in the opera-house. In no other form is the mortality rate so high; and yet it is not in opera that we always find the most striking examples of the dramatic in music. Consider only the element of *surprise*. The sudden sforzando, the leap to a distant key – in fact the dramatic interruption of the normal, continuous flow of the musical discourse – is familiar in Haydn's instrumental music, generally in a comic sense. Beethoven greatly extended this practice, although it often lies at the root of the scherzo or 'joke' movements which he virtually invented. An instance of Haydn's more serious use of a surprise-effect is the sudden fortissimo which greets the appearance of the light in *The Creation* and so delighted his first audiences. This is of course 'literary', in that its prompting is extra-musical; and Beethoven was to make surprise of all kinds one of the salient features of his style. In the theatre the most obvious example is in *Fidelio*, where the sudden sounding of the trumpet on the battlements announces the arrival of the Governor and the rescue of Florestan and Leonora. Coming in the middle of a passage of the greatest dramatic tension, when Leonora has just disclosed her identity, its effect in the opera-house is never-failing. But transpose it, as Beethoven does in his Leonora overtures, to the concert-hall and only the mental reconstruction of the operatic situation saves the effect from being dulled after repeated hearing, the more so because in the overture the situation is carefully prepared by the unison passage in the strings which leads up to it. This provides a more satisfactory setting from the purely musical point of view, but kills the effect of surprise which is the point of the trumpet-call in the opera.

The most famous of all Beethoven's surprises is the false horn-entry in the first movement of the *Eroica*. But no one would claim this as one of the beauties of the work; it is rather like the characteristic wart or mole on a great man's face.

The direct antithesis of these dramatic surprises, which are sometimes simply dynamic but more often involve tonal contrasts, lies
in Gregorian chant on the one hand and so-called atonal music on
the other. This is merely to say that it is tonality which has hitherto
been most fruitful in providing the surprises and the dramatic
contrasts of Western music. Until recently one of the greatest
pleasures provided by music lay in the variation of the expected by
the unexpected, the alternation of simplicity and complication,
often to be equated with the diatonic and the chromatic. It lay in
fact in the different individual's uses of a commonly accepted idiom.
No amount of familiarity seems to deaden the delight caused by
the ingenious manipulation of tonality which gives such variety to
the music which lies between Bach and Wagner. After the familiar
tonal language had been stretched to breaking point, first in *Tristan*
and then in *Parsifal*, the field of possibilities proved to be not extended but restricted. It was by rigorous restriction of his field that
Debussy obtained novel effects – the whole-tone scale, for example,
represents a drastic diminution – and the later complete and conscious rejection of tonality has meant the rejection of what had, for
two hundred years, been the composer's chief means of varying and
enlivening his work. In order to obtain dramatic contrast or variety
in an idiom from which key-relationships have been banished,
dynamics are often employed; and it is significant that the great
climax of *Wozzeck* is not marked by any daring chord or series of
chords but by a single note, played in unison but with a horrific
crescendo by the whole orchestra.

If violent dynamics are, on the whole, characteristic of the music
which loses most by being well known, conversely a restricted
dynamic range marks music which may be supposed to gain almost
indefinitely from increased familiarity. The appeal of this music is
either primarily to the intellect or else to a highly developed musical
sense in which the intellect plays a large part. Who could say that
he is wholly familiar with Bach's Art of Fugue or compute the
number of hearings after which the intellectual appeal of this music
would be deadened by familiarity? Are there even many who can
boast of such familiarity with Beethoven's last quartets that they
are near to exhausting their interest, in the way that interest in, say,
the same composer's fifth symphony may be exhausted? And many

would certainly make the same claim for the best polyphonic music of the sixteenth and seventeenth centuries.

These are special, isolated cases which do not come the way of the majority; but there is one composer on whose final rating there has never been anything like final unanimity, who may possibly have benefited by the fact that much of even his best music has been comparatively rarely performed. Apart from a few overtures, the *Fantastic Symphony* and the *Requiem* no other works of Berlioz are in the normal repertory. When we hear a recording or an occasional performance of *Romeo and Juliet*, *Harold in Italy*, *The Damnation of Faust* or *The Childhood of Christ*, even of *The Trojans*, we are struck by the intense power and beauty of passages here and there, by the original if often unsatisfactory design of the whole work and by the extraordinary juxtaposition of pathos and bathos. What would our feelings be if not only these works but *Lélio*, the *Funeral and Triumphal Symphony*, *Benvenuto Cellini* and *Beatrice and Benedict* were in the normal, week-by-week repertory of our orchestras and opera-houses? Berlioz's name would, I believe, sink very much below the point at which he is rated by his admirers, if not quite so low as that which he is assigned by his detractors. We forgive, or even overlook, the faults of one who pays us an occasional visit, surrounded by the aura of his grand poet's manner and his reputation. His sweeping enthusiasms carry us away; and even when we catch glimpses of unmistakable prosaic trousers and often quite a seedy frockcoat beneath his glittering bardic robes, the charm works – so long as it is not too often repeated. Subject Berlioz's music to the same test of familiarity as that to which we subject that of Beethoven and Chopin, Brahms or Tchaikovsky, Romeo's love-music and the Queen Mab Scherzo, three or four numbers from each of the choral works and half a dozen from *Les Troyens* might well prove imperishable, but the proportion of alloy to pure gold might become painfully plain. Berlioz, then, profits from our lack of familiarity with his music. The great peaks – and how beautiful they are! – seem greater and the valleys and plains between never quite lose the charm of unfamiliarity.

The whole problem of familiarity, interesting to the connoisseur, is of vital importance to the professional performer. How is it possible to infuse the same vitality into the three-hundredth as into the first performance, not of a leading role – not Aida or the first violin part in a Mozart symphony, but the role of Ramphis or the viola part in the same symphony? Or think of the pianist who has been playing the *Waldstein* sonata and Chopin's studies for thirty years, year in year out, and travelling from one end of the world to the other while he does so. Many start as infant prodigies, familiar with the notes of the repertory long before they can understand their full significance, and familiar with very little else, and these suffer all their lives from this *déformation professionnelle* or professional 'twist', as Szigeti calls it in his memoirs. We are all familiar with the performer whose playing can be called, as a cruel critic called Melba's singing at the end of her life, 'uninterestingly perfect and perfectly uninteresting'. The price of complete technical mastery is sometimes little less than the performer's soul. This is the direct outcome of that peculiar development of our musical life, little more than a century old, which we call 'concert-giving', and especially of its most recent developments as a commercialised business on a world-wide scale. The modern standard of technical perfection in instrumentalists threatens to breed a race of performers highly developed as technical automata, as were the castrati singers of the eighteenth century. In fact the fable of Paganini's pact with the devil has a hundred modern counterparts.

3 The Romantic Agony in Music – I

Seasons of decadence and seasons of renewal are no more sharply defined in the arts than in nature. Natural they are, too, and thus no subject either for tragic lamentation or moralistic invective. Pathos they certainly have, and an individual beauty of their own, as real and touching as the beauty of autumn or of old age. And so if I speak of decadence, it is in the factual, French sense of the word rather than in the disapproving English, or the comminatory Russian sense. True, old age has its unlovable foibles, as December has its fogs, and not all the music of this, any more than of any other period, is wholly admirable. Our business, however, is to understand why it is as it is rather than to find fault with it for what it is not. The fact of the decadence – the falling away and falling apart of music between the death of Wagner in 1883 and the outbreak of the First European War in 1914 – is surely un-assailable. During those years music went through convulsive changes which were at the same time the death-throes of one era and the birth-pangs of another, for the two are indistinguishable in the history of the arts. One fact stands out clearly: that the musical language which had been slowly ripening and expanding for three hundred years had reached its term. Further expansion in the same direction was impossible. There could only be a variety in the spending and enjoyment of accumulated wealth followed by the gradual contraction and final decay of the language. In the history of music Wagner occupies much the same position as Virgil occupied in the history of the Latin language, setting a pattern of perfection as a craftsman and intimidating his successors by the unsurpassable wealth and splendour of his language, crowning one great epoch and overshadowing another.

It is hardly an exaggeration to say that in the thirty years which separate *Parsifal* from *Der Rosenkavalier* there was no real *development* of the traditional musical idiom. Strauss is still consolidating Wagner's victories and exploring their full extent. His use of tonality – the crux of the whole 'linguistic' problem, as we shall see – seldom goes beyond what Wagner had at least adumbrated in *Tristan* or *Parsifal*. Seen in retrospect, his music contains nothing that can shock or puzzle the good Wagnerian. Nothing technical, that is to say – no chord or progression of chords, no *linguistic* puzzle. But there was a great and significant change in the use to which the language was put. Indeed here there was little less than a revolution.

During the nineteenth century music was dominated by idealism. It was universally accepted that music was a language of the emotions; and, until the last decade of the century, nobody questioned that what it conveyed or expressed, and the effect that it made upon the listener, should represent an enhancement of his moral being, an elevation of the mind through the senses. The heroic and the lyrical might find the most widely different forms of expression, and there was room for comedy on every level; but music had no 'fleurs du mal'. The rejection of the traditional categories of good and evil and the deep-lying scepticism of all that concerned the human will had found clear and strikingly beautiful expression in literature nearly half a century before the effect of this revolt was felt in music. Baudelaire had indeed divined a kindred spirit in Wagner, but long before he died Wagner had come to new terms with Christianity and idealism. Music did not become *fin de siècle* until the nineteenth century was in fact very nearly over, whereas the 'end' had begun almost a generation earlier in literature.

For it was literature, which had been making steadily larger inroads on the domain of music since Beethoven's death, that largely determined the forms assumed by music in the last decade of the nineteenth and the first decade of the twentieth century. Realism could hardly find a parallel in music, although it more than touched

Puccini and, in his symphonic poems, Strauss. But the Symbolists, themselves deeply affected by the music of Wagner, in their turn inflamed the imagination of composers; German expressionists, Russian neo-mystics and French impressionists – both painters and poets – contributed more to music than extra-musical forces had ever contributed in the past. Wagner's ideal of the *Gesamtkunstwerk* – the work in which all arts should be combined – haunted the imagination of composers; and symphony and chamber-music were comparatively neglected for opera, symphonic poem, song, cantata and ballet – any genre in which music was not required to stand alone, obeying its own laws and forming its own structures.

One reason for this lay in that loosening, almost to dissolution, of the sense of tonality, which Wagner had brought about. It was tonality that gave the large musical structures shape and coherence, and tonality had lost its binding power and could no longer be relied on to give a sense of direction. The composer then either looked outside music to literature for a ready-made shape for his music, or he contented himself with small works, in which colour and texture were his prime concern. This turning away from the architecturally conceived totality to concentrate on the constituent parts is, according to Nietzsche, the characteristic of a decadent art:

> Life no longer resides in the whole. The word gets the upper hand and jumps out of the sentence, the sentence stretches too far and obscures the meaning of the phrase, the page acquires life at the expense of the whole ... life, *equal* vitality, vibration and exuberance of life are pushed back into the most minute structures, the rest is poor in life. Everywhere paralysis, distress and torpor, or hostility and chaos, always becoming more striking as one ascends to ever higher forms of organisation. The whole has ceased to live *as* a whole; it is composite, summed up, artificial, an unnatural product. (*Der Fall Wagner*)

Nietzsche is writing of literature but the same fragmentation of the language, the same disproportion and exaggeration can be found in music. Idealism discarded and realism soon exhausted, the composer turned naturally to sensualism in its more exalted forms or to mysticism; and for both of these courses Wagner once again provided a precedent. Very roughly speaking Puccini, Strauss, Debussy and Ravel on the one hand, in their different ways, followed the first course, which makes music a form of the higher hedonism. On the other hand, Mahler, Scriabin and Delius each, in equally different ways, seeks to attain in his music an ecstasy which transcends the senses and is mystical, whether it be in a Christian, an esoteric or a pantheistic sense. Each of these composers was faced at the outset of his career, and more pressingly as he advanced, with the fact, felt often as an overpowering emotional burden, of coming at the end of a great period. For composers realised very soon that Wagner was not so much the beginning of a new era of musical history as the end-figure of a Golden Age. And since no creative artist in the nineteenth century could be content, as eighteenth-century composers had been, to work simply to a received pattern or formula, it was natural, and indeed inevitable, for each of these composers instinctively to search either for new ways of using a language already disintegrating or alternatively to fashion a new language composed of ancient or exotic elements.

Common to all the music of this period is a new complication of texture and a minute, filigree-like attention to detail. The wide, bold architectural span has disappeared and life, in Nietzsche's phrase, is 'pushed back into the most minute structures'. Just compare for a moment Puccini's workmanship with Verdi's: it is the technique of the miniaturist or the jeweller compared with that of the fresco-painter, a matter of 'exquisite touches', subtleties of detail and refinements of timbre which disguise or reconcile us to the decline in the *quality* of Puccini's dramatic vision and melodic invention compared with that of Verdi.

In *Bohème*, in *Madame Butterfly* and later in *The Girl of the Golden West*, Puccini provides us with an example of another characteristic of a declining art – the confusion of genre and the disproportion of means to end. He lavishes all his care and skill on subjects so humble, so lacking in what had hitherto been understood as nobility, so easily within the intellectual and emotional range of the *homme moyen sensuel*, that they would have served earlier generations only as operetta plots. The exquisite cherry-blossom scene in *Butterfly*, for instance, is operetta, almost tea-shop music written by a sensitive artist and a great craftsman.

In the same way Alban Berg was later to treat what are in reality *grand guignol* subjects as though they were great tragedies; and a crazed private soldier and a nymphomaniac woman, the hero and heroine of his two operas, have lavished on them all the care and psychological penetration accorded by earlier generations to an Alceste, a Leonora, an Otello or a Boris. Thus, too, Schoenberg in *Pierrot Lunaire* expends on a handful of sensationally morbid poems the same wealth of academic resources as the fifteenth-century Netherlanders expended on the text of the liturgy.

The relationship of Richard Strauss to Wagner is not unlike that of Puccini to Verdi. In Strauss, too, we find the minute workmanship, only here on a gigantic scale, and the same decline in quality, the same coarseness of moral fibre, the same search for new, at all costs striking effects still to be obtained within the old Wagnerian idiom. The hero of *Ein Heldenleben* stands to Siegfried very much as Puccini's Mimi stands to Verdi's Violetta, and each represents a sharp declension in the ideal. Strauss's hero is a vulgarian and a sensationalist compared with Wagner's Siegfried. He proclaims his heroism as shamelessly and as self-consciously as Mimi her sweet 'little woman's' innocence.

With Strauss sheer cleverness – self-conscious skill used for sensational purposes – makes its appearance in music. In *Salome* Strauss deploys all his skill in manipulating a vast orchestra, his contrapuntal facility, his inimitable gift for melody of a certain, highly sensual kind, to titillate his audience with the spectacle of the degenerate little princess's attempts to seduce an ascetic John the Baptist conceived in the flat, oily tones and conventional colours of the ecclesiastical oleograph. It is 'piquant', if anything so unmistakably German can be suitably described by a French word, and Massenet had already chosen an exactly similar subject in *Thaïs*. In the *Sinfonia Domestica* we find the same confusion of genres and the ludicrous disproportion between means and ends. Here we have a huge orchestra and music in which the texture is recklessly complicated, a medium and style which would need no enlarging for a work depicting the Last Judgment . . . and all devoted to a day in the domestic life of a one-child family of the German upper-middle-class in the year 1903.

In France the post-Wagnerian ferment, the sense of exhaustion coupled with a hectic musical vitality, brought entirely different results. Wagner was the climax of a specifically German phase of musical history and the French had other, if musically less fertile traditions. Debussy, then, was hardly tempted to continue in the mood of Wagnerian intoxication through which he passed as a young man. But how was he to escape? He was dazzled by the sensual magnificence of Wagner's music, the spellbinding power of 'the wizard of Bayreuth', and this was the last characteristic which he was to shed in his long search for an idiom at once new, personal and French.

Debussy experimented with a number of widely divergent styles before he discovered his own individual idiom. The Pre-Raphaelite painters and Whistler, the Russian nationalist composers and the exotic music of Java all contributed to what was, eventually, the most original and perfected of all the 'decadent' styles. Significantly it was Maeterlinck who enabled him to find the 'tone of voice' which was peculiarly his own. For Maeterlinck the human will was an illusion and an oriental 'Fate' was responsible for the motions and gestures of those shadowy creatures who replaced the autonomous, flesh and blood characters of the old drama. Pity is their highest virtue and a care not to tread on each other's dreams.

Pelléas represents the *ne plus ultra* of the anti-heroic style, and it was achieved within twenty years of Wagner's death, while Strauss was still busy with *Ein Heldenleben* and Puccini engaged on his gallery of fair, frail women and their pathetically ephemeral loves. For he, too, had reduced the virtues to pity and *pathos* – the emotion aroused by the spectacle of a fragile, uncomprehending humanity (preferably feminine) fighting a hopeless battle for its little share of happiness against hopelessly superior, and fundamentally inhuman, forces. This spectacle was to dominate the minds of Puccini, Strauss and in a later generation, Alban Berg. In this sense Mélisande, Salome, Elektra, the Marschallin, Marie and Lulu are all 'sisters under the skin', little victims of a cruel and incomprehensible fate – old age, neurosis, a 'bad family history', anything rather than the sense of personal responsibility which was the stuff of the old drama, whether tragedy or comedy. And to express their doomed hopes and voluptuous sufferings there were the rich, glittering, sounds and the long, dying cadences bequeathed by Wagner, with every note and phrase given its maximum of sonorous beauty and expressiveness; or the discreet short-breathed whispering, the perfectly tasteful prosody of Debussy. It was a heavily curtained, luxuriously cushioned world in which the most refined sensibilities were sedulously soothed or delightfully outraged. Music wore the velvets, satins, and brocades with which Wagner surrounded both his person and his music. A long autumnal sunset illuminated the whole musical scene, delighting the sensualists with its amber glow and inspiring in the neo-mystics a mood of pleasurable philosophical pessimism or exciting apocalyptic imaginings of a new world-order, in which reality should be finally superseded and transcended. Everyone knew, and no one quite believed, that the end was imminent; and meanwhile it was still possible to indulge in much the same fantasies, the same charades, masques and wild speculations as had entertained the court and the *beau monde* on the eve of the French cataclysm just over a century earlier.

4 The Romantic Agony in Music – II

Nineteenth-century music after the death of Beethoven is starred with individual styles which increasingly obscure and finally replace the common idiom of music as it was known in the eighteenth century. First Beethoven and then Wagner expanded the language of music; but although between them they shadow the whole century, the style and idiom of each remained obstinately personal. Those composers who willingly submitted to their influence too often found themselves mere imitators, adopting the manner and phraseology of the masters without their intellectual or emotional vitality. There are passages, for instance, even in Brahms's first ymphony and the operas of countless post-Wagnerian composers which give the impression of men of small, or at least average, build dressed in the clothes of giants and making gigantic gestures whose meaning they cannot quite implement. Wagner's idiom looked for a time like becoming the universal musical language of European music. That this was believed by many to be inevitable is implied, after all, in the phrase 'music of the future'; and the same claim has been made, at least implicitly, in our own day by Schoenberg and his disciples.

What actually happened in the years after Wagner's death was a great acceleration in the 'fragmentation' of musical styles, an even greater emphasis on the individual, personal musical character of each composer. Many of the most typical composers of this era started as comparatively conventional figures, using the Wagnerian or some other by now traditional idiom and only developing their new, personal musical languages later in their careers, in some cases quite suddenly and deliberately.

Debussy's early songs and piano pieces are not much more than a personal amalgam of elements which can easily be assigned to Massenet, Grieg or Wagner; and they bear less relationship to mature, fully individualised music of *Pelléas* than, let us say, the second symphony of Beethoven bears to the seventh. In the same way Scriabin's early piano pieces, in which the style and often the ideas closely resemble Chopin's, have very little connection with the *Poem of Ecstasy* or the late sonatas. The extremest example of all is furnished, of course by Schoenberg, who in a comparatively short space of time deliberately invented a new grammar and syntax for himself.

The invention of new languages – either for private use, as in the cases of Debussy and Scriabin or for all who cared to avail themselves of the new discovery, as in the case of Schoenberg – was thus a mark of the years between 1890 and 1914. But many composers who had neither the inclination nor the ability for such extreme measures, found another, less drastic escape from the unpleasant realities of the musical situation. Faced with a dead-end and the choice between merely disguising the facts or accepting some radical alteration in the language of music, even some of the most distinguished chose the policy of disguise. The choice has respectable historical precedent. The charades, the pastoral make-believe, with which the French court beguiled the long years spent in waiting for the revolution which they had neither the power nor, fundamentally, the wish to avert, were undertaken in the same spirit; and at the very time of which we are speaking the Russian ballet, whose European successes were partly due to the impasse in which music found itself, was the most significant production of the last years of the Russian Empire.

Societies on the brink of collapse concern themselves, ostrich-like, with other, less important matters than their own fate; and a future Tacitus may well draw attention to the fact that we surrendered India in the same year as the Sadler's Wells Ballet made its first, highly successful visit to America.

Charades, then, play an important part in this last phase of a musical era, the years of the decadence; and it is interesting to observe the various travesties adopted by composers. In France there was a long tradition of exotic imitations or pastiche, both in literature and to a lesser extent in music. Montesquieu's *Lettres Persanes* and Voltaire's *Contes*, Victor Hugo's *Orientales* and Leconte de Lisle's Greek and 'barbarian' poems, Félicien David's *Désert* and the Spanish, Indian or German settings of the most popular operas of Bizet, Massenet and Gounod – all these provided precedents of a kind. But when Debussy or Ravel assume a Spanish disguise in *Ibéria* or the *Rapsodie Espagnole* they do so in earnest, quite unlike Bizet in *Carmen*, who remains himself and an unashamed Frenchman. So that such a good Spaniard as Manuel de Falla, who marvelled at the identification achieved by Debussy and Ravel, found *Carmen* no more Spanish than a crude picture-postcard meant for tourists. For Bizet the exotic was merely a stimulus, for the later composers it was an escape.

When Mahler or Puccini turned to the music or the poetry of the East for inspiration, it was the gesture of world-weary men whose palates were jaded. Mahler found in Bethge's translations from the Chinese a pessimistic but aesthetically satisfying philosophy which exactly expressed his own autumnal mood. Puccini added two exotic women to his musical Don Juan's portrait-gallery – a *Mimi à la japonaise* in Cio Cio San and in Turandot a perverse, Chinese princess, who stands alone among his creations. There is little Oriental pastiche in the *Song of the Earth* and not much more in *Madame Butterfly*, or *Turandot*; but all three works show refined connoisseurs seeking to escape from themselves and the contemporary world in an atmosphere which stimulates by its novelty and unfamiliarity. Mozart was never more Viennese than when he set an opera in Turkey, and Wagner never more German than when his characters were Irish or Cornish. A later exotic opera, on the other hand, like Roussel's *Padmâvatî*, makes a real attempt to *be* oriental.

The composers we are speaking of found other travesties besides the exotic, for it is possible to escape by other than purely geographical means. There was the escape to the past – to the Middle Ages or the eighteenth century – and these were in a sense more promising musically, as they provided positive musical contrast with the contemporary, Wagner-dominated scene. The poetry of Verlaine suggested the elegant masked world of Watteau to Debussy and Fauré, and Richard Strauss found occasion for a return to a congenial eighteenth century in *Rosenkavalier* and *The Bourgeois Gentilhomme* music. Debussy even attempted a mediaeval 'atmosphere' in his music for d'Annunzio's *Martyrdom of St Sebastian*. None of this music is exactly pastiche but all of it testifies to a hankering after some earlier, imagined simplicity – Mozart in the case of Strauss, Lassus in that of Debussy – in exactly the same sense as Marie Antoinette playing milkmaid or shepherdess at the Petit Trianon. Since simplicity and reality of feeling were the great aims, it was obvious that composers could do better than remain within the conventional borders of civilisation, whether it were French or Chinese, of the eighteenth or the twentieth century; and the most common and universal of all disguises was that provided by the great anonymous 'folk'.

Here was an escape indeed from the over-cultivation of civilised personality to primitive anonymity, from the hothouse to the hedgerow. Vincent d'Indy fell on this music as on the antidote to a poison; for Holst it was no less intoxicating than the Wagnerian potions with which his whole musical organism was saturated. Some composers, like the couple in Turgenev's *Virgin Soil* (and sometimes with the same result) threw in their whole lot with the 'folk', adopted homespun as the everyday wear of their compositions and confined their whole musical diet to the small beer and local cheeses, as it were, of the musical past. The modes provided for them the solution to the problem of tonality, the flattened seventh became as much an obsession as the Wagnerian chords of the ninth or thirteenth.

In most cases, however, the influence of folk-song was gradual and partial. It was one among many movements of 'return to the past' which led to the rediscovery of the great polyphonic composers of the sixteenth and seventeenth centuries, of Lully and Rameau (so much admired by Debussy) in France and of Purcell in England. Like literature in the Alexandrine age, music became antiquarian and composers were proud to assume the functions of the scholar and even the editor, in addition to their purely creative activities. It is hard not to see in this a weakening of the purely creative impulse and, although these antiquarian movements proved of great importance in the formation of a new aesthetic and a new musical idiom, they must in themselves be regarded as typical hall-marks of a decadence.

Even in the list of escapes and disguises, however, folk-song represented a fast-dying, and in many parts of Europe already dead form of popular music; but there were other still vital although musically debased forms. The circus and the music-hall; in France the *café-concert*; in Hungary and Russia the gipsy bands; in Germany and England the brass-band – these were still unpolluted by the sophistication which had fallen like a blight upon music in its more serious forms. The hankering after escape in this direction had already showed itself in so staunchly traditional a composer as Brahms who, beside his interest in folk-song and old polyphonic music, showed his practical interest in gipsy music in his 'Hungarian' pieces. These were, in his case, a mere side-show to the main musical spectacle. In Chabrier and in the French composers who followed his lead, those who had grown up in the great early days of Diaghilev's Russian ballet, fair and circus scenes, the deliberate assumption of a musical *canaille* provided escape and disguise of a sophisticated realistic, urban kind very different from the rustic simplicities of folk-song. Here there was at least the suggestion of a bridge between the composer and the everyday world, a diminution of the gap which yawned between composer and common man in the music of Debussy, Mahler, Schoenberg or Scriabin.

With the advent of jazz to Europe during the 1914-18 war and the tentative flirtation of serious musicians with the negro folk-music, it looked as though the wheel had turned its full circle. Pamina, tired of Tamino's high sentiments and flowery speeches seemed to be thinking regretfully of Monostatos. Not that even the negro represented the *ne plus ultra* of simplicity. Composers of the mid-nineteenth century had attempted to think themselves into the child's mind – Schumann unsuccessfully, Mussorgsky and Bizet with a surer instinct. Now, at the latter end of a long musical civilisation, Ravel, Debussy and Mahler escaped in their different ways to the nursery. The *Mother Goose* suite and the *Children's Corner* are works on a scale commensurate with the child's mind: but Mahler, with a less sure stylistic instinct, embodies shreds of nursery sentiment even in his symphonies and in the fourth substitutes a 'once-upon-a-time' for the finale in which tradition and aesthetic propriety alike demand to find at least some revelant conclusion to what has gone before – no child's play either, in Mahler's case. Here we find once again the confusion of genres, that aesthetic chaos which I mentioned earlier as one of the hall-marks of decadence.

Can escape and travesty go further? There remained the animal world, invaded with no very serious musical intentions by Saint-Saens and Chabrier in the 80's and with considerably more art by Ravel in his *Histoires Naturelles* and Poulenc in his *Bestiaire*. Finally the most radical and sensational of all travesties was first assumed by Erik Satie, who dared to present his music stark naked – *l'art dépouillé*, as it came to be called by his enthusiastic followers, who formed for a time something approaching a school of musical Nudism. Satie's music does not parade its nakedness without a good many of the selfconscious jokes and gestures with which a similarly 'disguised' guest at a fancy-dress party might seek to conceal his embarrassment. Music, like the human body, can only afford to appear stripped in public if its basic forms, lines and textures are solid and irreproachable; and too much of this 'stripped art' reveals a poor, squinny structure and undernourished contours, the musical counterparts of the blue, greenish or ashen nudes who abounded in the pictures of the period.

The end of an artistic era shows many symptoms of failing vitality, need for artificial stimulants and general restlessness of mood which suggests comparison with the sickness or ageing of a human being. But the real, and hopeful, parallel is rather with the changing seasons of the year in their natural cycle. The birth of a new creature is not implicit in the old age and death of the individual; but spring is, by a natural cycle, implicit in the withering and decay of autumn and winter. It is that very decay or decadence which furnishes the material from which the young seed draws its nourishment; and two generations later we can see how deeply, how organically rooted in the immediate past were all those composers whose novel and apparently revolutionary experiments seemed so shocking in the years between the Wars. It has been a stormy spring, certainly, following on an exceptionally long and

beautiful autumn, whose glow still remains for many music-lovers
the overwhelming musical experience of their lives. Debussy's exquisite hedonism and Strauss's cynical sensuality, Rachmaninov's
luxurious despair, Scriabin's self-induced ecstasies, and Mahler's
and Delius's beautifully tinted nostalgia – they may all have pointed
to the end of an era, even of a civilisation; but those who live in a
silver age look back with awe and veneration upon their golden
forebears, just as in the Dark Ages silver shines with very little less
lustre than gold.

5 Verlaine's 'Art Poétique'

The French Romantic poets were for the most part indifferent or even hostile to music. It was positively unpleasing to Victor Hugo; and Théophile Gautier to whom, as an unwilling music-critic, much must be forgiven, declared that he preferred silence. It was only with Baudelaire that music entered the consciousness of French poets as anything more than a repository for vague metaphors. Baudelaire was a Janus, a Parnassian with one face turned backwards to the Romanticism which he echoed and the other forward to the Symbolism which he foreshadowed, in his poetry. Thanks to Baudelaire's essay on *Tannhäuser* Wagner found a foothold in Paris, and amongst the poets rather than the musicians; and Wagner's music and Wagner's aesthetic theories were eventually to cause almost as much ferment among the poets of the late 80's and 90's as among the musicians.

The dominant characteristic of French artistic life in the last quarter of the nineteenth century was this mutual exchange of ideals, ideas and even techniques; so that we find on the one hand a poet, Mallarmé, becoming a Wagnerian initiate and apostle and on the other hand a musician, Debussy, forming his style on the analogies which he instinctively drew with painters – the Pre-Raphaelites or Puvis de Chavannes – or with a poet like Verlaine. This 'correspondence' between the arts had already been proclaimed by Baudelaire, imagining Nature as a vast temple, a 'forest of symbols' (fateful word) in which 'scents, colours and sounds

echo each other'. 'Scents fresh as children's bodies, sweet as the
oboe, green as the meadows.' But in this fusion, or exchange, one
art came gradually to predominate; and that art was music.

Even in isolated England Walter Pater was to write, in 1889, of
music as 'the typically perfect art . . . the ideal of all art whatever,
precisely because in music it is impossible to distinguish the form
from the substance or matter, the subject from the expression'.
And it was an easy step from regarding music as an ideal to regarding it, as Mallarmé came to do, as a kind of unfairly privileged
usurper among the arts, or a storehouse whose doors were fairly
open to all comers from the other arts. 'Il faut reprendre à la
musique son bien' – each art, says Mallarmé, must recover its
property from music.

This gradual emergence of music as the ideal language of the
artist represents a reaction against the preponderance of fact over
fiction, and documentation over imagination, in the 'realistic' or
'naturalistic' art of the day, best known to us from the novels of
Zola and the stories of Maupassant. Music could not photograph
life nor preach a social gospel. Music is not, except in the very
vaguest sense, *about* anything. 'What it says is how it says it', in
John Lehmann's neat phrase. And it was this freedom from 'content', this identity of the thing expressed with its expression, that
poets and painters envied, the ideal which found a typically wayward and personal expression in Verlaine's *Art Poétique*. Few poets
have been less didactic by nature than Verlaine, and it is safe to
say that none has written an Ars Poetica in such strange surround-
ings as the prison at Mons, where Verlaine wrote his *Art Poétique*
in the spring of 1874. Three years earlier the first of Zola's Rougon-
Macquart stories had been published, and two years later there
was to appear Mallarmé's poem *Prélude à l'après-midi d'un faune*.
Poison and antidote, whichever way you choose to regard them,
were to continue to appear together for twenty years or more.

Verlaine's poem, a mere nine quatrains, has all the qualities
which it inculcates in the poet. Musical beauty before all else,
fastidiousness, a power of suggestion rather than a statement of
fact, the wedding of the precise and the vague in the choice of
images, and the employment of shades (*nuances*) rather than brilliant
colours. Wit and cleverness, the easy laugh and verbal acrobatics

he avoids like the plague; eloquence he silences with a blow. Only rhyme, against which he warns the poet, he uses himself. His plea is for freedom, of which music is to him the pattern, naturalness, humility; and he is equally hostile to the heavy, over-emphatic rhetoric and gaudy colours of the Romantics and to the formal wit and intellectual peacocking of the eighteenth-century poets – all 'eloquence' or 'literature'.

De la musique avant toute chose,
Et pour cela préfère l'Impair
Plus vague et plus soluble dans l'air,
Sans rien en lui qui pèse ou qui pose.

Il faut aussi que tu n'ailles point
Choisir tes mots sans quelque méprise:
Rien de plus cher que la chanson grise
Où l'Indécis au Précis se joint.

C'est des beaux yeux derrière des voiles,
C'est le grand jour tremblant de midi,
C'est, par un ciel d'automne attiédi,
Le bleu fouillis des claires étoiles!

Car nous voulons la Nuance encor,
Pas la Couleur, rien que la nuance!
Oh! la nuance seule fiance
Le rêve au rêve et la flûte au cor!

Fuis de plus loin la Pointe assassine,
L'Esprit cruel et le Rire impur,
Qui font pleurer les yeux de l'Azur,
Et tout cet ail de basse cuisine!

Prends l'éloquence et tords-lui son cou!
Tu feras bien, en train d'énergie,
De rendre un peu la Rime assagie,
Si l'on n'y veille, elle ira jusqu'où?

O qui dira les torts de la Rime!
Quel enfant sourd ou quel nègre fou
Nous a forgé ce bijou d'un sou
Qui sonne creux et faux sous la lime?

De la musique encore et toujours!
Que ton vers soit la chose envolée
Qu'on sent qui fuit d'une âme en allée
Vers d'autres cieux à d'autres amours.

Que ton vers soit la bonne aventure
Eparse au vent crispé du matin
Qui va fleurant la menthe et le thym . . .
Et tout le reste est littérature.

What a revolution in poetry Verlaine's poem implied it is difficult for any but a Frenchman to grasp. English poetry has, except under French influence, been a much freer, less formal art, subject to far fewer rules and able to dispose of a much wider vocabulary, a greater variety of rhythms and metres. Even stranger is the fact that Verlaine should, in 1874, have taken music as his ideal of a free art, unencumbered by emotional eloquence or intellectual formalities. It is quite certain that no composer then living would have understood Verlaine's poem or, had he understood it, felt the smallest sympathy with the ideals it expressed. What in fact happened was that music during the next quarter of a century, gradually assumed the character attributed to it by the poets; so that in the 90's music began to be written which did in fact correspond to the ideal promulgated by Verlaine. The music written in France, as elsewhere, during the 70's and 80's had all the characteristics that Verlaine most deplored. It was eloquent, highly-coloured, generally symmetrical and always vividly and obviously emotional; it had little subtlety of atmosphere and made small use of the half-lights or the precision-in-vagueness preached by the poet.

In fact it was exactly twenty years after Verlaine wrote his *Art Poétique* that the music which he had imagined was first heard, when Debussy's *Prélude à l'après-midi d'un faune* was played at a concert of the Société Nationale. Debussy was the friend of writers and painters rather than of musicians, whom he regarded with a certain naïve superiority. Like many of his friends, he was still in 1894 partly under the sway of Wagner; but he had realised that Wagner represented the end, the climax of a great epoch rather than the starting-point for a new conception of music. That conception he was gradually to realise for himself, helped by what he saw taking place in the sister arts. The nearest he ever came to expressing it in words was to say that he wished all his music to sound 'as though it were improvised', an ideal which Verlaine would certainly have echoed. Debussy knew the *Art Poétique*, of course (he had published settings of Verlaine's poems as early as 1888); and reading through the poem with Debussy in mind, we shall find that almost every verse suggests some passage of Debussy's music. It even seems as though the clearest illustration of what Verlaine was aiming at in poetry is to be found not in words, but in the music which was written under his indirect influence. Debussy was not alone among composers, though Verlaine's ideals find their clearest and most complete expression in his music. Fauré's settings in *La Bonne Chanson*, though more traditional in syntax as well as in feeling, were wholly in accord with the poet's aesthetic; and even such a faithful pupil of Massenet as Reynaldo Hahn came near, in his Verlaine songs, to catching the note of understatement, the half-lights and the unpretentious wayward lyricism of the poetry.

'Music before all else', wrote Verlaine, 'and to obtain the effect of music choose the asymmetrical rather than the symmetrical, the odd rather than the even, vaguer and more evanescent, unweighted and unresting.' How Debussy obtained this effect can be seen in his pianoforte prelude *Des Pas sur la neige* – with its short, broken melodic figures, its limping rhythm and its avoidance of strong affirmations of tonality.

'Be fastidious in your choice of words', Verlaine continues. 'There is nothing lovelier than the grisaille music of a song in which vagueness is mated with precision.' The colour grey fascinated Debussy. His orchestral Nocturnes were originally planned as studies in a single colour 'what a painter might call a study in grey', he wrote, with obvious reference to Whistler. And again, in speaking of his music for *Pelléas* he refers to 'a sort of grisaille'. This really implies a form of continual understatement, an avoidance of all dramatic touching up with colour, all artificial emphasis. Debussy's setting of Verlaine's own *Colloque sentimentale* is a good example. There is no hint of rhetoric, no moment of emotional self-indulgence in the whole piece, whose fluid lines and

Chinese economy of characterisation are wholly in Verlaine's spirit. The fastidiousness of that setting represents only one side of Verlaine's ideal – the side certainly most imitated by Debussy. There was another, humbler and more popular side. Verlaine defended poetry against the pundits and the wits, and his *chanson grise* had none of the aloof mysteriousness of Mallarmé. Reynaldo Hahn caught this humbler, more popular note in his Verlaine settings, which he properly called *Chansons grises* – and in *En Sourdine* the fastidious delicacy of the opening gives way to a perilous but successful approach to the commonplace which has countless parallels in Verlaine's best poetry.

When Verlaine hints to the poet the images that should stir his fancy, he chooses three that are apparently commonplace – 'Fair eyes from behind a veil, the trembling light of noon, the blue haze of stars in a warm autumn sky' – but each of these poetic commonplaces is qualified by imprecision – the eyes are *veiled*, the midday light *trembles* and the stars are a *haze*. You will remember how Debussy in *La Mer* suggests the growing light over the sea and how he only suggests the blaze of noon in the very last bars.

'More and more subtlety of shading – not colour, only nuance, for nuance alone mates dream with dream and flute with horn.' No composer who, like Debussy, followed the painting of his French contemporaries and learned from them, as well as from the poets, could be called a faithful follower of this counsel of Verlaine's, one which Verlaine himself often failed to follow. But how Debussy mated flute with horn we know from his *Prélude à l'après-midi d'un faune*, the work in which he achieves supremely the dream-atmosphere, the simplicity and the vague voluptuousness which were Verlaine's ideal.

Three verses of the *Art Poétique* are devoted to castigation. 'Avoid at all cost the murderous shafts of wit, the clever sally and the cheapening laugh that brings tears to the eyes of Poetry – and all the garlic-seasoning beloved of kitchen-maids. Take eloquence and wring its neck and, in this forceful mood, read Rhyme a stern reproof. Unwatched, there are no lengths to which she will not go. Oh! who will chronicle Rhyme's offences? Was it a deaf child or some idiot savage who first chiselled this pinchbeck jewel, that rings hollow and false beneath the poet's file?'

Debussy, too, was in open revolt against the logical discourse, the witty points and balanced periods inherited from the music of the eighteenth century. Garlic – the strong, popular flavour of 'local colour' – was abhorrent to his naturally fastidious palate. Bizet's *Carmen* was no more to him than the highly-coloured Spain of the picture-postcards and when his imagination took him South of the Pyrenees the sights, the sounds, and the smells conjured up by his music had all the 'precision-in-vagueness' demanded by Verlaine, as in *Soirée dans Grenade*.

'Take eloquence and wring its neck.' Perhaps, but what a slaughter among the composers of the nineteenth century this meant for Debussy! And Rhyme – the regular, comfortable recurrence of stresses and assonances, the rhythms which set the untutored foot 'beating time'! It meant an end, as far as Debussy was concerned, to music's power of mass-suggestion and communal aspiration, a turning of the back upon so much that was considered sacred, including some of the great things in Beethoven, such as the finale of the ninth symphony.

Neither Beethoven nor, for that matter, Bizet were 'deaf children' or 'idiot savages' to Debussy; but in his search for a new approach to music he had, instinctively, to turn his back on them. 'Music again, and always music! Let your verse be the winged creature that escapes from the soul as she soars to other skies with other loves, be the adventurer's banner unfurled in the morning air, sweet with mint and thyme – and all the rest is literature.' This soaring quality, this refusal of earth-bound creatures to remain earth-bound, this shining, morning air, that Verlaine demands of poetry found its expression in music too. But not the music of Debussy so much as that of Fauré. His setting of Verlaine's own poem of spring 'L'hiver a cessé', in *La Bonne Chanson*, has the fresh earthiness, the humility and the lyrical abandon which form the complement to Debussy's exquisite and severely controlled art.

Part II

Musicians and Music

_1_ Mozart and his Age

'As Death, if we come to consider it closely, is the true goal of our existence, I have formed during the last few years such close relations with this best and truest friend of mankind, that his image is not only no longer terrifying to me, but is indeed very soothing and consoling.'

Leopardi? Tolstoy's Pierre Bezukhov in Masonic mood or even Goethe's young Werther? No, but an artist who has much in common with Leopardi, a Masonic sympathiser like Pierre and a contemporary of Werther – Mozart, aged thirty-one, with four more years to live. It would be difficult to name another eighteenth-century character in any field of human interest who is so alive in the imagination, so firmly established in the affections of the twentieth century. Why?

The musician has a hundred answers, but Mozart's music does not appeal only to those with a musical training. It may be that his apparently instinctive, 'natural' mastery of the craft of music is divined by many who themselves have no expert knowledge; and there is certainly something intoxicating in the spectacle (or the sound) of an extremely complex and difficult operation performed with absolute self-assurance and ease. Mozart's spirits, too, whether high or low, stir our immediate sympathy. The emotion aroused in us by Beethoven's heroic defiance of fate and cosmic questionings is tinged with scepticism; his simple and robust good humour is far removed from our more sophisticated sense of well-being.

Mozart is a vigorous dialectician but his arguments are conducted in the manner of the best conversation, without rhetoric or moralising; and he takes his subjects, as it were, from every level of human experience, not only the highest. Without preaching, declaiming or even adopting an unmistakably serious manner he covers the whole range of normal human emotion. He can be frankly frivolous – a relief, no doubt, to him and certainly to us. Yet even his most sustained frivolities, such as *Così fan Tutte*, contain moments of tenderness and glimpses of unearthly beauty to be found in no other composer.

This human wholeness, this uninhibited and unembarrassed ability to move over the whole human scene and to look beyond it, are infinitely attractive to present-day audiences, uncertain of everything and often lop-sided in their emotional attitude to life. (It is the lop-sidedness of the Romantics that makes them, in a different way, attractive.)

What was the secret of this integral humanity of Mozart's, which is also the secret of his appeal to us? No man ever had a less well balanced education: in modern jargon, he had 'specialised' before he was six. And his reflections on death while still a young man would be universally considered nowadays to show a morbid streak in his character.

Are they not, though, evidence that Mozart had 'seen life steadily and seen it whole' at an age when most men see little more than what is immediately in front of their noses? And do not his high spirits and his wit draw their special character and strength, his tender or reflective moods their deep poetry from the implicit recognition of the true nature and, as it were, proportions of human life? Humility is just that: the undramatised acceptance of the truth. This unspoken, clear-sighted humility combined with an unparalleled musical gift accounts for much of Mozart's greatness and the power of his music today.

We are all the more surprised, then, if we come upon what seems clear evidence of Mozart sharing the eighteenth-century's insensibilities – in the case of *Don Giovanni* we might even say callousness.

Is it merely because we have become more humane, more squeamish, that the double humiliation of Donna Elvira by Leporello is almost intolerable? Or can it be that our idea of Leporello needs correcting?

His name of course, means 'hare' and he is, basically, the cowardly servant of a noble master, the type we know best in Sancho Panza but one that is common in Spanish and Italian literature from the Renaissance onwards. He is shrewd and resourceful where his own or his master's interests are concerned, good hearted though hopelessly venal. He is generally shown on the stage as a rotund, stocky peasant, the anti-type of his tall, aristocratic master. We know that he is married and unfaithful to his wife. If his calling his master by the affectionate diminutive 'Don Giovannino' suggests that he is considerably the older of the two, his phrase 'l'amico' ('our friend') emphasises his independence, which he will assert with considerable impudence until threatened by his master with violence or contemptuously bought with money. In fact, though he stands much nearer to the clownish Papageno, there is something of the Figaro in him as well.

At the very opening of the opera he complains of his life as a servant and says he would like 'to play the gentleman'. After the murder of the Commendatore his comments are insolent and coarse, and his 'I'm playing the noble lord too' when rebuked by his master for pinching the bottom of one of Zerlina's friends, is the reply not of a yokel but of a smart gentleman's gentleman who can imitate his master plausibly and probably wears his cast-off clothes. We must, I believe, see him in this light if we are to tolerate either his 'catalogue aria' or his successful replacing of his master with Donna Elvira.

It seems to me possible that Mozart may be pointing the way at the opening of the first scene, and that the gait of 'Notte e giorno faticar' may contain something of an insolent strut, which we can find again at the opening of the catalogue aria. The very opening words of this are insolent – 'Madamina' is insultingly familiar from a servant to a woman of Donna Elvira's breeding – and I feel sure that this whole aria demands a Leporello only a little older than his master, a flashy parody in looks and figure, only distinguished to the casual eye by his round cap, poor quality cloak and lack of a sword. The comic gestures with which singers unfailingly illustrate the nature of Don Giovanni's conquests are quite unnecessary, for

Mozart has done this in musical terms that need no underlining.

That Elvira tolerates Leporello's account of his master's exploits is a measure of the fascination that Giovanni exercises over her. This fascination is made quite clear in Act II scene 2, where she responds to his renewed love-making in spite of all she knows. Here we have an even stronger suggestion that Leporello is physically a close parody of his master, and perhaps his humble counterpart 'below stairs'. When the two change clothes, Leporello should be able to give a reasonable imitation of his master's love-making, so that the audience can understand Elvira's mistake and not be forced to regard the whole thing as a rather unsavoury pantomime. After all, Giovanni observes: 'She won't recognise you, if you don't want her to' and himself imitates Leporello well enough. In any case neither we nor Elvira should be insulted by the farce of a cringing peasant in a feathered hat masquerading successfully as his master. There is no warrant for this in Mozart's music. In fact Giovanni himself finds Leporello's love-making so convincing that he feels obliged to interrupt it by a ruse.

No doubt Leporello is all 'hare' at his next appearance, when his impersonation is discovered and his pleas for mercy become incoherent with sheer fright. But in the churchyard scene we are reminded by Don Giovanni himself that he was mistaken for Leporello, a further argument in favour of their physical resemblance; and his master laughs impatiently at Leporello's plea that he cannot read – which might well have been true had he been the traditional Sancho Panza yokel.

When he is caught gnawing a pheasant bone while serving his master's dinner, Giovanni refers to him as a *marrano*. Whether this is simply a term of abuse (as it came to be in Italian) or whether it preserves any trace of its original Spanish meaning of 'a newly baptised Jew or Moor', is hard to decide; but the fact that this was an accurate description of da Ponte himself suggests that he may have used the word wittingly. I am unaware of any Jewish claims to Leporello, and have never seen him represented as an African rather than Iberian type; but once again the word suggests an urban not a rustic character. *Marranos* changed their faith for social advancement, so that we are brought back to a Leporello with a streak of the Figaro in him. Nobody feels any sense of impropriety, let alone indignation, when Figaro impersonates the Count in the last act; and although Leporello's situation with Elvira is both more serious and more delicate, it should cause us neither embarrassment nor indignation.

Leporello is not the only Mozart character generally misrepresented on the modern stage. Marcellina in *Figaro* is an even more extreme, if less important case. She is normally played as a woman in her late fifties, though Sadler's Wells has presented her as a kind of Queen Victoria in widow's black and at least sixty. This custom has presumably arisen from two considerations – the fact that she is Figaro's mother and that Susanna mocks her for her age.

At what age are we to suppose that Dr Bartolo seduced Marcellina? Let us give him the benefit of any doubts and say eighteen. And how old is Figaro? Certainly no more than twenty-five. This would make Marcellina forty-three, an age which the eighteen-year-old Susanna would certainly mock as an 'old' woman by the standards of the Spanish eighteenth century. But it is completely wrong to exaggerate this and thereby to make her determination to marry Figaro preposterous. Marcellina should be at least a reasonably preserved woman bent on making the best of her appearance and more likely to arouse laughter by dressing too young than by voluminous black and grandmotherly hats. Here in fact is a case in which modern producers have too often reduced a character to the status of a commonplace music-hall type, and Marcellina needs restitution.

Since age is so variable a consideration and singers are no longer the race of outsize monsters that they too often were in the past, producers should consider very carefully whether traditional representations are really justified either by the facts of the drama or by the necessity imposed by the available human material.

The human age-cycle starts and ends, at least in civilised countries, later than ever before, even if we take into account the modern child's insistence on adopting the externals of adult life two or three years earlier than these were accorded to his parents. We have therefore come to think of old age as only starting at a time of life when earlier generations expected to be senile, if not dead. How old, for instance, was Falstaff in his St Martin's summer, when his prosecution of two simultaneous love-affairs was a cause of congratulation to himself and of incredulous amusement to his neighbours? Boito's libretto gives us a clue in the opening scene of Act III, where Falstaff comments ruefully on his first grey hairs; and yet how often we see the part played by a singer in a white wig and looking at least sixty-five. Falstaff, like his later Austrian re-incarnation, Baron Ochs, should be in his very early fifties, running to seed and to fat (though with the characteristic drinker's belly, the German *Bierbauch*, rather than an all-over monster) and with the same *bon vivant*'s leer as Ochs. If Mrs Ford and Mrs Page are to be imagined in their early thirties, married at seventeen and already in their own and the world's eyes matrons, Falstaff must be at most twenty years their senior.

2 Beethoven and the Revolutionary Ideal of Liberty

Towards the three points of the trident which the French Revolution aimed at the heart of the old régime, Beethoven's attitude throughout his life was always unambiguous – though that is not to say that it was always the same, or that his understanding of Liberty, Equality and Fraternity was that of the politicians. For Beethoven was a rebel, but not a revolutionary. He judged the laws and conventions of the society of his day by a wholly subjective standard, that of his own nature. His exuberant and powerful character would have found any system likely to win general acceptance with the rest of mankind irksome and full of illogical anomalies. His passionate belief in Liberty never faltered, though it changed in character; but it was in the first instance a wholly natural, instinctive egoism, the emotional reaction of a high-spirited, hugely talented youth increasingly aware of his exceptional gifts and irritated by the difficulties and frustrations which lay in the way of their development. Growing up in the Rhineland, he spent his most impressionable years far nearer the site of the ultimate conflagration than any of his subsequent Austrian friends; but he never, so far as we know, took the smallest interest in political theory. At the age of twenty he did indeed write a cantata on the death of the Emperor Joseph II, the 'enlightened despot' whose measures for curbing the power and influence of the Church won him a halo among the progressive thinkers of the day. And that Beethoven regarded him as a champion of Liberty may possibly be suggested by the fact that he embodied some of the music of this cantata in *Fidelio*. But the young Beethoven's unwillingness to submit himself to any kind of external discipline; his passionate, instinctive rejection of the notion of equality; and his absorption in his music together formed an effective bar to his ever becoming a revolutionary in the practical or political sphere.

How closely Beethoven at the age of thirty seemed to prefigure Nietzsche in his scorn for the feeble and ignorant of any class can be seen in a passage of a letter written to Zmeskall – 'I don't want to know anything about your system of ethics', he wrote. 'Strength is the morality of men who stand out from the rest, and it is mine.'

How far he was from the revolutionary dogma of Equality the whole tone of his life, his music and his letters testify. Even in 1825, two years before his death, he could write: 'Our age needs powerful spirits to lash these wretched, small-minded perfidious scamps of men.' Of the poor Zmeskall himself: 'I rate him and those of his species' – Zmeskall was a minor court functionary – 'only according to what they can do for me. I regard them purely and simply as instruments on which I play as I please.' When the elegant Abbé Gelinek, worsted in a pianistic duel by Beethoven, complained 'There is a devil in that young man' he was nearer to the truth than he knew, only it was Milton's Satan, a being of supernatural splendour and vigour, not Goethe's Great Denier.

If we place side by side with the Nietzschean protestations of the young Beethoven the equally passionate protestations of love for humanity, either in the Heiligenstadt Testament of 1802 or in a passage such as the following from 1811, we have an unpleasant sense of unreality: 'Never since my childhood has my zeal to serve poor suffering humanity relaxed. Never have I accepted any reward for this. I need no other than the feeling of well-being that always accompanies a good action.' Is it Rousseau speaking, we wonder? or Adolf Hitler laying the foundation-stone of a new block of workers' flats? No, it is Beethoven, who believed always and with all his soul in Liberty – at first as a practical principle for his own life and then with increasing depth and vision as a spiritual ulti-mate; never believed in Equality; but learned to find in the *idea* of *Fraternity* the emotional satisfaction which was denied him in its ordinary, personal forms. The Heiligenstadt Testament, where

broken pride stammers for the first time, was the immediate outcome of Beethoven's first real facing of his personal tragedy, his
deafness. It was years before he achieved complete resignation,
years during which he confessed that he 'sometimes cursed his
Creator'; but the old Nietzschean spirit never returned for long
nor with the same confidence. The works which appeared in the
years immediately following this complete realisation of his deafness, with all that it meant in disappointment of his hopes for
private happiness, touch deeper levels of experience than anything
that he had written before. In the third symphony he answered the
mood of the Heiligenstadt Testament with an affirmation of life at
its highest natural level, that of the Hero; and in *Fidelio* the breadth
and depth of his human sympathy showed that to him, more perhaps than any other artist, could be applied the παθήματα μαθήματα
of Aeschylus – he indeed learned through suffering.

The libretto of *Fidelio* came to Beethoven from France, where
it had been set by Pierre Gaveaux under the title of *Leonora or
Conjugal Love*, in 1798. The story was based on a historical incident
which took place in Touraine during the Terror – when presumably it was from the hands of the local revolutionary committee,
not from a prison of the old régime, that the prototype of Leonora
rescued her husband. It was enough to Beethoven that the story
combined the ideals of personal liberty and conjugal devotion. He
was only prevented from giving the work the title of *Leonora* by
the fact that Paër had already used it for his setting of the same
libretto, produced in Dresden in 1804 but not in Vienna until 1806,
the year after *Fidelio*. On the other hand Beethoven certainly knew
and admired Cherubini's *Water-Carrier*, produced in Vienna in
1802, and this deals with a similar case of conjugal devotion and
heroism.

It is a frequent complaint that *Fidelio*, the drama of human
liberty, opens with a disappointing scene of commonplace domesticity in the manner of the old French *opéra comique*; and that only
the restless agitation of the disguised Leonora suggests that this is
not simply a sentimentalised scene of everyday working-class life.
In the first place we should not forget that the *opéra comique* in
France had been the chosen musical form of the Encyclopédistes
and all 'advanced' thinkers since the 50's of the eighteenth century;

that it had been used as a vehicle for social criticism for even longer; and that, in a rather new form, it was, with the ode, the most favoured musical form of the French Revolution, just as (again with the ode) the programme symphony has been the favoured form of the Russian. Those who find the opening scenes of *Fidelio* disappointing might in any case ask themselves – did not everyday life continue apparently unchanged on the very threshold of Auschwitz and Dachau? Are there not doubtless today, prim rooms with pots of geraniums in the windows and prison-officers' daughters in love with their fathers' assistants, at the gates of concentration-camps or optimistically named 'rehabilitation-centres'? There is no more effective way of presenting the horror of imprisonment than by first showing freedom, not in forms of impossible splendour but in the humble shape in which it presents itself to the ordinary human being. The quite unheroic character of Rocco is equally right dramatically. He is an affectionate father, mildly avaricious but fundamentally 'decent' and a victim of his circumstances, which leave him, like thousands of his successors today, a choice between 'collaboration' with odious and criminal inhumanity and a heroic resistance beyond the powers of most human beings. (Silvio Pellico's moving picture of his gaoler in the Austrian political prison of Spielberg bears an astonishing resemblance to Rocco.) It is only with Pizarro that we meet the stage character of the revolutionary pamphlet or propaganda play, a mere impersonation of Tyranny decked out in black cloak and jackboots – the Capitalist, with cigar and astrakhan collar, of the early Soviet posters. Not even Beethoven can make this figure live; and so we have a reversal of the usual situation, in which villains are live (and even sympathetic) characters, while the good are insipid and unconvincing. We in fact measure the evil which hangs over Florestan's prison not by Pizarro's expression of it but first by the reactions it provokes in Leonora and then in the incredulous, stammering gratitude with which the prisoners greet their few moments of light, air and comparative freedom. These express far more than Pizarro's histrionic rantings, in which apoplectic fury almost topples over into the comic gobbling of the enraged Osmin. But before that, in the orchestral introduction to the prison scene, Beethoven makes darkness audible and gives a voice to solitude. Into this breathing, sighing, palpable darkness, in which the irregular drum-beats of Florestan's heart make an effect worthy of Edgar Allen Poe, there rings the cry of human agony – Florestan's 'God! this awful darkness'.

The actual saving of Florestan by the last-minute arrival of the Governor links *Fidelio*, whose first act opened by a scene from the French *opéra comique*, with the rescue-operas which won such popularity in France during the Revolution. (Beethoven certainly knew one of the most famous, Cherubini's *Lodoiska* of 1791, which was given at Vienna in 1802.) The trumpet announcing the Minister's arrival corresponds exactly to the soft wood-wind or string figure which announced the *deus ex machina* in the old *opera seria*. But with what a difference of effect! Pizarro has raged, Leonora has revealed her identity – Berlioz remembered Schröder-Devrient brandishing a pistol in Pizarro's face, her arm trembling and laughing hysterically – and she is threatening to shoot when right out of the key the trumpet gives the first signal, far away on the battlements. As it dies away the original movement returns to the music, but the four singers are paralysed and hardly do more than stammer. But they remain in the tonality of the trumpet-call and it is only after the second, louder signal and Jaquino's breathless, spoken announcement of the Minister's arrival that the previous movement and the tonality of the scene are restored. This irruption of the new world of daylight and freedom upon the night of tyranny and injustice has its counterpart in the violence with which Beethoven interrupts his movement – the sudden, forcible contrast between four voices with the orchestra fortissimo and the single distant trumpet, and then the speaking voice with its literally melodramatic effect – for this was borrowed from the French *mélodrame*, the form characteristically favoured by the Revolution.

In the last scene the emphasis shifts soon from the glorifying of the Minister as the personification of Liberty to Leonora as the personification of conjugal fidelity and devotion. Here we are reminded of the old *opera seria*; for *Fidelio* ends like *Orfeo*, in a static scene of rejoicing, only Beethoven wrote German choruses instead of French ballet music. *Fidelio* stands, in fact, like its author, between two operatic worlds – between Gluck and Weber – but not only chronologically. Geographically, as it were, scenes from the French *opéra comique* or melodrama alternate with formal Italian

scenes such as Leonora's in Act I and Florestan's in Act II. It was
the combined forces of national feeling and romantic sensationalism
which enabled Weber to mould the similar heterogeneous elements
of *Der Freischütz* into an artistic whole in 1821. Beethoven in 1805
achieved unity under the spell of the revolutionary ideals of liberty
and humanistic idealism which – in the words of Romain Rolland
– were, rather than the libretto, the real French contribution to
Fidelio.

3 Beethoven in Human Terms

No hero has been more fantastically misrepresented, more assiduously idealised than Beethoven; and it is easy to understand why.

The extreme disparity between an artist's works and his personal life is still a mystery to psychologists and a stumbling-block, even an offence, to simple people; and in no case is the disparity more extreme than in Beethoven's.

His first biographer, Anton Schindler, was painfully aware of this and solved his problem simply by destroying 264 of 400 'Conversation Books' left by the composer. Like all those who knew Beethoven personally, Schindler was completely under the spell of his personality. He adopted all his hero's attitudes (even when these were manifestly illogical) and saw to it that posterity should have a portrait of the man Beethoven which tallied exactly with that demanded by the composer of the *Missa Solemnis*, the ninth symphony and the last quartets – the persecuted friend of humanity misunderstood by haughty aristocrats and boorish relations, poor and lonely and the victim in his relations with women of an unattainable ideal of purity.

This picture in its full naïveté has for some time been rejected. Beethoven has not, to my knowledge, suffered from the attentions of a 'debunking' biographer – the exact equivalent of the adolescent who, in a rage of disappointment at the discovery of his parents' humanity, rejoices to emphasise their failings and vices – but the proverbial feet of clay have long been uncovered.

Now, however, we have a truly adult portrait of the composer from two Austrian writers, psychologists by profession and trained musicians as well (*Beethoven and His Nephew*, by Richard and Editha Sterba), who have taken great pains to investigate what has hitherto been the most mysterious, and they now show to be the most important emotional relationship in his life.

Their first task was to establish, as far as the scanty evidence makes possible, the character of Beethoven's relationship to his parents and two brothers. They have not found it difficult to show that he was bullied by a father whom he despised; and they find in this fact the explanation of his rebelliousness, his violently aggressive attitude to authority in any form, even when that authority was demonstrably just or took his side.

The relationship with his mother is much less easy to establish; but that it was negative and unhappy is suggested by his violent misogyny and the fact that his erotic relationships were exclusively with women whose unattainability seems to have been part of their attraction. In the famous 'Immortal Beloved' letter, the authors point out, it is the composer who insists on parting and renunciation. Was the letter, in any case, ever sent?

All Beethoven's affection, and a large surplus of his unsatisfied erotic feelings, seem to have been centred on his two commonplace and rather unprepossessing brothers. This was noticed as strange even by his contemporary admirers, who were embarrassed by the alternation between demonstrative affection and bitter hostility in his attitude to both Karl and Johann.

His affection was violently possessive and turned to hatred when the brothers married, but this hatred was nothing in comparison with his insane persecution of their wives, who became the chief objects of his misogyny. Since he was well known in Vienna and had powerful friends, whom he completely dominated emotionally, he was able to enlist the authority of the law on his side and, in the case of Karl's wife, to rob her in effect of her child.

Dr and Mrs Sterba find in Beethoven's obsessive attachment to this nephew, which lasted from 1815 until the composer's death, the characteristics of motherhood rather than fatherhood; and this point of psycho-analytical detail is not wholly convincing to the layman, though it is skilfully woven into the theory that 'the polarity between the male and female principle' was the strongest incentive to his creative activity.

The stormy history of this relationship has been traced in the greatest detail through the 'Conversation Books', legal documents and the accounts of contemporaries; and it forms the most pathetic document of the destructive effects of jealousy.

Beethoven invariably quarrelled with anyone of any age or either sex for whom Karl showed the smallest affection. He did his best to instil in the child dislike and distrust of his mother, an easy-going and amazingly long-suffering woman who retained her son's affection in spite of everything and was rewarded by ceaseless persecution at the hands of Beethoven, who called her 'the Queen of the Night', plainly casting himself for the role of the benign, all-knowing Sarastro. Dr and Mrs Sterba make it abundantly clear that Karl's attempted suicide was the direct result of Beethoven's cruel harrying and emotional blackmail; and after that crisis and the resulting change in Karl's attitude to his uncle, Beethoven never recovered, dying within a year.

The day on which a child realises for the first time that his parents are human beings, with no unique powers or virtues and no immunity from the most trivial and unheroic failings, is the day on which he ceases to be wholly a child.

But although this is a universal experience in the life of the individual, society has only recently begun to realise that its heroes and 'great men' are in fact as truly human as the parents whose role they in a sense take over in adult consciousness.

To the ordinary layman it is absolutely inconceivable that these years of legal wrangling, petty jealousies, pettier household economies (unnecessary, for Beethoven was not really poor at this time), spying and quarrelling were in fact the same years in which the *Missa Solemnis*, the ninth symphony and the last string quartets were written.

The authors of this book never for one moment undermine our admiration of Beethoven's music, but they administer a very strong and bitter dose to our childish love of idealisation. It is a wholly healthy dose, but I suspect that there will be some wry faces and bitter protests from those who still prefer historical truth liberally diluted with sugar. The hagiographical instinct has nowhere shown itself stronger than in the records of Beethoven's relationships with women. Here, too, the believers in a romantically wronged and misunderstood superman have received a rude shock from the thirteen hitherto unknown letters from Beethoven to the Countess Josephine von Deym recently published with a commentary by Dr Joseph Schmidt-Görg.

All but one of the letters are undated, but we know the exact period at which they were written – from the summer of 1804 to the autumn of 1807 – and in many cases internal evidence makes it possible to establish their order and approximate dates.

Josephine von Brunswick was born in 1779, and was thus nine years younger than Beethoven. She was a younger sister of that Therese von Brunswick whom Thayer believed to be the 'immortal beloved' and of Franz von Brunswick, to whom the 'Appassionata' sonata was dedicated, as well as a cousin of Giulietta Guicciardi. Beethoven met her first in May 1799, a few months before her marriage to the middle-aged Count Deym, who died in 1804, leaving her with three children and a fourth born shortly after his death. Both Therese and Josephine were Beethoven's pupils, and it was perfectly natural for him to maintain a correspondence with the young widow, who spent her time between Vienna and her family's home in Hungary. But the character of the letters themselves makes it clear that this was not simply an affectionate relationship between teacher and pupil, or fashionable composer (for Beethoven was that) and music-loving young aristocrat. These are quite unambiguous love-letters, and since we have a number of Josephine's letters and other papers, it is possible to reconstruct with considerable plausibility the character of the relationship.

That Beethoven was wholly serious and indeed deeply stirred does not surprise us. All the direct evidence that we possess of his relations with women confirms his fidelity to the high principles he professed in matters of sexual morality. The obverse of this idealism is to be found in his extreme hostility to all women whom he suspected of moral laxity, and in the coarseness and violence of his behaviour towards them. What is more surprising is that Josephine herself seems seriously to have considered the possibility of marrying Beethoven. In a crucial passage in one of her letters she confesses her love for Beethoven and the 'goodness of his character', but makes it clear that she can never 'satisfy this sensual love' (*diese sinnliche Liebe befriedigen*). 'I should be obliged to do violence to sacred bonds, were I to listen to your entreaties.'

Since Josephine was a widow during all the years of this correspondence and both her social position and Beethoven's principles make it extremely improbable that he was asking her to become his mistress, these 'sacred bonds' can only refer to some other ties. These were almost certainly her children, to whom a marriage with Beethoven might not have proved advantageous. When she did eventually remarry, it was to the Baltic Baron von Stackelberg, who was educating her children successfully and seems to have made marriage the condition of continuing his work as tutor.

Josephine's papers show that she was a serious and deeply idealistic young woman, with very high ethical standards, and perhaps too strong an inclination to self-sacrifice. On Beethoven's side we find the same protestations of ideal and undying love that we know from his other letters to women, and also the same insistence on his own suffering, the same fatalistic attitude which almost seems to conceal a wish that the whole affair should come to nothing. There is pride in his refusal to be kept waiting by her servants when he visits her, and rage with those of her circle who were plainly afraid of her marriage to a commoner, even a commoner of genius.

Dr Schmidt-Görg points out that Beethoven's passion for Josephine was contemporary with his work on *Fidelio*, and it is more than possible that the character of Leonora, in which the desire for self-sacrifice is the predominant trait, was connected in the composer's mind with her. The reference in one letter to her having 'renewed his ties with life' is almost certainly to the despair which overcame him in the autumn of 1802, when he first took full and conscious stock of the fact of his deafness. Was it the ever-recurrent realisation of this crippling and humiliating handicap that caused Beethoven always to acquiesce, often it seems with relief, in the failure of his marriage projects? Certainly Josephine von Deym could have understood the agony of mind expressed in the Heiligenstadt Testament very much better than Beethoven's brothers to whom it was addressed. But did he perhaps realise that the sympathy of a tender-hearted and idealistic woman for a deaf

genius, even an unbounded admiration of his character and works
was no foundation for the only marriage that he could envisage, a
passionate union of equals in which pity could have no part whatever? It may be so, and that the Promethean pride which attracted
women to Beethoven also prevented him from ever forming more
than a tentative and unhappy connection with any of them.

Certainly the complaints in these letters are without exception
those of wounded pride rather than of passionate devotion unre-
ciprocated. 'Believe me, my suffering is much greater than yours –
much, much greater,' he writes. 'I cannot express to you how
deeply wounding it is for me, with my inner consciousness of
having sacrificed so much for virtue and duty, to be placed on a
level with wretched creatures, even in thought or the sligthest
suspicion.'

Like any other woman, Josephine could not bear to let her
admirer go, even when she had decided against marrying him, and
her last letter has a coquettish note that was not lost on Beethoven.
After asking after his health and happiness, she goes on 'or does
my friend Beethoven (may I call you that?) think that I have
changed?'

'Thank you,' he wrote with unusually fine irony, 'for still wishing
to appear not to have forgotten me even if this is largely at the
prompting of others. You ask me to tell you how I am. You could
not have put a more difficult question, and I prefer to leave it
unanswered rather than to answer it too truthfully.'

No further internal evidence is needed to date this as the last
letter of the correspondence.

4 Carl Maria von Weber

No universally acknowledged 'great' composer of the last century is represented in the modern repertory by so few works as Weber, and few composers so narrowly escaped failure to find themselves eventually counted among the immortals. All composers, all artists indeed, pay a certain tribute to the fashions of their day; and many cast their finest inspirations in forms which never achieve permanent or universal validity. Bach, Handel, Mozart and Beethoven could write music as ephemeral as the film-music of today, and the music of some of the greatest operatic composers – Monteverdi, Handel, Lully or Gluck – has frequently aged with the form in which they cast it. But Weber is unique in having achieved a position among the great although *all* his work is open to one or other of these main objections. He wrote a mass of songs and chamber-music, almost all 'occasional' or designed for brilliant display; and the best of himself he poured into his stage music and into two operas, one of which is – in the words of Alfred Einstein – 'subject to ridicule on every stage except the German', while the other is burdened with a libretto which would sink the music of even the greatest genius. And yet Weber is not a figure of merely historical or local importance. His best music has unique qualities which are still recognised today, and universally recognised, so that we ask ourselves what he might not have achieved if his life had been different while it lasted and if it had not ended at forty.

IM E

Carl Maria von Weber – the 'von' a pathetic fabrication of his ludicrous father – was born sixteen years after Beethoven, in 1786, and he died a year earlier, in 1826. This father (uncle of Mozart's wife) was a crazy, stage-struck beau with fantastic ideas of his social status, who insisted on dragging his family from one petty German court to another and his youngest son, Carl, from teacher to teacher, in the hope of turning him into an infant prodigy. As if this unsettled life were not enough to ruin the young Weber, his father's plans went near to succeeding and Carl Maria found himself a theatrical conductor at eighteen, and something very near a hack composer. His musical career was variegated with attempts to make a fortune by lithography (which nearly cost him his life when he drank nitric acid by mistake) and by a spell as comptroller of the household to a dissolute duke at the court of his even more dissolute brother, the King of Württemberg. This ended in imprisonment and then banishment and a return to music as a profession, to restless journeyings up and down Germany and eventually to conductorships at Prague and, for the last eight years of his life, at Dresden.

This episodic, flashy existence was that of a hundred minor composers of the late eighteenth and early nineteenth century. But in Weber's case a kind of glamour was cast over it by his personality. It was not only his romantic excesses in wine and women, his poisoning, his imprisonment, his consumption and early death that made him an early type of the new 'romantic' artist of the nineteenth century. Unlike the little court-composers and theatrical conductors of the eighteenth century, whom he resembled in the exterior course of his life, Weber was never content to be simply a musical tradesman, a craftsman. Indeed an absence of solid craftsmanship from his work earned him the contempt or disapproval of Beethoven and Schubert, it accounts for Grillparzer's blank misunderstanding of him and Goethe's snobbish disregard. But, in exchange, Weber's determination to be something more than a mere musician, to be a poet in sounds as well as a literary artist and a German patriot too, gives the best of his music a penetrating intensity and a freshness whose bloom never faded even when its novelty passed. It was this quality which caused Berlioz to idolise Weber and made first his old friend Meyerbeer and then, supremely, Wagner flatter his memory in the sincerest of all ways, by imitation.

The Abbé Vogler, Weber's chief teacher, has been described as 'one of the most devastating of musical humbugs'. He had been a great traveller, reaching not only Spain, Portugal, Greece and Africa, but even, it is said, Armenia and Greenland. He made experiments in organ-building, developed a system of harmony based on acoustics, composed a Swedish opera and a Paradigm of the Ecclesiastical Modes (whatever that may mean) and wrote a small library of theoretical books. One attributed to him (and certainly its title suggests the author) is an *Ästhetisch-kritische Zergliederung des wesentlich vierstimmigen Singesatzes des vom Knecht in Musik gesetzten ersten Psalms* – or 'An aesthetic-critical dissection of the real four-part writing in Knecht's setting of Psalm 1'. His appearance was described as that of 'a large, fat ape'. Not, in fact, a teacher to inspire confidence, possibly in great part a charlatan; and yet two of the pupils of his old age at Darmstadt, Weber and Jakob Beer (later to be known as Giacomo Meyerbeer) made operatic history, and cherished the kindliest and most reverential memories of their old master. Already at Darmstadt Weber dreamed of the creation of a real German opera, comparable with the opera of Italy and France, not simply the humble, popular *Singspiel*; and when Meyerbeer achieved his first successes in Italy, with operas modelled on Rossini, his former friend wrote a sad letter of remonstrance, reminding him of their old ideals and, with no corresponding success of his own to show (for *Der Freischütz* was not yet written), still pleading for loyalty to the cause of German opera.

It was as a German patriot outraged by Napoleon's defeat and humiliation of his country that Weber first became known to the general public. Beside being something of a virtuoso as a pianist, Weber played the guitar and accompanied himself in his own compositions. Many of these were Italian canzonettas, and Weber's singing was one of his social assets rather than a serious musical activity. But when, after the dark days of Napoleon's victories, he set to music young Theodore Körner's patriotic songs, Weber's fame spread beyond musical circles. Körner was killed in the battle of Gadebusch at the age of twenty-two and his name and verses were thus lent something of the heroic glamour which attached to

those of Julian Grenfell or Patrick Shaw-Stuart after the 1914-18
War. Weber's music in these *Lyre and Sword* songs looks back to
the songs of Gluck rather than forward to those of Schubert; but
his *Prayer during Battle* and *Lützow's Wild Hunt* achieved a popularity with successive generations of young Germans and it was to
copy out the *Hunt* that Wagner bought his first music-paper. The
folk-song element – the other vein of originality in Weber's songs
– found its fullest expression, of course, in *Der Freischütz* and in
the songs it is still a quaint flavour rather than a deliberately
pursued aesthetic policy.

Again and again we find this primacy of the theatrical in everything that Weber wrote. It is more than the expression of a dramatic
temperament. The theatre and theatrical life were in Weber's
blood, and it is difficult to say whether his unfaltering choice of
the 'brilliant' and the 'effective' was conscious or, as I think more
probable, instinctive and natural, at least by what we call 'second'
nature. Meyerbeer we know to have been quite deliberate in his
theatrical effects, but it is possible that both he and Weber were
not simply fulfilling a demand of the fashion of the age but were
also carrying on something which they had learned, perhaps by
example rather than precept, from old Vogler, whose whole existence smacked of the theatre. The very forms of Weber's instrumental music often reflects the flashy, episodic nature of the talent
which he expended upon them. There are too many 'grand' variations or pot-pourris, rondos and romances are too often Hungarian
or Sicilian, moments are 'capricious' and polonaises unfailingly
'brilliant', while empty-headed variations (exclusively melodic) and
concertos for individual players are in disproportionate abundance.
Out of all this occasional or 'social' music a few pieces stand out
and have survived, but each of them bears serious blemishes. Take
the four piano sonatas. In an autobiographical sketch Weber
speaks of 'these accursed keyboard fingers which, by dint of ever-
lasting practice, at last acquire a kind of independence, a wilful
reason of their own and are unconscious tyrants and despots of
our creative forces'. And so we find them. Again and again the
thread of genuine musical thought and feeling is interrupted by
pure finger-juggling, rocketing scale or arpeggio figures, lavishly
ornamented tonic-dominant see-saw or 'brilliant' dotted rhythms

supporting a poor, conventionally operatic melody. Sometimes extraneous interest is provided, rather as in Meyerbeer's operas where each act has a revue-like sequence of 'novelties'. Thus the last movement of Weber's first piano sonata is a moto perpetuo, the second has a Menuetto capriccioso and the fourth a tarantella finale. Compare even the best – no. 2 in A flat – not with a Beethoven piano sonata, but with Schubert, and though Weber has poetic ideas, it is impossible not to feel the inferiority of his whole approach – glittering, superficial and 'social', the *style galant* of the restored monarchies of Europe, a Congress-of-Vienna style. Even in the Concertstück the deeply expressive opening gives place first to the rather too easily raised storm of the *Allegro passionato*, with its interminable dominant seventh arpeggios; and then in the interests of the 'programme' first to the naïvetés of the C major march and finally to the empty finger-music of the *Presto assai*.

The Concertstück was one of the youthful Liszt's earliest battle-horses and Mendelssohn included it (with the *Invitation to the Dance* and the C major Polonaise) when he played to Goethe on 24 May, 1830. How vivid an impression it made on Mendelssohn's own piano style can be seen from two works, both dating from 1832 – the G minor piano concerto and the *Capriccio brillante* for piano and orchestra. Schumann showed in *Carnaval* that he knew the Menuetto capriccioso of the first piano sonata and, in general, it may be said that Weber's piano style formed the foundation of much of the 'brilliant' piano writing of the next generation. But, whereas Weber too often exploited brilliance for its own sake, Schumann and Liszt made it the vehicle of a new poetry and only Mendelssohn's lesser piano works continue the Weber tradition unaltered.

The *Invitation to the Dance*, far less essentially pianistic in character, is really a miniature symphonic poem (Weber himself provided a very nearly phrase-to-phrase programme) and it has lived in Berlioz's orchestration rather than in Weber's piano original. Its origin lay in one of those polite musical parlour games with which Weber amused his dilettante patrons – sitting at the piano and improvising musical illustrations to scenes or tales suggested to him by members of his drawing-room audience. In fact the *Invitation* is the first of a series of 'apotheoses of the valse' which ended (we may now be permitted to hope) with Ravel's *La Valse* almost exactly a hundred years later.

To look for Weber's true physiognomy in his instrumental music is tantamount to looking for a poet to reveal himself in the small talk, however brilliant and occasionally profound, with which he may grace a cocktail party. If it is in his poems that we look for the poet, it is in his operas that we must look for Weber. It was there, in the opera, that every circumstance of his life and every trait of his character, inherited or acquired, would lead us to expect him to reveal himself. And yet, even here, what a disappointment at first sight! Of ten operatic embryos the first two have disappeared (Weber once said to Schubert that a composer's earliest operas were like puppies: they should be drowned) while the third and fourth exist only in isolated numbers. In *Silvana* there are only occasional hints of the mature Weber's style and *Abu Hassan*, light-handed and witty as it is, still belongs essentially to the eighteenth century. *Die drei Pintos* exists only in fragments. . . . All that remains is *Der Freischütz*, a single masterpiece; *Euryanthe* – potentially Weber's greatest music but indissolubly wedded to a nonsensical libretto; and *Oberon*, a hastily written work, a cross between romantic rescue-opera and fairy play, only remembered for its magnificent overture which is perhaps Weber's greatest single achievement, some fairy music and one big dramatic scene for soprano. It is really with this ill-assorted and patchy baggage that Weber has won immortality.

The historical importance of *Der Freischütz* in the development of German opera can hardly be exaggerated. Here, out of French melodrama and romance, Italian bel canto and German folk-song Weber succeeded in creating what Mozart had adumbrated in *The Magic Flute* and Beethoven (using the same ingredients) had hardly bothered to achieve in *Fidelio* – a full-scale German opera, with the same direct appeal to national sentiment as Verdi, Glinka and Smetana were to sound in their different countries. The spoken dialogue and the plain humour of the old *Singspiel* are still there and so are the stock characters – a timid, modest Virtue wooed by Youth, handsome but weak and led to the verge of ruin by fair-spoken Villainy: the flighty soubrette, the Pious Hermit and the Just Prince. But surrounding them, as never before, and casting a warm, new light over their familiar features is the atmosphere of the unmistakably German countryside, suggested by Weber not only in dances and choruses originating in German folk-music but in the romantic forthrightness and simplicity of the characters. Each of these reflects in a different way that idealising of the national character which every nation loves to find in its popular art. For *Freischütz* was immediately, as it has remained, a great popular work. It was thinking of *Freischütz* that Wagner, addressing Weber's spirit, cried: 'Today the Briton does you justice, the Frenchman admires you, but only the German can love you; you are his, a beautiful day in his life, a fragment of his heart.' Or a latter-day nationalist like Hans Pfitzner could compare Weber's 'national mission' with that of Luther or Bismarck. We may leave such extravagant outbursts to those whom they may concern, among whom Weber is not to be found. Non-Germans may miss some of the overtones of Weber's music, but they will find the same melodic power, the same freshness of orchestral colour, the same magic rehabilitation of familiar forms as delighted Berlioz. With Berlioz we may agree that Weber's supreme gift is instrumental rather than vocal and that where, for example, he entrusts a melody on one occasion to a member of the orchestra (most probably his favourite clarinet) and on another to the voice, it is the instrumental singer whom Weber favours. To take a single example, it is the clarinet in the overture that we remember, not Max in the Wolfschlucht, when we hear that most magical of melodies rising over the boiling tremolando of the strings.

In *Freischütz* Weber found the only coherent and truly musical libretto of his life. Its naïve horrors and naïver pleasures are as real and as valid within their own universe as the naïvetés of Haydn's *Creation*. But in *Euryanthe* Weber was confronted with the wholly unreal cardboard figures of a fourth-rate lady novelist's imagination. Here are the absurdities of *Robert the Devil* and *Lohengrin* in all their unredeemed crudity, and in fact both Meyerbeer and Wagner used the music of Weber's *Euryanthe* as a quarry. If there is truth in the old quip that *Rienzi* is Meyerbeer's best opera, it might with equal truth be said that *Lohengrin* is Weber's. How Weber, the first of the literary-minded musicians of the nineteenth century and himself a writer, ever came to accept Helmine von Chézy's libretto is a mystery; and the fact that, hotch-potch as it is, *Euryanthe* contains some of Weber's finest music is a proof of how easily ignited, how deeply saturated with musical ideas he was. Mediaeval chivalry attracted him, as the gipsy and oriental worlds had attracted him, by its remoteness and also by the dramatic possibilities in the extravagant contrast between radiant virtue and blackest vice. There is no hint of symphonic thinking in the concerted numbers of *Euryanthe*, any more than in any other work of Weber; and yet it was the suggestion of a new balance between music and drama which so excited Wagner in this score. Take only the purely instrumental poetry of the mysterious muted passage in the overture, or the introduction to Act II, where the orchestra speaks – as later in Wagner – with greater eloquence than any singer.

Euryanthe served as a kind of trailer or prospectus for some of the most effective scenes in nineteenth-century opera – the finale of Act II, with the heroine unjustly accused and humiliated in a huge public scene, looks forward to *Traviata* and *Otello*, through Meyerbeer and Halévy; Lysiart and Eglantine closely foreshadow Friedrich von Telramund and Ortrude and the hunting horns in Act III contain a hint of Tristan. In *Oberon*, written when Weber was dying, the poetry of orchestral colour far outweighs any other element in the music. The fairy horn-call, the gossamer patterns of the wood-wind, the distant trumpet fanfare, the warmth of the divided cellos, and the velvet softness of the clarinet melody alternating with the idealised theatrical bustle of the strings and their own passionate melody – all these in the overture steal the thunder of the rest of the piece. Even Rezia's 'Ocean, thou mighty monster' culminates in a melody which the strings have already sung far better than any soprano can sing it, for the simple reason that it is an instrumental, not a vocal melody. Rezia's greeting of the sunrise contains the germ of Brünnhilde's awakening at the end of *Siegfried*. We can even find the Sword motive and Isolde waving her scarf to Tristan, in this scene. In fact Weber stands behind the young Wagner, not only as a musical model but as an inspiration, a living reminder of the potential greatness of German opera.

Anyone insensible to the particular quality of Weber's early romantic charm might claim, with some show of justice, that he did nothing but what was better done by his successors – might reasonably counter *Freischütz* with *The Bartered Bride*, *Euryanthe* with *Lohengrin* and the fairy music of *Oberon* with Mendelssohn's *Midsummer Night's Dream*: the piano music with that of Schumann, Liszt and Mendelssohn: and the songs with those of any of the great Lieder writers. But such a critic would show himself a poor judge of musical character, for Weber's melody and the colour and texture of his orchestral writing have unmistakable personality. It is this that ensures him his place among the immortals even if, in Alfred Einstein's words 'in the semicircle that holds the niches of Bach and Handel, Haydn and Mozart, Beethoven and Schubert there should at least be distinctions in the size of the heads' and Weber's be smaller than the rest. Yet, we do not love people for the size of their heads and Weber's ill, eager face with its hectic, melancholy smile will never lack friends and admirers.

5 Giacomo Meyerbeer

A hundred years after Meyerbeer's death his name can be read a hundred times in the pages of opera-histories for every single time that it appears on the hoardings outside an opera-house. It is, indeed, a name generally dishonoured among musicians, though more by vague generalisation than by detailed criticism. The aesthetic canons of today are as different as possible from those of the French 'Grand Opera', which Meyerbeer stabilised and perfected, if he did not invent; and although those canons in many ways resemble those of late seventeenth-century Italian opera – which laid quite as much emphasis on the spectacular element – the French 1830's have decidedly less historical interest for scholars. And so historians are usually content to saddle Meyerbeer with the responsibility for the most conventional passages in the early or middle works of Wagner, Verdi and Bizet without a thought of how this convention was first formed and then came to be accepted by men of such intrinsic originality. Every age numbers some Meyerbeers among its most admired composers – artists, I mean, who will be remembered less for their own works than for the influence they exercised on their successors, for having created the convention which provided the starting-point of new discoveries.

Meyerbeer was a cosmopolitan, and this accounted for much of his music's popularity during his lifetime and for its disappearance so soon after his death. Like Handel, he was German by birth and Italian by early adoption and training, yet eventually exercised his

mature powers in still another country, whose traditions and tastes
played a large part in determining his mature style. By 1864, when
he died, national self-consciousness was already strong in the music
of Wagner, in the then Bohemia, and in Russia; and six years later
the Franco-Prussian war stirred a wave of this same nationalist
feeling even in France, where Meyerbeer's music had been most
admired and performed. Meyerbeer disappeared from pre-eminence
with the Second Empire, and Western Europe was not to acclaim
another cosmopolitan composer until Igor Stravinsky's Russian-
French-American career came to repeat the pattern laid down by
Handel and by Meyerbeer.

The world into which Meyerbeer was born – on either 5 or
23 September, 1791 (accounts vary) – was that which also produced in the same generation the poet Heinrich Heine and, less
than twenty years later, Felix Mendelssohn. Meyerbeer's father,
Jakob Herz Beer – a member of a Jewish banking family in Frank-
furt – had established himself in Berlin, where he married Amalie
Wulf, daughter of another successful Jewish business house, with
many international connections and a strong interest in the arts.
As the eldest of four sons in a rich and cultivated family, Jakob,
who later added 'Meyer' to his name at the request of an uncle, was
given every encouragement, including the best teachers available,
when he showed his remarkable musical gifts. He studied the piano
with Franz Lauska – not with Clementi, as Grove states, though
Lauska himself may well have been a Clementi pupil – and composition with Zelter, the friend of Goethe who was also to be
Mendelssohn's teacher; and with Bernhard Anselm Weber. This
Weber – no relation of Carl Maria – was a friend of the famous or
notorious Abbé Vogler with whom he toured as a pianist, and he
had profited during a stay in Vienna from the friendship and advice
of Salieri, the rival of Mozart and the friend of Haydn and Beethoven. Before Meyerbeer was twenty, therefore, he was in contact,
direct or indirect, with most of the distinguished musicians in the
northern and central European musical world. When in 1810, on
his master Weber's advice, he was sent to Darmstadt to study with
Vogler himself, he found as one of his fellow-pupils his contemporary Carl Maria Weber, who was to play so important a part in
the eventual creation of German opera. Meyerbeer, already a highly

gifted pianist, here continued his studies in composition which issued, after two years, in some settings of Klopstock, and an oratorio entitled *God and Nature*, which was performed at Darmstadt and obtained him the position of court-composer to the Duke. But he was already attracted to the opera, and it was the failure of this first attempt in this field – the biblical *Jephtha's Vow* given at Munich in 1812 – and the comparative success of his comedy, *Host and Guest* at Stuttgart the following year that proved turning points in his career. The music of *Jephtha* is blameless and dull, but *Host and Guest* – aided no doubt by Meyerbeer's excellent connections and long purse – was accepted for production in 1813 at the Kärntnerthor Theatre in Vienna, where Meyerbeer went to oversee its preparation and also to make an appearance as a pianist.

The account in his letters of his journey down the Danube by steamer, delayed only by the bad weather and a truly extraordinary number of amorous adventures, shows Meyerbeer at twenty-two gifted, handsome, rich, ambitious and lacking only a sense of direction – the lack that was, in a sense, to be his undoing all along. Meanwhile, however, a concert of Hummel's which he attended the evening he arrived in Vienna, made such an impression on him that he set aside the first months of his stay in Vienna to re-fashioning his own technique. His recital, when it took place, won him golden opinions, among others those of Moscheles, and there is little doubt that Meyerbeer could have made a career as a concert pianist. His opera, on the other hand, was a failure; and he seems to have felt a musical provincial in Vienna – a general sense of humiliation that was objectified on the famous occasion (which we have no reason for believing apocryphal) when he played the bass drum in a performance of Beethoven's *Battle of Vittoria* and was pulled up by the composer with the harsh but shrewd comment that 'he never had the guts to come in properly at the right time'.

It may well have been to escape this feeling of failure that on leaving Vienna, Meyerbeer paid his first visit to Paris. Very little is known of these months spent in Paris during 1815, but there can be no doubt that his impressions of the Bourbon Restoration and of the Spontini régime at the Opéra further stimulated his ambition. Nevertheless he was still, beneath his sophistication, a puzzled and undecided youth and something of a chameleon; and Salieri's advice to him in Vienna – to go to Italy and study opera in its home country – easily persuaded him. Italian music in the spring of 1816 meant Rossini; and forty years later Meyerbeer was to remember the enchantments of those first months:

> I was attracted (he wrote to Dr Schucht) quite independently of my will, by these delicate meshes of sound [Rossini's music, that is]. I seemed to be imprisoned in a magic park from which I neither could nor would escape. All my faculties, all my thoughts were becoming Italian; after I had lived there a year I felt like an Italian born. . . . That so complete a transformation of my inner life should have the most essential influence on my style of composition may be readily understood. I did not wish, as people imagine, to imitate Rossini or to write in the Italian manner, but I was obliged to compose in the style that I adopted *because my state of mind compelled me to do so.*

Meyerbeer's 'state of mind' was, indeed, a stronger factor than either his musical character or his musical convictions – both of which were weak – and between 1817 and 1824 he wrote six operas indistinguishable from those of any Rossini-imitator and correspondingly popular in Padua, Turin, Venice and Milan where they were given. His old friend C. M. Weber, who had confided in Meyerbeer his hopes for a national German opera, was heartbroken and wrote frankly: 'It makes my heart bleed to see a composer of creative ability stoop to become an imitator *in order to win the favour of the crowd.*' The accusation coming so early in Meyerbeer's career and from so sincere a friend, is significant.

Before the last, and certainly the most interesting, of these Italian operas – *Il Crociato in Egitto*, given in Venice in 1824 – Meyerbeer returned for a short time to Berlin; but his ambition, only temporarily satisfied by what were after all the merely provincial successes that he had enjoyed in Italy, prompted him to return to Paris; and in the event it was Rossini himself who made this possible, by offering to stage *Il Crociato* at the Théâtre Louvois. Without the castrato Velluti, the last of his kind, for whom Meyerbeer had written a principal part, *Il Crociato* was not a success in Paris; but Meyerbeer's time there was crucial because during it he met the librettist Eugène Scribe, who had already started his immensely successful collaboration with Auber. When Meyerbeer returned in 1826 to Berlin, to his father's death-bed, he took with him the first draft of what was, five years later, to be *Robert le Diable*. This was announced as early as May 1827 as 'a comic opera in three acts'. But the next years were to be filled for Meyerbeer with too many personal events for him to devote much time to composition. Soon after his father's death he married his cousin, Minna Mosson, and the death of his boyhood friend C. M. Weber in 1826 was followed in tragically quick succession by the deaths of the first two children that Minna Meyerbeer bore. And so it was not until 1830 that Meyerbeer returned to Paris with the completed score of *Robert*. Its performance was postponed first by the July Revolution and secondly by the composer's unexampled demands in the way of rehearsals, which lasted for five months. For Meyerbeer, at nearly forty, had had enough of qualified successes and was determined to leave no detail to chance, no effect unconsidered either in the music or the production. It may be that his domestic tragedy – so like that which Verdi suffered in his first marriage – had broken Meyerbeer's nerve; but there is no doubt that, for whatever reason, he had already developed many traits of that anxiety neurosis which was to haunt him for the rest of his life and to embitter even his greatest successes. Pathologically shy and nervous, he spent such money as did not go on subsidising production of his works, in the purchase of privacy, eventually developing such a horror of being buried alive that he left instructions that he was not to be buried for several days after his death and that bells were to be attached to his hands and his feet. His pursuit of popular success may be regarded as another facet of this desire for reassurance.

If I have so far dealt in some detail with Meyerbeer's life, it is in order to show what were the musical influences to which he was exposed as a young and impressionable man, and to search for any indications of how we should explain the character of the four big operas which engaged him for the remaining thirty years of his life and form the basis of his reputation. Although solidly grounded by Zelter and Bernhard Anselm Weber, he had turned instinctively to the more liberal and adventurous harmonic teaching of the Abbé

Vogler. This permitted a then unexampled freedom in the use of chords of the seventh, ninth and eleventh on any degree of the scale, without modulation, and even countenanced chromatic alterations of these chords and their inversions. There was more than a streak of the charlatan in the old Abbé, who indulged in mystifications and exotic experiments of doubtful artistic character in his organ recitals – thunder storms, the 'Fall of Jericho' or 'variations on a Hottentot theme' – and even in his compositions. The fact that these mild charlatanries impressed the public and increased Vogler's reputation was certainly not lost on so bright-witted and ambitious a boy as Meyerbeer.

His sense of failure when he first competed in the international musical arena at Vienna and his easy successes in Italy, as little more than a pasticheur of Rossini, had combined to make him cynical about the public, whose approval he nevertheless craved, with all that instinctive, illogical craving that can afflict a natural 'insider' who by the mere accident of birth finds himself marked from the start as an 'outsider'. This was in fact the position of every member of the Jewish community, and it must be borne in mind, whether we are seeking to explain Mendelssohn's wonderfully successful, apparently instinctive conformism, Heine's exhibitionist aggressiveness, or Meyerbeer's anxious but indomitable determination to bribe his way out of the golden ghetto into which he was born.

It happened that events in Paris provided him with just the opportunity that he needed, at exactly the right moment in his career. The last superintendent of the Parisian theatres before the July Revolution was a certain Vicomte Sosthène de la Roche-foucauld, immortalised by Théophile Gautier as 'the unfortunate and virginal viscount who lengthened the skirts of the dancers at the Opéra and with his own patrician hands applied a modest plaster to the middle regions of all the statues'. His régime was not unnaturally a financial disaster for the Opéra, despite two enormously successful productions, Auber's *Muette de Portici* (or *Masaniello*) in 1828 and Rossini's *William Tell* in 1829. The first artistic concern of the new régime of Louis Philippe was to ensure the Opéra's solvency; and its administration was therefore, for the first time, entrusted to a 'director-entrepreneur, who shall manage it for six years at his own risk and fortune' – it was in fact farmed out for private exploitation; and the new director was frank in his aims. Dr Louis Véron had considerable experience in the fields of publicity, including journalism and medicine, and he tells us in his memoirs[1] that it was this experience, rather than any (in fact non-existent) musical qualifications, that he urged at his interview with the Minister of the Interior.

> I was permitted to explain in a few words how a brilliant and skilful direction of the Opéra might be valuable politically at the beginning of a new reign. It was desirable that the foreigner should be attracted to Paris by the fine performance of musical masterpieces, and that he should find the boxes filled with an elegant and tranquil society. The success and receipts of the Opéra should be a testimony to the government's stability.

Véron's candidature was backed by an advance of 200,000 francs from Rossini's close friend, the Spanish banker Aguado, and once successful, Véron embarked on a publicity campaign worthy of the great American art-tycoons whom he anticipated in so many other ways. His whole existence became advertising copy – 'his carriage, his horses, his dinners, even his cravats' and of course his personal relationships of all kinds. He surrounded himself with a court of influential businessmen and literary hangers-on, among whom he paid especial attention to the journalists on whom he relied for publicity and, in the event, for favourable notices. The kind of works that he was to give to the public depended, of course, on what public he wished to attract. The social upheaval following the July Revolution had brought prosperity to a new and powerful middle class – 'men of business, men in the professions, politicians seeking distraction from their daily worries and anxious to prove that money could take the place of birth'. These were in no sense connoisseurs of music, but neither were they complete Philistines. They were, however, enormously open to the appeal of what would now be called 'glamour' – the suggestion of a world of fabulous sensual delights and easy emotional excitements, of physical splendour and aristocratic magnificence all within their reach for the expenditure of a comparatively small fraction of their new-found

[1] Véron, Louis, *Mémoires d'un bourgeois de Paris*, 1856-7.

money. Véron skilfully sharpened public interest by removing the 'no admittance' sign from the stage door of the Opéra and making the Opéra balls as luxurious and as easy to attend as possible. This was the world inhabited and described by Balzac,[1] who must indeed have known it well, since he was one of the habitués of the famous *loge infernale* who were said to have had opera-glasses made 'that enlarged objects thirty-two times and from which the dancers' tights kept no secrets'.

The opera for such a public must clearly be spectacular in every way. Only lavish display of vocal and every other kind of charm would convince the aesthetically simple-minded, purse-proud bourgeois that he was getting his money's worth; and Véron already had pointers to the direction in which public taste could be exploited. Rossini had been called in to regenerate the art of singing in France as early as 1824, when he became director of the Théâtre Italien; and with the example of the great Italian singers whom he introduced to Paris, a new generation of French artists was growing up – including the sopranos Cinti-Damoreau, Maria Malibran and Dorus-Gras, the tenor Adolphe Nourrit and the bass Nicolas Levasseur. It was singers of this calibre, well qualified to deal with Rossini's spectacularly florid, yet strictly defined vocal writing, that made the success of his *Moïse*, *Comte Ory* and *William Tell* and of that most prophetic of all French operas of the 1820's – Auber's *Muette de Portici*. The revolution in the scenery and production at the Opéra, demanded by the tastes of the new public, had already been brought about by Louis Daguerre (inventor of the *daguerrotype*) who specialised in panoramic lighting-effects, Edmond Duponchel, an enthusiastic and ingenious inventor of magnificent historical sets; and Pierre Cicéri, who had even been sent by the government to a performance of Pacini's *Last Day of Pompeii* to observe La Scala's presentation of the eruption of Vesuvius, which appears also in Auber's *Muette*. Véron's chief conductor at the Opéra was the same Habeneck who took such pains with the first performances of Beethoven's symphonies in Paris, while the ballet was led by Marie Taglioni and Fanny Elssler. Véron, characteristically, economised by lowering the pay of the rank and file of the Opéra – members of the orchestra, the chorus and the corps de

---

[1] See *Gambara* (1839) and *Massimilla Doni* (1839).

ballet – but never objected to the high fees demanded by his principals.

Since Meyerbeer left Paris not long after the failure of his *Crociato* in September 1825 and did not return until 1830, he was not in fact present at the first performances of either *Muette de Portici* or *William Tell*, though he undoubtedly saw them later and knew their music. In any case he had in Eugène Scribe a friend and a collaborator who was intimately connected with the new régime at the Opéra and librettist of *La Muette*. Meyerbeer and Scribe agreed in rejecting both classical myths and already existing stage plays as operatic subjects. Scribe himself was an enormously adroit theatrical carpenter, with the eye of a lynx for the vagaries of public taste and a psychological flair for what the new theatrical public would enjoy and understand. A taste for the Gothic tale of 'mystery and imagination' which had invaded France well before the Revolution of 1789, received a new stimulus during the Restoration, when the public no longer had the exciting realities of the Napoleonic wars to occupy their imagination. The popularity of Weber's *Freischütz*, even in its mangled form as *Robin des Bois*, and Boieldieu's *Dame Blanche*, with a libretto by Scribe based on Walter Scott's *The Monastery*, are clear evidence of this taste in the opera-house. That Rossini could enjoy such a success with *Le Comte Ory*, in which Scribe parodies the whole Restoration taste for mediaeval, Walter Scottish pageantry and sentimentality, is a sure indication of how strong this taste had been. The grotesque and macabre tales of E. T. A. Hoffmann, too, which Meyerbeer doubtless knew in the original German, obtained an instantaneous success in France when they were translated. In fact the opera with which Meyerbeer returned to Paris from Berlin and which had its first performance on 21 November, 1831, after five gruelling months of rehearsal, during which Meyerbeer took advice from any member of the Opéra staff who chose to proffer it, was an extremely clever concoction designed to appeal to all these shifting currents of taste and to provide something novel and piquant into the bargain.

When Wagner later attacked Meyerbeer in his notorious pamphlet, 'Das Judenthum in der Musik', his chief charge was that, from sheer Jewish rootlessness and lack of national tradition,

Meyerbeer had for the first time made 'what the public wanted' the *primary* consideration of his operatic aesthetic – that whereas many other composers had borne popular taste in mind and allowed it to modify their musical utterances, in Meyerbeer's case this 'popularity' was the sole determining factor. It would of course be quite possible to admit this to be true of Meyerbeer – and the enormous popularity of his works with one generation, and their swift disappearance from favour when taste changed, would bear out Wagner's theory at least in part – without accepting Wagner's ridiculous generalisations about composers of Jewish origins. It is certainly quite as ridiculous to speak as though the peculiar position in which sons of rich Jewish banking-houses in Germany as Meyerbeer, Heine and Mendelssohn grew up during the first two decades of the nineteenth century had no effect at all on their characters. A ghetto is none the less a ghetto for being paved with gold and lined with bank-notes; and to find every door open to one's money except one – and that the door leading to social acceptance as an equal – is a bitter and humiliating experience that will leave no young man of spirit unmarked. Heine's whole life was a tortured shuffling between defiance and unsuccessful attempts to take on French national colour as a protection. And he showed his worst side to his own people such as Meyerbeer, from whom he accepted much-needed money to act as a kind of publicity agent, only to turn and make fun of his patron and his pretensions. Mendelssohn's apparently instinctive and flawless conformism was achieved, perhaps, by refusing to penetrate below the surface of a happy family life and a successful career; or alternatively his character and his genius may have been so well adjusted to each other, and to the purely formal demands of his art, that the impulse to confront the shadow-side of life – his own life or life in general – never appeared to him except as a symptom of illness or fatigue. Meyerbeer, on the other hand, when he came to write his *Robert le Diable* had nearly reached forty without the thirty years of 'promise' – as a young pianist, a grand ducal protégé and a local Italian operatic light – ever having been crowned by unqualified success. He was the victim of tantalisation, unsure (like many rich men) of how much he owed to his money even that measure of success that he had enjoyed, and spurred on, perhaps, by domestic tragedy to make sure once and for all of capturing the most important of all operatic publics.

When he saw the new conditions at the Paris Opéra, where money could buy everything – quality as well as quantity, lavish sets and productions as well as first class singers and endless rehearsals, and good press notices into the bargain – he recognised his chance. I think it would be unrealistic to say that he was wholly uninfluenced by an instinct – an instinct more probably than a conscious desire – to conquer the society that accepted his money but in the last resort refused him, to compensate himself for the countless occasions when he had been made to feel different, an outsider. The operas that he wrote after 1830 are the works of an obsessional would-be insider, for they contain (as Mendelssohn said with distaste after seeing *Robert*) 'something for all tastes' – and that includes trained musicians and genuine music-lovers as well as all varieties of groundling. What Mendelssohn found these operas lacked was 'a heart' – by which he meant, no doubt in the first place, a 'true German heart'. And we must remember that he, like many Germans before and since, was humiliated and affronted by French cultural pretensions and by the style and glitter of Paris, which made him feel at the same time provincial and morally superior. Meyerbeer conquered Paris by wearing a French mask, just as Lully and Gluck had done before him. There was nothing disreputable in this, or in the Italian elements of his style, which could easily be paralleled in Gluck's Paris operas. His case was, however, different from Gluck's in two important ways – first in that he was writing for an uneducated and sensation-hungry public, whereas Gluck was writing for the court and the educated middle classes; and second, that Gluck, for all his flexibility and willingness to compromise on occasion, was a man of strong basic character and convictions, whereas Meyerbeer had neither. He commanded an excellent conventional technique of composition, which meant then, as now, a great facility in imitating accepted models. What was original in his music was not its actual character but the combination of ideas borrowed from Spontini, Rossini and Auber and the theatrical effectiveness with which this combination was presented. For these operas are not primarily, still less exclusively, *musical* works; and it is unfair to Meyerbeer to judge them as such.

They are in fact what Wagner called a *Gesamtkunstwerk*, though not quite in Wagner's sense – theatrical entertainments in which stage spectacle, ballet, lighting, sets and 'machines' form quite as integral a part as singing and orchestral music. 'Musico-dramatic historical pageants' would be a clumsy but less misleading way of describing them than 'operas'; and the Baroque mythological musical entertainments given in seventeenth-century Italian courts provide the closest historical parallel.

Characteristics of Meyerbeer's mature works

The four operas on which Meyerbeer's reputation rests 1 or perhaps I should say rested – can be considered together, from the stylistic point of view. They are *Robert le Diable*, produced in 1831; *Les Huguenots*, produced in 1836; *Le Prophète*, produced in 1849; and *L'Africaine*, produced after Meyerbeer's death in 1864, in the last of several versions, revised by Fétis (the only instance to my knowledge of a composer having his work 'finished', at least in this sense, by a critic). The other works written by Meyerbeer during this last period of his life need hardly detain us, but they should perhaps be mentioned here. One of them was connected with the official post of Generalmusikdirektor in Berlin, which Meyerbeer held from 1842-9. *Ein Feldlager in Schlesien*, written for Jenny Lind deals with an imaginary incident in the life of Frederick the Great and is made the occasion for a glorification of the army. It was described by one critic as 'das typisch preussische Hoffestspiel, mit riesiger Aufmachung, militärischem Prunk, sentimentalem Hurra-patriotismus und familiärer Hohenzollernbeweihräucherung' – 'a typical Prussian court work, with giant expense, military glitter, sentimental jingoism and familiar adoration of the Hohenzollern dynasty'. Meyerbeer rewrote this work for Vienna as *Vielka* and for Paris as *L'Etoile du Nord*, in which form it was admired by Berlioz in 1854. He found it 'wonderful in point of truth, elegance and freshness of ideas. By the side of the most alluring, coquettish devices are to be found startling complications and striking touches of passionate expression.' The other minor work was also an opéra comique *Dinorah* or *Le Pardon de Ploermel*, remembered today if at all only for the 'shadow-song' beloved by an earlier generation of coloratura sopranos. *Dinorah*, however, takes us back to the first of the big four, *Robert le Diable*, where the influence of the old opéra comique is still strong.

Meyerbeer was well aware of the French middle class's attachment to their national form of opera, with its inheritance from the eighteenth century – wicked baron and virtuous milkmaid; peasant lover, also more or less virtuous but more noticeably a ninny or Sancho Panza figure; scenes from 'innocent' peasant life contrasted with the reprobate luxury of the rich; and a plentiful indulgence in primitive descriptive music – ding-dong choruses for the church bells, reapers' choruses in which they whet their scythes in the orchestra and so forth. To combine this tradition with the new historical-tableau or pageant type of opera seemed an obvious recipe for success; and Meyerbeer used it in *Robert* and again, less obviously, in *Le Prophète*.

The characters of Alice and Raimbault in *Robert* are set quite apart from the grand world of Robert, Count of Normandy and his mephistophelean protector Bertram. Alice is a Micaela, sent with a letter from his mother to reclaim Robert from his wicked ways; and Raimbault, who gets into trouble by singing a ballad about Robert the Devil, is made a butt for Bertram's grim humour – just as the cruel baron in the traditional opéra comique plays like a cat with the bumpkin whose betrothed he means to seduce (Don Giovanni and Masetto, in fact). In *Le Prophète* the situation of Berthe and Jean, the peasant lovers persecuted by the wicked Count Oberthal, is exactly that of Lucia and Renzo in Manzoni's *Promessi Sposi*. Berthe and Jean's old mother, Fidès, stand out by their simple would-be unaffected rhythms and melodies, though Meyerbeer cannot resist giving these a showy and ingenious frame.

I wanted to mention this opéra comique element in Meyerbeer before discussing the general characteristics of his chief operas because it is found only in two of them and is very often disregarded by those who write about his music as though it were simply a highly seasoned *ragoût* of Rossini and Auber. Each of the four chief operas is very long. Louis Philippe's purse-proud bourgeoisie wanted a good run for their money, and plenty in quantity as well as what they regarded as quality. Scribe, who played a very large part in determining Meyerbeer's mature style, knew his public perfectly. They were to be given five acts – with a ballet, or chief scenic attraction in Act III and the sentimental *clou* in Act IV, which must culminate in one of the monster *morceaux d'ensemble*, with chorus added – such as the blessing of the daggers before the St Bartholomew massacre in the *Huguenots* or the coronation of the prophet John in Munster Cathedral in *Le Prophète*. Act V brings the *dénouement*, with retribution for the guilty and death or quasi-apotheosis for the virtuous, and probably a transformation-scene, a spectacular and edifying death or a *deus ex machina*, as in *Les Huguenots*.

Each scene of each act provides some kind of diversion, generally visual, for the groundlings – 'something for all tastes', as Mendelssohn observed bitterly. *Robert* has an exciting gambling scene in the first act (not lost on Verdi or Massenet in *Traviata* and *Manon*); a *valse infernale* and a titillating scene of mild sadistic character between Bertram and Alice, followed by the ballet of spectral dissolute nuns, who tempt the hero; a scene in which with the magic golden bough Robert first sends the Sicilian court to sleep and then wakes them; and finally a cathedral wedding. *Huguenots* and *Prophète* go much further in such matters. *Huguenots* opens with an 'orgy' of Catholic noblemen, enlivened by Marcel's *pifpaf* imitation of a battle. This is followed by a ballet of bathing beauties and a spectacular emotional scene in Act II; Protestant rataplan chorus and Catholic litanies, gypsy dances, curfew, duel and wedding procession in Act III; blessing of daggers and love duet in Act IV; massacre and royal appearance in Act V. As the King of Prussia tartly observed of this opera 'Catholics and Protestants cut each other's throats and a Jew sets the proceedings to music'. Perhaps Meyerbeer's boldest inventions in this line were the ballet of skaters, the coronation scene, the solemn exorcism and the catastrophic final explosion in *Le Prophète*. Selika's death under the upas-tree in *L'Africaine* is a tame conclusion to such a list.

Now there is no doubt at all that one of the main interests in these great jamborees is visual, for reasons that I have already gone into. But we cannot assume simply for this reason that the music is negligible. In fact it can hardly have been that, if it was admired so much, as it was, by Berlioz, Bizet, Gounod, Verdi, Wagner and Tchaikovsky. These men all had reservations about Meyerbeer's music, but they nevertheless paid it the sincerest of all compliments – the tribute of imitation, as I hope to show.

What in fact were Meyerbeer's gifts and qualifications as a composer?

He was no great melodist – Vasco's 'O Paradis sorti de l'onde' from *L'Africaine*, always quoted as evidence of his melodic gift, is the only solo number that has really survived from all four of these operas. For the most part Meyerbeer was content either to imitate Rossini and Auber (who was often himself imitating Rossini) or to borrow the melodic forms of the opéra comique and contrast their simplicity with the Italian-style decoration of the 'grand' airs. He was, however, skilful at concealing this poverty of melodic invention, either by striking instrumental accompaniment or by strongly stressed dramatic character. A good instance of the former is Raoul's opening air in the first act of *Les Huguenots* – 'Plus blanche que la blanche hermine', which is accompanied by a single instrument and that the then unheard of *viola d'amore*. An instance of the strong dramatic character of melody masking its intrinsic poverty is Raimbault's ballade from *Robert* which Wagner plagiarised for Senta's ballad in *The Flying Dutchman*.

If Meyerbeer had no striking gift for inventing great solo melodies, such as opera has always thrived on, the same cannot be said of his ensembles and choruses, where he was supported by his remarkable harmonic sense and that ability to build up to a great dramatic climax from a single germ idea – a gift which has been compared, rather generously I think, to that of the symphonist. These great ensembles and choruses of Meyerbeer's are musically the most striking features of his operas – huge tableaux in which he may combine as many as seven principals and a large chorus, playing one body against the other like the ripieno and soloists in a concerto. One of the most striking of these is in the second act of *Les Huguenots*. The finale opens with representatives of Catholics and Protestants swearing eternal peace, at the instigation of Marguerite de Navarre, four male soloists with male chorus. The scene is introduced by pianissimo tympani (the parallel between this scene and the Prelude to *Rigoletto* cannot be fortuitous); otherwise the orchestra only plays with the chorus. The soloists sing in octave unison and then at the height of the excitement break into an unaccompanied prayer, upon which the chorus calls down heaven's blessing. This is followed immediately by Raoul's outrageous refusal of Valentine, which introduces the main body of the finale – always called by Meyerbeer 'strette', using the word in its secondary, general sense of 'bringing the accents closer together and thus producing a climax of excitement' as Grove puts it. Most magnificent of all these set-pieces, though not perhaps as strikingly unified in character as the one to which I have just referred, is the scene of the Blessing of the Daggers in Act IV. This is carried out by three monks, while the Catholic leaders stand by, and the note of fanaticism grows in the chorus as the monks move from group to group assuring them that the Catholic cause is just and that 'Dieu le veut!' – no heretic is to be spared. The dotted rhythm, and the recurring figure with which it is connected, are very characteristic of Meyerbeer, as are the theatrical alternations of the fortissimo chords of E major with pianissimo chords of A flat major – the sort of enharmonic sequence (it is not a modulation) that dazzled Meyerbeer's contemporaries. The thundering out of the E major theme in unison, with its threatening triplets was to become a commonplace (we find it as late as Verdi's *Otello*, in the duet which ends Act II), but must have made an overwhelming impression when it was first heard.

We have already referred on several occasions to Meyerbeer's harmony, and I want to say something more about this. He belongs of course – none more obviously – to what may be called the diminished-seventh school of operatic composers; but he went further than that. His harmonic boldness was, of course, strictly superficial and decorative, not in any sense organic; but it has been the rule of history that harmonic expansion has taken place by chords which were at first considered exotic or merely decorative being accepted eventually in their own right as organic; or by chords heard at first in what seemed to the ear bold succession eventually being accepted simultaneously. There is an interesting example of this in the Exorcism scene in *Le Prophète*, where Jean, having publicly denied his own mother, forces her to admit that she was mistaken in claiming him as her child. First comes a fairly obvious repetition of the same phrase mounting by semitones – (Puccini was to do the same thing on a much grander scale in *Turandot* of course). Then, while Fidès is fighting with herself, a high tremolando in the strings introduces a sequence of chords whose roots lie an augmented fourth apart. It was to be just over fifty years before Ravel dared to place those chords in even closer juxtaposition in *Jeux d'eau* and another ten after that before Stravinsky positively relished their dissonance in *Petrushka*.

A great many of Meyerbeer's most effective harmonic *coups* are dramatically placed chords of what Gerald Abraham has called the 'Russian' sixth, owing to its popularity with Russian composers – the chord of the dominant seventh on the flattened sixth of the scale. There is a spectacular use of this chord in the Cathedral scene in *Le Prophète* where it is characteristically employed to give interest to the melodically conventional solo of Fidès, the Prophet's mother. The same harmony is prominent in 'O Paradis' in *L'Africaine*. *Le Prophète* was first given in Paris in 1849, the year in which Liszt revised his A major piano concerto, which opens with exactly this progression. Whether the Russian composers were influenced by Meyerbeer (whose *Prophète* was first given there in 1852) or by Liszt's concerto would be hard to say. The most famous instance of the progression, which became a commonplace with Rimsky and Tchaikovsky, is in the letter song from *Eugene Onegin*.

Another instance of this progression in a very different context throws a slightly sinister light on Meyerbeer's influence as a harmonist. Histories of music generally blame Gounod for introducing the particularly oleaginous kind of harmony connected with the more mawkish Victorian hymn tunes; and in effect it was he who was responsible for introducing it into England in his much admired 'sacred' music – 'Redemption', 'Mors et vita', and a whole heap of 'sacred' songs. But where did he find it? There is no trace of chromatic harmony in his delicately written early works, *Philémon et Baucis* and *Sapho*. It is not until *Faust*, in 1859, that Meyerbeer's influence becomes strong in his music – in the whole character of Mephistopheles, in the church scene and the final 'apotheosis', as well as most unmistakably in the ballet. The 'Russian' sixth harmony is crucial in Faust's 'Salut, demeure chaste et pure' and again in the Jewel Song. But what are we to say when we find Vasco in *L'Africaine* actually producing what is to all intents and purposes a full-scale Victorian hymn-tune of the Gounod type, only going off the ecclesiastical rails in the excursion into Russian sixth territory. *L'Africaine* was produced in 1865 and it was in the 70's, while he was living in London as a refugee from the Franco-Prussian war, that Gounod started his infiltration of cathedral organ-lofts and provincial festivals. The poison he brought with him – if we may speak melodramatically – was, I believe, of Meyerbeer's brewing. What it became in other hands we can see from Wagner's *Tristan*, whose harmony no doubt owes something to Spohr and to Chopin, but perhaps also something to Meyerbeer. One of the crucial harmonies of the Tristan love-duet is, indeed, just this same Russian sixth again, and in the same key and position as it occurs in the central scene of *Le Prophète*.

Only slightly less important than Meyerbeer's harmony is the influence of his orchestration. Spontini was the first to introduce the characteristically Napoleonic idea of orchestral *grandiosity* for its own sake. When *La Vestale* was produced in 1807, there was a joke current in Paris about a deaf man advised by his doctor to go to a performance of this opera to cure his malady. The two men went together to the Opéra and after a particularly loud orchestral outburst the deaf man turned in delight to his neighbour: 'Doctor', he cried, 'I can hear.' But the doctor did not answer; for what had cured his patient had deafened him. The Spontini tradition was followed by Auber in his *Muette de Portici* and by Rossini in *William Tell* and was naturally accepted by Meyerbeer as part of his arsenal of 'effects' to astonish and delight his audience – or *épater le bourgeois*, as Théophile Gautier expressed it. The practice of marking each beat, or at least each strong beat in the bar, with the cymbals; the unleashing of sudden fortissimo chords of the dominant seventh in the brass; using the heavy brass to double the basses of the chorus, often with trombone triplets, or even with chords off the beat – all these are practices of Meyerbeer's which persisted at least as late as the triumph scene in *Aida* (1881) and Tchaikovsky's *Sleeping Beauty* (1889), where Carabosse's entry is pure Meyerbeer.

Meyerbeer had a special predilection for the bassoon, as Gluck had for the oboe and Weber for the clarinet, and there are countless instances in these operas where the instrument's characteristic hollow, nasal tone and somehow unwieldy agility are spot-lit. The most famous is no doubt the Anabaptist sermon at the beginning

of *Le Prophète* – the 'Ad nos ad salutarem undam' that Liszt was to
borrow for variations. The three preachers sing in octave unison
with the bassoons.

The cor anglais solo in *Robert le Diable* and Meyerbeer's frequent
use of solo tympani (as in the passage from *Les Huguenots* described above), bring us to the vexed question of the priority of
novelties in orchestration between Berlioz and Meyerbeer. The
two men were friends of a kind; Meyerbeer needed the good will
of Berlioz the critic and Berlioz admired a great deal in *Les
Huguenots* and *L'Etoile du Nord* as well as isolated features of other
works. Probably his attitude is best expressed in the letter he wrote
to his sister after the first performance of *Le Prophète* in 1849:

> I hope that Meyerbeer has the good sense not to take amiss
> the four or five reservations I put into my ten columns of praise.
> I should have liked to spare him the pain... but there are
> certain things that must absolutely be said out loud. ... I
> cannot let anyone think that I approve, or even condone, the
> compromises that *such a master* [notice that expression] makes
> in favour of the bad taste of a part of the public. ... This score
> contains some very fine things side by side with feeble and
> detestable ones. But the splendour of the *show* will win accept-
> ance for everything.

Meyerbeer probably became acquainted with the *Symphonie
Fantastique* at the time that *Robert le Diable* was being rehearsed
at the Opéra, that is to say, between June and November 1831.
The *conception* of both works is so characteristic of the mood of the
day that we do not need to suppose any further connection. Jacques
Barzun makes the non-committal, but heavily weighted observation
in a footnote that 'the opinion of those competent to judge, from
César Cui to Arthur Hervey, supports the view that Meyerbeer
drew heavily on Berlioz's melody, instrumentation and dramatic
conceptions'. Yet if we accept this, to say the least of it doubtful,
proposition, we find ourselves attempting to explain the best of
Meyerbeer in terms of Berlioz – a very difficult task – rather than
the worst of Berlioz in terms of Meyerbeer, which is very much
easier. Meyerbeer was certainly an inveterate borrower of ideas;
but all his best scenes show exactly that purely *theatrical* skill that

Berlioz never wholly achieved, or only after Meyerbeer's death, in *The Trojans*. That Meyerbeer borrowed individual ideas of orchestration is probable – the cor anglais solo in *Robert* perhaps, the echoing 'pastoral' clarinets in the prelude to *Le Prophète* almost certainly.

That Meyerbeer, or anyone else, ever 'drew heavily' on Berlioz's highly individual *melodies* seems to me out of the question. When we come to Berlioz's debt to Meyerbeer, we are confronted simply with a list of the passages in which Berlioz most nearly surrendered his individuality and conformed with the conventions of his day – the Brigands in *Harold*, Friar Lawrence's oration in *Roméo et Juliette* and the entrance of the Cardinal in *Benvenuto Cellini* are obvious examples. To recognise the immeasurable superiority of Berlioz as a composer it is not necessary to ignore, or skate over, his petty indebtedness to his contemporaries, and Meyerbeer, great eclectic though he was himself, exercised a remarkably strong and wide influence on the dramatic music written between 1835 and 1880. We have already caught Wagner cribbing from *Robert* in *The Flying Dutchman* and Verdi probably unconsciously repeating an effect from the *Huguenots* in *Rigoletto*.

Before coming to the *general* nature of that influence I should like to trace in rather more detail the scenes in which that influence is most often found, and give some familiar examples.

The *supernatural treated as a theatrical effect*, the 'demonic' or the 'angelic', the cathedral or the witches cavern, prompted a Meyerbeerian stock response. The evil chatter of the wood-wind, the tremolando strings or tympani roll, sudden fortissimo brass chords of the dominant seventh on the one hand. And on the other the harp arpeggios, the organ in a blaze of what the Germans call 'Scheinkontrapunkt' (the perfect examples of which are to be found in the prelude to the *Huguenots* and the Coronation scene in *Le Prophète*) and 'celestial' hymn-like four-part writing in the wood-wind as in *Lohengrin* – it is all very familiar. Do not let us bother with operas such as Halévy's *La Juive* and Wagner's *Rienzi*, frank imitations of Meyerbeer. But think of Elsa's wedding procession in *Lohengrin*, with Ortrud and Telramund the melodramatic embodiment of evil; of the celestial voice at the end of Act III of *Don Carlos*, where the whole scene is strongly marked by Meyerbeer's influence; of the apotheoses in *Les Pêcheurs de Perles*, *Faust* and *Mireille*, all modelled on the hymn from *Le Prophète*; of Gounod's Mephistopheles and Ourrias (in *Mireille*); the temple scenes evoked in *Pêcheurs de Perles* and actually presented in *Aida*; Berlioz's demons in the *Damnation*, Mussorgsky's satanic Jesuit Rangoni in *Boris*, and the whole confrontation of sacred and secular in Saint Saëns's *Samson et Delila* – right down to Massenet's *Thaïs* of 1894, where the climax of the ballet is a drawing-room waltz entitled 'La Perdition', directly descended from the 'Valse infernale' of *Robert*.

Another preoccupation of Meyerbeer's for which he found singularly apt expression was a certain slightly fatuous kind of *courtly elegance* – the charming frivolity of the Catholic noblemen and Marguerite de Navarre's ladies in the first act of *Les Huguenots*. The dotted rhythms, *ben marcato*, the cadences that suggest a bow or a hand-gesture, the elegant triplets and slightly affected staccato phrases all combine to evoke the courtier. There is the entry of Raoul, the hero of *Les Huguenots* – a Protestant, it is true, but sadly tainted in his manners by the deplorable example of the Catholic court. Verdi turned to this kind of music for Gustav and Oscar in *Ballo* and the Duke in *Rigoletto*, just as Bizet did for the Duke in *La Jolie Fille de Perth*; and minor French and Italian opera is full of examples.

Meyerbeer's influence is nowhere stronger on Verdi than in *Aida*, not even, I think, in the operas specially written for Paris. Verdi knew that *Aida* was to be a kind of occasional 'court' opera in the first instance; and the strong element of display suitable for the occasion prompted his return to the Meyerbeerian idiom. In one case he even borrowed an idea of Meyerbeer's. Ines's 'Adieu mon doux rivage', in which she says good-bye to Lisbon, was to recur to Verdi's mind when he made Aida think with nostalgia of her Ethiopian home.

Perhaps Amonasro is the most Meyerbeerian single character in *Aida* and his 'Su dunque! sorgete egizie coorti!' could almost have been written by Meyerbeer at his best. How strongly this affinity was felt by contemporaries is shown by Vincent d'Indy's contempt-uous dismissal of the whole of *Aida* as 'that Meyerbeero-Wagneroid bore'.

When we come to consider the wider aspects of Meyerbeer's influence on his contemporaries and the next generation, we are confronted with the difficulty of distinguishing between the composer and the spirit of the age, the *Zeitgeist*, which he so perfectly embodied. The whole romantic aesthetic of shocking, dazzling, astonishing is summed up in his work. Berlioz, who was by no means untouched by it himself, summed it up in a great tirade:

> high C's from every type of chest, bass drums, snare drums, organs, military bands, antique trumpets, tubas as big as locomotive smokestacks, bells, cannon, horses, cardinals under a canopy, emperors, queens in tiaras, funerals, fêtes, weddings . . . jugglers, skaters, choirboys, censers, monstrances, crosses, banners, processions, orgies of priests and naked women, the bull Apis and masses of oxen, screech-owls, bats, the five hundred fiends of hell and what have you – the rocking of the heavens and the end of the world, interspersed with a few dull cavatinas here and there and a large claque thrown in.

What, then, are we to say of certain aspects of Berlioz's own works – where we have a high C sharp, military bands, antique cymbals, a cardinal under a canopy, a queen on a funeral pyre and the five hundred fiends of hell? Are these the 'influence' of Meyerbeer or simply more moderate examples of the same general aesthetic as Meyerbeer's? And what are we to say of Liszt's virtuoso paraphrases, transcriptions and studies in 'transcendental' virtuosity? They are exact instrumental parallels to what Meyerbeer achieved in the theatre and were perhaps inspired by this, as well as by the example of Paganini. We happen to know what Chopin thought of *Le Prophète*, to which he dragged himself a few weeks before he died, from a note in the diary of Delacroix, who visited him the next day and spoke of Chopin's 'horror of this rhapsody'. Yet the E major middle section of the big A flat major Polonaise, with its ostinato octave figure is a comparatively quiet and tasteful example of what Liszt displayed with fewer inhibitions in *Funerailles*, and both are quite in Meyerbeer's spirit.

Have Meyerbeer's latter-day champions – Joseph Conrad, who preferred him to Wagner, Constant Lambert and Bernard van Dieren among musicians – really any case to make against the

oblivion which has in fact befallen his music? Is he in fact an
unjustly neglected composer? I should answer emphatically 'no'.
Despite some fine individual scenes and a handful of effective
rather than really powerful arias, his importance is entirely historical. I have enjoyed a grand production of *The Huguenots*, but
the production was as important as the music and that for us today
is a serious condemnation of any opera. I should not go so far as
Vaughan Williams and maintain that any music worth performing
is worth performing badly. But it is a fact of everyday experience
that the greatest music survives the most extraordinary maltreat-
ment; and as the essential quality of the music itself deteriorates,
so the quality of performance becomes more and more important.
We have only to remember what a persuasive advocate Beecham
was of second and third rate music. In the case of Meyerbeer
performance was everything. That is why he was willing to spend
limitless sums, to consult the cleaners and the claque-members
before deciding the final form of a scene; to hire the greatest singers
and to insist on the most sumptuous productions – because without
these things his works were no more than pasteboard façades, his
characters are voices rather than three-dimensional human beings.
Great men borrowed ideas from him and turned them to greater
things; that was his true destiny and nothing more.

6 Fryderik Chopin

Three great Poles have caught the imagination of the world and left their imprint clearly marked in their respective fields. At the time of the Renaissance Jan Kopernik revolutionised the science of astronomy, in the seventeenth century Jan Sobieski altered the course of European history by finally removing the threat of Turkish invasion, and one hundred years ago Fryderik Chopin ushered in a new era – a new sensibility served by a new technique – in the history of the pianoforte, and indeed of music itself. Of the three, Chopin alone has achieved a complete personal immortality, a name which is almost synonymous with Poland itself to the many who know little or nothing of the bitter complications of Polish history. His reputation has been probably less subject to the fluctuations of fashion than that of any other composer, for no serious critic has tried to impugn his perfection as an artist and even the distorted features which his cult-image has assumed have pleased the vulgar in whose likeness they have been drawn. On the other hand, no composer, except perhaps Beethoven, has suffered more cruelly at the hands of his interpreters and devotees; and unintelligent love, as always, has proved capable of inflicting wounds which no enemy, however vicious, could conceive.

Until comparatively recently even Chopin's warmest and most intelligent admirers were ready to admit that the perfection of his art was intimately linked with its restricted scope, and to claim for their hero no more than one of the first places among writers for the pianoforte. To have known and observed so scrupulously his own limitations, they would say, was but another proof of his genius; and they might feel happy that Goethe had said so, in more general and elegant terms, before them. But scholarship in the last twenty years has shown that, however restricted the field in which Chopin chose to exert himself, the boldness and novelty of his harmonic language place him in the very forefront of his contemporaries (not excluding Berlioz, Liszt or Wagner) as an innovator; and that much which appeared violently controversial when developed at length and in the large by a mammoth orchestra had been present, unrecognised because untrumpeted, in Chopin's comparatively modest piano pieces. Thomas Mann's Adrian Leverkühn, having first paid tribute to the legend of Chopin's morbidity ('the sublime incest of his fantastically delicate and seductive art'), still found that 'it surpasses in despairing beauty of sound all the *Tristan* orgies . . . without the bullfight character of a theatrical mysticism robust in its corruption'.

This unemphatic, 'hidden' quality of Chopin's genius was the more remarkable for being in complete opposition to the tendencies of the age and the place in which he lived. Although he arrived in Paris in 1831, with what we should now call a transit visa only, it was six years before he reached his ostensible destination, London, and then only for a short visit. From 1831 to his death in 1849 Chopin was never away from Paris for more than a few weeks and never really happy then, except during visits to Nohant, while his relationship with George Sand provided him with that form of family life tinged with romantic emotion which he found most congenial to composition. French artistic life has seldom been more devoid of the French qualities – logic, sobriety and balance – than in the 1830's. The musical world, it is true, was filled with foreigners, and it was Liszt, Meyerbeer and Thalberg rather than Berlioz who set the tone. But whether the artists were French or foreign, Parisian artistic life was noisily aggressive, full of the new devices of advertisement and much given to the extremes of sentiment traditionally shunned by French art, if not by French artists.

Chopin, half French and half Pole, was far more traditionally French than his noisier contemporaries. His father was a Lorrainer, but had left home at the age of sixteen and was settled in Poland from the age of seventeen to his death at seventy-three; and Chopin never visited, perhaps was not even aware of the existence of, his French relations. He was whole-heartedly a Pole, read little but Polish literature, spoke French with a Polish accent to the end of his life and was generally at his easiest and most open with his own compatriots. In his smaller works, especially the mazurkas, he drew on the memories of his boyhood, memories of actual experiences in a real Polish countryside. In his larger works the vision of an idealised Poland, intensified by his absence and the thought of her sufferings, brought out all the chivalrous nobility of his character and that mixture of sorrow, regret, resentment and repentance which the Poles call *żal* and which Liszt believed to be the fundamental emotion in Chopin's character. It was an emotion that seldom found expression in his conversation, but it appears in the entry in his diary after the fall of Warsaw to the Russians in September 1831: 'O God, do You exist? You do and yet You do not take vengeance. Have You not had enough of these Muscovite crimes or . . . or are You Yourself a Russian?'

Yet, paradoxically, it is not the Chopin of the mazurkas, the ballades or the scherzos who has won the popular imagination, not the Polish Chopin so much as the French Chopin, the salon composer *in excelsis* of the waltzes and nocturnes. And this elegantly frail and aristocratic Chopin has, of course, been credited with suitably frail and aristocratic *amours*. The publication of his letters should have been sufficient to explode this popular delusion. From them it is perfectly clear that as a boy Chopin was humorous, vivacious, enterprising and quite reasonably extrovert. The verbal jokes, the pet names, the mixture of languages and the occasional coarseness all recall the young Mozart. There is no suggestion of morbidity, excessive sensibility or ill-health, though his constitution was obviously never robust. He writes to Jan Matuszyński in 1825, when he was fifteen:

Did you see at Sibylla a brick taken from the house of Copernicus, from his birthplace? I've seen the whole house, certainly a little profaned at present. Imagine, Jasio, in that very room where the famous astronomer received the gift of life stands now the bed of some German who probably after eating too many potatoes often emits many zephyrs; and on those bricks, of which one was sent to the great ceremony of Pulawy, crawl many bedbugs.

That might be the young Mozart writing from Italy; and the vein persisted, though only in his relations with his own countrymen and never – hence the one-sidedness of the traditional portrait – with his French friends and least of all with Liszt, whom he never whole-heartedly liked or trusted. In 1839 he wrote to Fontana of a 'luncheon of sphinx's beard and a parrot's kidneys sprinkled with eggs from the microscopic world', and the nonsense vein recurs in his letters to his family.

Of the three famous and posthumously romanticised *amours* it is quite clear from his letters that Konstancja Gladkowska was no more than a boyish affair of calf-love. For Delphina Potocka he almost certainly had no more than great admiration, as for a beautiful and musically accomplished compatriot. There remains Maria Wodzińska, to a member of whose family we are indebted for the novelettish *Three Romances of Frederick Chopin*. There is no doubt that Chopin was in love with her and that the lapsing, rather than breaking, of their unofficial engagement was a real blow to him, serious enough to make a lasting impression but not to withstand George Sand's determined efforts at consolation immediately afterwards.

Many thousands of words have been written about Chopin's liaison with the woman whom George Eliot considered a martyr, Baudelaire nicknamed *le prud'homme de l'immoralité* and Nietzsche *die Milchkuh mit schönem Stil*. What brought them together was a quality which they had in common, a physical diathesis which was also responsible for the remarkably short duration of their physical relations (probably only a few months of 1838). George Sand, needless to say, explained in print the circumstance which, more than any other, drove her from lover to lover in search of emotional and physical satisfaction. 'When my brain is on fire with voluptuous thoughts my body remains as ice.' For different reasons – perhaps connected with the consumption which already had a firm hold on his system in 1838 – Chopin was plainly no more ardent than she, except in the realm of the imagination where the two lovers could enjoy the Platonic 'pattern' of that physical ecstasy which was so charily bestowed on them in fact. Before a year was up their relationship had taken on a mother-and-son colouring which was only to be disturbed by occasional fits of jealousy until George Sand's vilely spoiled children created a permanent misunderstanding between them. Chopin certainly owed some of the happiest and most creative periods of his life to this strange woman, and the sensual experience which he was largely forced to undergo in fact went wholly to enrich his music, whose voluptuousness is the more powerful for its astonishing chastity of expression and suggestion. The version of the story by which George Sand exhausted Chopin by her excessive physical demands has no shred of evidence to support it and the famous discreet simile – *comme un vin trop capiteux détruit des vases trop fragiles* – is nothing but literature. Equally, though more fantastically, wide of the mark is, of course, Hadow's suggestion that there existed nothing more between the two than 'a pure and cordial friendship', a suggestion that caused Rémy de Gourmont such malicious anti-Britannic pleasure. It was Hadow who accused Chopin of 'want of manliness, moral and intellectual', but his own reading of the facts had a good deal of the provincial old maid about it.

There is little doubt, on the other hand, that Chopin's health affected his musical expression. Not that either his life or his music showed the smallest trace of that hectic quality common with consumptives. In fact he was the least hectic of his artistic contemporaries, and if we take the names of a random gathering at his rooms in the 1830's – Heine, Meyerbeer, Nourrit, Hiller, Delacroix, Mickiewicz and George Sand – he must have stood out for the regularity of his life and the balance and restraint of his art. But consumption certainly sharpened his sensibilities comparatively early and finally exacerbated them beyond bearing. This influenced his musical taste, so that he only played a few of the works of Beethoven with pleasure, though he was an ardent admirer and constant player of Bach and Mozart. (He was unaccountably silent about Schumann, who had hailed him as a genius from he start, only vouchsafing that 'Carnival' was 'not music at all', a compliment which Schumann returned in writing of the last movement of the B flat minor sonata.) An entry in Delacroix's diary under 22 April, 1849 reveals his opinion of Meyerbeer's music:

> After dinner to see Chopin, a man of exquisite heart and I need not say, mind. . . . He had dragged himself to the first performance of *The Prophet*. His horror of this rhapsody!

Alone among contemporary pianists, he completely rejected the leonine manner, all the self-dramatisation of the Titan-virtuoso. Liszt's claim that Chopin 'loved to hear his music played with all the vigour that he himself lacked' is probably a reflection on his own insensitiveness and a tribute to Chopin's ironical tact. Yet Liszt realised that what he called the Oriental politeness and modesty of the Poles, Chopin included, was quite misleading, a conventional way of speaking which also provided an element of mystification instinctively sought in all relationships, at least with foreigners. This restraint of manner and the extreme sensitiveness of the consumptive combined with Chopin's natural pride to account for his popularity with the *beau monde*, in which he was accepted on much more nearly equal terms than any other contemporary musician – to the jealous rage of his colleagues, not even excluding Liszt. 'Everyone instinctively treated him as though he were a prince', which is, after all, different from being treated as a lion.

His dislike of violence in any form, a natural trait greatly exaggerated by illness in his later years, probably provides the explanation for what have been considered mysteries in his life. Why, if he loved both his country and his family so devotedly, did he never return to Poland? The truth is probably that, like many artists, he shrank from all that was distressing and painful, and he instinctively avoided seeing with his own eyes what the failure of the rising of 1831 had meant to Poland. He could visualise it well enough, from the letters and conversations of his friends, and he could express his sympathy and indignation, provide consolation and inspiration in his music. In the same way, he never sought to unravel, still less to rectify, the tangled emotions which led to his break with George Sand. It was 1847; he had only two more years to live; and the squalid scenes of violence at Nohant were too much for him. George Sand had chosen to attribute to a misunderstanding all the force of a deliberate insult, and Chopin was wounded in his pride as well as in his affections.

His final journey to England in 1848 was probably at bottom a flight from the upheavals of the revolution in Paris quite as much as a desperate attempt to make some more money. George Sand certainly thought so when she wrote of Chopin that he was 'a character incapable of modifying itself to any upheaval in society'. He left Paris on 16 February, eight days before Louis Philippe, and returned on 23 November, just a month before Louis Napoleon was elected President. He was miserable in England, ill of course but also desperately bored and guilty that he could not enjoy all the kind arrangements made for him by Jane Stirling. The gushing of the women, who crowded round the piano and always, without fail, cooed that his playing was 'leik (*sic*) water': the men with whom he was forced to sit 'two hours at table, look at them talking and listen to them drinking' – it all bored and depressed him to such an extent that he wrote of his experiences, 'whatever is not boring is not English'. In this mood his only weapon of self-defence was malice, and his letters are often amusing when they are not pathetic:

> Among the notabilities was Lady Byron, with whom I am on very friendly terms. We converse like the goose with the sucking-pig, she in English and I in French. I understand why she bored Byron.

Once again, boredom. But by Mrs Grote he was not bored, and he has left a thumbnail sketch which instantly conjures up the picture of that timeless phenomenon, the progressive hostess *à l'anglaise*:

> Mrs Grote is a very kind woman, though eccentric and a good deal of a Radical. She talks in a bass voice and does not wrap the truth in cottonwool.

The photograph of Chopin made in 1849 does not suggest that he was a suitable recipient for her unwrapped home-truths.

In the dedication of his *Modeste Mignon* 'to a Polish woman' Balzac apostrophises the Countess Hanska in glowing terms which would have suited perhaps more aptly her more famous compatriot:

Fille d'une terre esclave, ange par l'amour, démon par la fantaisie, enfant par la foi, vieillard par l'expérience, homme par le cerveau, femme par le cœur, géant par l'espérance, mère par la douleur et poète par tes rêves.

This inflated rhetoric might have embarrassed Chopin, but it suggests very well the contradictions in his own character. The fascination exercised by Poles in the literary and artistic world of the 1830's and 1840's can be seen not only in contemporary accounts of Chopin but in Balzac's infatuation for Mme Hanska and Liszt's passion for the Princess Sayn-Wittgenstein. The mingling of Polish and Latin blood had brilliant but not wholly happy results in Chopin and also in the Italian poet-composer Arrigo Boito, son of an Italian painter and the Polish Countess Jozefina Radolińska. Chopin's easy and excellent relations with his French friends were in almost all cases superficial, and it is only necessary to look at his letters to see how much nearer to him were quite undistinguished Poles like Grzymala and Fontana. This characteristic of divided allegiance, the consciousness of having to choose – between Poland and France for Chopin, music and poetry for Boito – handicapped both men, and it is a handicap often suffered in one form or another by the children of two very different races. Typical also is the fact that both, in the last resort, refused to make the choice – that Chopin insisted on the anomalous role of Polish patriot domiciled, but not exiled, in France and that Boito wrote his own operas and other men's libretti. We should be thankful that there was no division of allegiance in Chopin's creative expression. André Gide quotes Chopin as

one more example of the truth, which I take to be proven, that almost all the *grands esprits* ... almost all the creators, almost all those who have risen above the mass are the products of hybridisation or at least transplanting.

At any rate, the disadvantages of his position were paid for in his life, and his work was enriched by the blend of the Latin with the Slavonic.

In the comparisons between the arts beloved by earlier generations it was as accepted a thing to bracket Chopin with Keats as

Mozart with Raphael. Such comparisons are, of course, only incidentally illuminating and only within a very restricted range. A rich, florid manner, swirling draperies, conscious grandeur and theatrical treatment of religious subjects are characteristics common to Liszt and, say, Tiepolo; but how little of Liszt, or Tiepolo, this reveals! With Chopin, however, it is possible to find an extraordinarily close contemporary parallel in Giacomo Leopardi. He was born and died exactly twelve years earlier (1798-1837), and he was also consumptive. Like Chopin, he used a limpid idiom closely modelled on the classical to express that warmly personal and often desperate emotion which we associate with the word romantic. He was a passionate Italian patriot in the idealistic rather than the political sense, and as indignant with Italian supineness as Chopin with Polish suffering. An unhappy childhood and physical deformity gave him a bitterly pessimistic view of the world, which was aggravated by the grotesque contrast between his amorous disposition and his disastrous physique; and in this his experience of life was very different from Chopin's. But in the combined richness and purity of their style, the alternation between nostalgic melancholy and vivid resentment, the intense but diffused sensuality combined with lyrical idealism there are extraordinary similarities between the two men. Leopardi's shorter poems – 'L'Infinito', 'Alla luna' or 'A se stesso' – are perhaps the nearest equivalent in any other art to Chopin's Preludes. His night poems are close to the Nocturnes. In the longer poems, where the discursive intellect is almost always engaged, the general parallel with music of any kind is obviously less marked, but all of them contain lyrical apostrophes and moments of desperate lyrical *élan* which recall passages from the ballades or the sonatas of Chopin. Like Love and Death, the twin Divinities of Leopardi's own poem, these two poets are closely related and complementary in their differences. No parallels between different arts can go very far, but perhaps this goes farther than most.

The appeal of Chopin's music has hardly fluctuated in volume for a century; but his devotees have changed in character. It has been said that he is before all else a woman's composer because he combines voluptuousness with chastity – a reflection more interesting for the light it throws on its author's experience of women than for any illumination of Chopin's music. If many women prize Chopin highly it is because he speaks, gently and intelligibly and with an unmistakably individual voice, the language of the human heart in its simplest and most poignant moments; and this is what the large majority of women seek in any art. But is it really a matter for distinction between the sexes? Apart from the very few whose enjoyment of the arts is largely intellectual, what do any of us seek except some kind of communication between human beings? If Chopin is not on an equal footing as composer with Bach and Beethoven, it is because his experience of the human heart is less deep than theirs, or at all events less wide and varied. And yet . . . how many people, if they dared, would agree with Gide when he wrote in his diary under 30 October, 1927:

> How charming Alibert was yesterday when he exclaimed – 'I would give all Beethoven's symphonies – and when I say all I mean it – for a single Chopin ballade.'

With Gide, be it noted, rather than with Alibert. Devotion to Chopin need not be blind, but it can be as strong and as jealous as a personal friendship; and of how many artists is that true on the centenary of their death?

'The other day I went to see Dr Spurzheim's phrenological cabinet, shown by a young physician . . . that I possessed a taste for music and some imagination was obvious; the doctor found afterwards that I was rather covetous, loved order and little children, and liked flirting; music, however, he declared to be predominant.'

London in the last days of April 1829 and the brilliant twenty-year-old Jewish banker's son from Berlin, already acclaimed as a musical genius and now stealing a few moments for one of the most fashionable yet decorous amusements – phrenology. Four years earlier, as a boy of sixteen, he had received a letter from the aged Goethe, whom he had charmed by his lively intelligence, his fiery piano-playing and his romantic appearance:

> You have given me very great pleasure, dear Felix, with your valuable present. . . . I regard it as the graceful embodiment of that beautiful, rich, energetic soul which so astonished me when you first allowed me to make its acquaintance.

Which was nearer the truth – the young physician at Dr Spurzheim's phrenological cabinet, perfunctorily fingering the bumps on young Mendelssohn's head or the old poet caressing the dark curls and retrieving a moment of his own youth as he gazed into those liquid eyes with their oriental lustre? Mendelssohn just failed to live long enough to give an unequivocal answer to the question. His youth was artificially prolonged by an intense and jealously guarded family life, by a well-meaning but overwhelming father and by the isolation from reality effected by great wealth. And when, at thirty-eight, he died, it was hard to say whether it was of momentary exhaustion or whether perhaps he really had given all that was in him to give, like some early-flowering species that wilts in June.

No other composer, except perhaps Berlioz, comes so vividly to life in his letters or reveals himself so clearly in the choice of his correspondents. His family, his old master Zelter, Moscheles and Klingemann get the best of his letters; no single love-letter exists, nor any communication of interest with his own musical peers among his contemporaries, though he knew Schumann, Berlioz, Liszt and Chopin. It was not that he preferred the friendship of his artistic inferiors. His whole upbringing had inclined him to conceive of human relationships and human happiness in terms of the family, as son and as brother. Temperamentally incapable of the extremes of passion, he instinctively avoided the rough exchanges and possible thrusts of a friendship between equals. The dominant figure throughout his life was his father – the cultivated, kindly, ambitious Abraham who described himself as the son of his father (the philosopher and savant Moses Mendelssohn) and the father of his son. Every action, every composition was mentally referred to the judgment either of his father or of one of those reverend paternal figures – Bach, Zelter, Goethe, Cherubini or Spohr – toward whom he instinctively adopted a filial attitude:

> I could never appear as the opponent of a master of Spohr's standing (he wrote at the age of thirty-two) whose greatness is so firmly established; for even as a boy I had the greatest esteem for him in every respect, and with my riper years this feeling has in no way been weakened.

Hiller and Moscheles, the third-rate composers whose music he appreciated and helped to forward, were safe familiar figures in this patriarchal world; but 'one ought to wash ones hands after handling Berlioz's scores', Chopin's mazurkas are 'so mannered they are hard to stand' and Liszt's harmonies 'simply seem very stupid'. Indeed, those brilliant contemporaries appeared to Mendelssohn as gifted but incorrigibly naughty, unfilial boys. Liszt, it is true, like Meyerbeer, aroused in Mendelssohn a vein of apparently moral indignation in which it is easy to discern the note of envy:

> The superficialities are so tempting, people enjoy honours and money and decorations and cheers and orchestras and lack absolutely nothing. . . . I consider it ignoble, and if the present epoch demands this style and considers it indispensable, I will write oratorios.

Poor Felix! Felix Meritis, Felix the Deserving! His lifelong search for a libretto was perhaps no more than an instinctive refusal to measure himself with these wicked, successful Parisian gentry whom he was so ill-equipped to meet on their own ground. Perhaps he was wise to drop his sister Fanny's suggestion of the Nibelungenlied as a suitable subject for an opera. 'I scarcely remember what your allusion to the "sinking into the Rhine" stands for', he writes to her. It was just as well. *A Calm Sea and a Prosperous Voyage* was more Felix's mark than any Twilight of the Gods.

Indeed it is his natural physical delight in external objects, the sense of cloudless well-being, that inspires the most vivid passages in Mendelssohn's letters, as in his music. On his inexorable father's advice he was to 'put on the shelf that elfin and spirit life with which he had chiefly occupied himself in his compositions and to proceed to graver works'. His letters, too, become graver – and duller – and after the age of twenty-three there are very few of those pen-pictures which make the boy's letters such excellent reading. What professional writer could improve upon this description of a fine autumn day in London and the first outing after an illness?

> When we turned the corner and the sun shone on me and the sky did me the favour of being a deep blue, I had for the first time in my life a *feeling* of health, because I had never before done without it for so long. London was indescribably beautiful. The red and brown chimney-pots contrasted so sharply with the blue sky and all the colours glowed, the gay shops gleamed and the blue air poured out of every cross-street and enveloped the background. Instead of the green, fluttering leaves I last saw

from my gig I now saw red sticks, standing up stiffly, and only the lawns were still green. How beautifully the roses in Piccadilly gleamed in the sunshine and how full of vitality everything seemed!

Like all sensitive young Northerners, Mendelssohn had found his first visit to Italy a moral as well as an aesthetic experience. He was twenty-one, and had just attended the ceremony of the Austrian Crown Prince taking the oath as King of Hungary at Bratislava, a scene of exotic splendour which he describes with extraordinary vividness and excitement. A fortnight later he is in Venice, and from there he writes to his old master, Zelter, revealing just that sense of moral disturbance, that need for reassurance of his own standards, that the Northerner feels at his first contact with the south.

The aspect of the world at this moment is very bleak and stormy and much that was once thought unchangeable and permanent has been swept away in the course of a couple of days. It is then doubly welcome to hear well-known voices, to convince ourselves that there are certain things which cannot be annihilated or demolished, but remain firm and steadfast.

By the time he reached Rome, he had regained much of his equilibrium. Mendelssohn's impressions were always vivid and precise, but they never went very deep unless his carefully trained moral nature were affected. He writes with quite extraordinary sympathy of the religious ceremonies that he attended, able (as so few of his contemporaries were able) to feel the grandeur and poetry which even slipshod or tasteless singing could not destroy. Of the Papal Choir he writes that 'they do not sing particularly well, the compositions were poor, the congregation was not devout and yet the whole effect was heavenly. This was only due to the fact that they were singing in the central nave of St Peter's.' This receptivity, half moral and half aesthetic, the ability to experience the whole Roman scene as a masterpiece of the human spirit not invalidated by a multiplicity of jarring details – execrable houses, tasteless gardens and mediocre music – forms the strongest contrast with Berlioz's superficial hostility. Even so, the rich Berlin bourgeois in Mendelssohn, the elegant traveller with well-washed person and well-lined purse, reacted with priggish – almost missish – incomprehension to the unkempt artists in the Caffé Greco and to the easy-going amorality, the unrelieved squalor (as it presented itself to his German eyes) of the human scene in Naples.

For no hundred per cent racially pure German Aryan could be more German than this first-generation Lutheran of wholly Jewish origin. In Rome he attended the annual ceremony at which the Jews formally sought permission to inhabit the ghetto, and no comment suggests that he was aware of the smallest link between himself and these queer orientals. From England he expressed the time-honoured German opinion that the English understand nothing about Shakespeare; and he experienced the secular German feeling of irritation, in which admiration and a feeling of inferiority are inextricably mixed, for the 'cursing young Englishman, who was half sportsman, half peasant, half gentleman and altogether insufferable'.

Paris in 1832 – the Paris of Balzac, that is – he found interested in two subjects only – 'politics and sensuality, around which everything revolved'. But how intelligently he enjoyed the small vaudevilles at the Gymnase Dramatique (the theatre which plays so large a part in Balzac's *Illusions Perdues*).

It is extraordinary how one finds in all these little comedies such extreme bitterness and deep disgust, and although these are cloaked by the prettiest phrases and the liveliest acting, they become only the more conspicuous. Politics everywhere play the chief part . . . but the politics of the Gymnase take a light and ironical turn – referring to the occurrences of the day and to the newspapers, in order to excite laughter and applause, and at last you can't help laughing and applauding with the rest.

His German soul was revolted by the emigré compatriots he found in Paris:

I seldom see Heine, because he is entirely absorbed in liberal ideas and politics.

Heine was also doing some remunerative blackmail as Meyerbeer's Paris agent:

Heine has recently published sixty *Frühlingslieder*. Very few of them seem to me either genuine or truthful, but these few are indeed wonderful. . . . Börne intends to publish some new volumes of letters . . . all these gentlemen are abusing and reviling Germany and all that is German, and yet they cannot speak even tolerable French. I can't quite swallow this.

Not very logical, perhaps, but very understandable. Mendelssohn like Mozart, before him, felt at his most *teutsch* in Paris, or indeed anywhere out of Germany; but even so, he did not lose his sense of humour. Returning from Italy through Switzerland he describes himself as 'overjoyed to find myself once more among honest, natural people, who could speak German' but adds 'and swindled me into the bargain, quite infamously'.

Italy and France each caused a minor moral and emotional crisis in the young Mendelssohn; and from France he wrote the only letter in which he expresses a resentment, decorously controlled and only momentary, of that paternal guidance which shaped his whole life. His father was pressing him to find a French libretto for an opera, for Abraham Mendelssohn cannot have been indifferent to the phenomenal success of Jakob Beer, his fellow Berlin banker's son, now peacocking in Paris as Giacomo Meyerbeer. Felix writes stiffly:

Although I by no means agree with you in this opinion, still it would have been my duty to settle nothing without your express sanction. . . . I believed, however, that I was acting entirely to your satisfaction.

Much formal self-justification follows and then:

There is one thing which consoles me, and it is that if I were to rely on my own judgment, I should act again precisely as I have done now. . . . Pardon me for saying exactly what I think.

He was twenty-two and the catastrophe of his father's death was still four years distant. When it came, his character was already set in the paternal mould and all thoughts of real independence had long ago been rejected as unworthy disloyalties to his high vocation. He wrote to Pastor Bauer after his father's death:

The wish which of all others recurred to my mind every night was that I might not survive my loss, because I so entirely clung to my father . . . a sorrow which of all others, from my childhood on, I always thought the most acute. The loss was that of my only perfect friend during the last few years, and my master in art and life.

Within a few months of his father's death, Mendelssohn became engaged to his future wife, Cécile Jeanrenaud, whom he married in March 1837. The phrenologist had been right about his fondness for flirtation, which was no euphemism for philandering in his case, but an innocent exchange of admirations with members of the opposite sex. Even when he fell in love with Cécile Jeanrenaud, to whom he became sincerely devoted, his first reaction was to go away and think the matter over, which was no doubt wise, but not very flattering in a lover of twenty-seven. It is even doubtful whether we have missed any very illuminating letters by the fact that 'the minute details of the pure and elevated happiness which Mendelssohn enjoyed in his most intimate domestic relations are expressly withheld, as being the peculiar treasures of his family' – his brother's explanation of the absence from his published letters of any addressed to his wife, either before or after their marriage.

The tone of his other letters becomes less lively after his marriage, their content more factual. During those last ten years of his life he was excellently cared for, he was a fond husband and father, and an acknowledged composer of the first rank in Germany and, even more, in England. But he was steadily overworked. Already in the autumn of 1832 he had been threatened with what would now be called a nervous breakdown. He writes in March 1833 that the last six months have been 'a time of uncertainty, doubt and suspense, amounting to a malady and one of the worst, too'. And seven months after his marriage he writes to his brother of his 'longing for rest' and his disillusion with his activities as performer, conductor, organiser:

Very little remains of performances and festivals and all that personal stuff. People shout and applaud, but it passes so quickly without leaving a trace . . . once one has gone in, it is impossible to get out half way. . . . I dare not even withdraw, lest the cause

for which I stand should suffer. . . . If only I could devote myself more to what is my real mission – the composition of music
– and leave the performing of it to others.

That cry is heard again and again in the letters of his last years.
'If only I had more time for composition. . . .' Yet there are very
few discussions of music, his own or other men's, in any of his
letters at any period. Occasionally he shows a clear understanding
of his own weakness as a composer. In a letter to Moscheles 'he
speaks of his 'poverty in shaping new forms for the piano . . . how
I am to start writing a calm and quiet piece (as you advised me
last spring) I really do not know. All that passes through my head
in the shape of piano music is about as calm and quiet as Cheap-
side; and when I sit down to the piano and force myself to start
improvising very quietly, it's no use – by degrees I fall back into
the old ways.'

He did indeed. The *Capriccio brillante*, written in October 1832,
is one of many examples. The opening Andante promises so well,
with its soft harped chords and cantabile melody, but there is a
bare page of this 'calm and quiet improvisation' and then Mendelssohn's hands start rocketing about the keyboard in the same
empty, feverish way as Weber does in his piano music, only to land
in one of those commonplace 'brilliant' marches that Weber too
had affected.

In the same letter to Moscheles, Mendelssohn speaks of one of
his compositions as being 'only too tame', the very criticism which
has been levelled at such an overwhelming proportion of his music
since his death. But immediately he comes to the conclusion that
so much self-criticism is not good, that he must stick to his work,
which is the only way he knows of keeping well and happy.

During the last six years of his life Mendelssohn was burdened,
in addition to his work of composing, conducting and organising,
by unrewarding and exhausting duties which were pressed upon
him by the Prussian King Friedrich Wilhelm IV, and by the disappointment of seeing his cherished plans for the organisation of
an Academy of Music in Berlin rejected. Already at the end of the
London season in June 1842 he was complaining of dizziness and
complete exhaustion. His social success was certainly dazzling and

in a letter to his mother he recaptures for a moment his old power of vivid description and the ability to communicate his own intense excitement. He has been summoned to Buckingham Palace and received with the most flattering intimacy by the Queen and the Prince Consort. Not only did he play Prince Albert's private organ, but first the Prince and then the Queen herself sang for him, his own songs. 'Schöner und schöner' was the Queen's song, which she sang 'beautifully in tune, in strict time, and with very nice expression. Her only mistakes were two D sharps where the composer had written D natural.'

In his letters to publishers written during the last years of his life Mendelssohn shows as much interest in his editions of Bach's organ music as in those of his own music. Bach was indeed the one great musical passion of his life, and all his work as a conductor and administrator in Berlin, Düsseldorf and Leipzig was undertaken in order either actually to restore Bach's masterpieces to their rightful position in the modern repertory or at least to renew in Germany the attitude to music and the technical resources which would make such a restoration possible. It seems strange to us now, but he conceived his own oratorios as the legitimate modern descendants of Bach's Passions, Masses and cantatas; and perhaps at bottom it was the immense gulf separating the music of Liszt, Berlioz and Chopin from that of Bach, that really determined Mendelssohn's attitude to these composers. In the music of his own later years there is only one major instance of a return to that 'elfin music' which his father had advised him to abandon for 'graver things'. That is the violin concerto of 1844, whose adagio might well count as his swan-song, so perfectly does it express the serenity, the purity of heart and the virginal tenderness that were his most endearing traits. We should guess that no work, even of the facile Mendelssohn, can have been written with fewer heart-searchings or subjected to less correction once written! Yet nothing could be further from the truth; and a letter to the violinist Ferdinand David, written in December 1844, shows Mendelssohn indefatigably engaged on improving minute points of scoring and texture, humbly asking David's opinion, confessing that he is just 'groping around' and begging David and Gade not to laugh at him too much. Such humility in one of fortune's darlings is rare and must have formed one of the chief attractions of Mendelssohn's personality.

Felix Meritis indeed! and if the tragedy of his life lay less in its shortness than in its fundamental misdirection, that very misdirection was the result of an idealism, reinforced no doubt by vanity, but still wholly genuine. He wished to please so many and such reverend figures – God, his father, Zelter, Bach, King Friedrich Wilhelm IV, the British Public, Queen Victoria, Prince Albert – and to do so he must write Hymns of Praise, Reformation Symphonies, *Elijah*, *St Paul* and forget the waters lapping in Fingal's Cave and the fairies that dance in the *Midsummer Night's Dream* music, in the octet and once again in the finale of the violin concerto. It is impossible, after reading his letters, to bear a grudge against Mendelssohn – impossible, too, not to feel that he was nearer to being the 'beautiful, rich, energetic soul' divined by Goethe than the rather covetous, flirtatious man, fond of order and children, but predominantly musical, revealed by his 'bumps' to the young physician in Dr Spurzheim's phrenological cabinet.

8 Wagner's *Ring* as a Political Myth

Anyone who has attended even one performance of *The Ring* is aware that this is not simply opera written to a slightly different formula – that richer and heavier instrumentation, continuity of musical design and the characterisation of personalities or ideas by appropriate musical phrases are not the only traits which distinguish *The Ring* from other operas of the mid-nineteenth century. Every honest listener will have admitted, at least to himself, that though he wholly enjoys the grand lyrical and dramatic moments, there are long passages which he finds heavy going. And he is, on any showing, right; though it is not always recognised that the heaviness is the heaviness of Wagner's own Sieglinde in the second act of *Walküre*, the heaviness of a woman in the last weeks before she gives birth to a child. Wagner's music in *The Ring* is both heavy and big – with ideas: a weight with which no previous composer (except perhaps Mozart in *The Magic Flute*) had ever thought to burden an opera, and one with which few successful operas have been burdened since. The exact nature of these ideas is still disputed, often very hotly; and Wagner himself would almost certainly fail to give a coherent account of them, for they changed in significance according to his mood of the moment, according to his shifting beliefs about the world and man's place in it, and not least according to the technical exigencies of the stage presentation of the myth in which the ideas are embodied. When pressed, he spoke of the artist 'feeling himself in the presence of his own work, if it is true art, as though confronted by a riddle, about which he might have illusions like anyone else'. Nevertheless, in the circumstances of Wagner's life, in passages from his letters and in the history of the genesis of *The Ring* there are abundant hints.

Look for a moment at Wagner's life during the years in which he was writing *The Ring*. The first sketches of a Nibelungen drama date from 1848, when Wagner was opera-conductor at Dresden. In October of that year he sketched a 'Siegfried's Death'; and working backwards from this, through a 'Young Siegfried', he finally after much recasting and rewriting completed the poem of *The Ring* as we know it, which was printed in a private edition during February 1853. During these years between 1848 and 1853 Wagner led a most eventful life, both physically and spiritually. In 1848 he was an ardent political and social revolutionary and a friend of Bakunin; so that we find him, for example, making a speech to the National Democratic Association 'demanding the abolition of money and the extinction of the aristocracy'. When the revolution broke out in Dresden in May 1849, a warrant was issued for Wagner's arrest and he fled to Switzerland and thence to Paris, where he produced his pamphlet on *Art and Revolution*. Although the poem of *The Ring* was finished by the end of 1853, the composition of the music continued, with increasing distractions, until 1857, when Wagner abandoned it just before the end of the second act of *Siegfried*. This he did in order to work on *Tristan* and *Meistersinger*, which were both composed before *The Ring* music was completed by the finishing of *Götterdämmerung* in 1874.

The Ring as a whole, then, text and music, originated in the years between the middle-class, liberal revolutions of 1848 and the Paris Commune of 1871 – two resounding defeats for the revolutionary parties aggravated by Louis Napoleon's successful *coup d'état* and Bismarck's successful unification of Germany under the Prussian monarchy during the late 60's. Little wonder, then, if Wagner's revolutionary optimism was first damped and then utterly extinguished, if he turned from the romantic glorification of Bakunin and his ideals to the bitter and contemptuous mockery of them in *Eine Kapitulation*, with its *Republik, Republik, Republik, lik, lik* echoing Rossini's *William Tell*. We know from his own letters that the French *coup d'état* struck him as 'so absolutely incredible that it seemed to me the world was really coming to an end'. This shock followed hard upon his discovery of the writings of Schopenhauer, in which he found the very antithesis of the optimistic, 'progressive' yea-saying attitude to life – a death-devoted pessimism and that Buddhistic longing for Nirvana, which found its musical expression in *Tristan*.

These, then, are the facts of Wagner's life during the *Ring* years. It was to prove that they can throw light on the ideas of the drama that in 1898 Bernard Shaw wrote his *Perfect Wagnerite*. Shaw was in possession of all the main facts; he was also, as ever, in possession of a personal message. Inspired journalist as he was, with the instincts of the populariser rather than the original thinker, he interprets *The Ring* as an assortment of ideas picked up from Nietzsche and Marx, from Ibsen and the French socialist writers; and he makes an extraordinarily plausible case. For him, then, *Rheingold*, *Walküre* and the first two acts of *Siegfried* are social and political music-dramas of ideas, and the ideas are those of the 1848 extremists, with Bakunin at their head. The last act of *Siegfried* and the whole of *Götterdämmerung*, on the other hand, represent Wagner's return to opera, in which he appears as a teacher with a panacea, where before he was a philosopher stating a problem.

Shaw, then, sets forth the myth of the gold of the Rhine as the myth of 'capitalistic pluto-democracy'. He shows the birth-pangs of the new social and political order, of which we know that Wagner was dreaming in the late 40's, as symbolised in the story of the painful supersession of the old order of gods, giants and dwarfs by the New Man Siegfried – the Hero and the 'Freewiller of Necessity'. Each estate of the old order is reflected in the world-order of *The Ring*. The gods are 'the intellectual, moral, talented people who devise and administer churches and states'. The giants are the 'patient, toiling, stupid, respectful, money-worshipping people' and the dwarfs 'the instinctive, predatory, lustful and greedy'. For Shaw, as for all Wagnerian interpreters, the Wagnerian gods are in every way inferior to man, the 'heroic saviour' whom they call into being to rescue them. Godhead represents infirmity and compromise, manhood strength and integrity.

The plight of the gods is already manifest in *Rheingold*, where

Wotan is forced to have recourse to the lies of Loge in order to get possession of Alberich's hoard, of the Ring and the Tarnhelm. True legality perishes when Wotan breaks his word; and he is forced into further deception and tergiversation, which culminate in the killing of Siegmund, his own son and the first of the heroic race of men, as a sacrifice to Law, represented by Wotan's consort Fricka. According to Shaw, Wotan's predicament is the predicament of the churches, who have called in state organisation, the *raison d'état* (Loge) and Law (Fricka), to establish their ascendancy over the brute force of the giants and the dark, plutonic powers of the dwarfs, newly organised and suddenly grown infinitely more powerful under the leadership of Alberich. For Alberich is the factory-owner of Engels' *Condition of the Working Classes in England*, and Nibelheim is a factory of the 1840's, while by a typical Shavian quirk the Tarnhelm is 'a top-hat, which makes a man invisible as a shareholder and changes him into various shapes – pious Christian, subscriber to hospitals, benefactor of the poor, model husband and father'.

This parable is set forth with all Shaw's verbal and intellectual virtuosity; but it can also claim confirmation from much of what we know of Wagner's ideas and more of what we may plausibly infer. Writing to Röckel, the revolutionary friend of his Dresden days, he asks him to 'look well at Wotan, for he is the unmistakable likeness of ourselves and the sum of the present-day spirit, while Siegfried is the man we wait and long for – the man of the future whom we cannot create but who will create himself by our annihilation, the most perfect man I can imagine'.

But in his pitying and tolerant contempt of the disillusioned Wagner who composed the music of *Götterdämmerung* – the Wagner who also wrote the *Kaisermarsch* and made fun of the Commune – Shaw vociferously denies our inability 'to create the perfect man'. Wagner, he says in effect, saw in Siegfried (and in Bakunin, who was in many ways Siegfried's prototype) the logical heir of the Protestant revolution, carrying that revolution consistently forward to its next stage, which is anarchism. Wagner lost his faith in anarchism (and never, alas! proceeded to Fabian socialism), preaching instead the panacea of 'love', for which Shaw rates him soundly. But Shaw himself produces a panacea without which, he says, even socialism cannot put the world to rights. This is neither social reform nor sexual passion, but eugenics. 'No serious progress will be made', says Shaw, 'until we address ourselves seriously to the task of producing trustworthy human material for society.' Siegfrieds, then, can and must be bred by the state, and in the mating of Siegmund and Sieglinde, brother and sister, Shaw sees a kind of instinctive preservation of the purity of the heroic strain, a eugenic experiment *avant la lettre*.

The figure of Brünnhilde introduces a further complication into the myth, and strains both Shaw's interpretative faculty and, oddly enough for so versatile a craftsman of letters, his style. He describes her as 'the inner thought and will of godhead, the aspiration from the high life to the higher that is its divine element and only becomes separated from it when its resort to kingship and priestcraft for the sake of temporal power has made it false to itself' (a sentence, surely, of less than Shavian elegance and clarity). She is, in fact, 'the real Wotan', his 'better self'; and when he is caught in the toils of his own 'law' and 'desire for necessary power' he is forced to part with Brünnhilde. The flames with which he surrounds her at the end of *Walküre* are the invention of Loge, and Shaw insists that, like all Loge's inventions, they are pure fiction, though sufficient to deceive all but the Heroic Man. He compares them tellingly to the fires of Hell – 'those frightful flames which have scared mankind for centuries from the Truth and have not heat in them to make a child shut its eyes. They are mere fantasmagoria . . . and nothing ever has perished or will perish eternally in them except the churches, who have been so poor and faithless as to trade for their power on the lies of a romancer.'

The relationship between Wotan and Loge, on the one hand, and between Wotan and Brünnhilde, on the other, is envisaged by Shaw as a dramatisation of the same dilemma in which Dostoevsky imagined his Grand Inquisitor, though Shaw does not draw this parallel. Both Wotan and the Inquisitor represent the state and the state church which need Loge, the Lie, and are bound, in the very interests of law and religion, to persecute the truth when it appears – to kill Siegmund and to punish Brünnhilde. Whether this dilemma ever presented itself clearly to Wagner himself is very doubtful. We must not forget, as Shaw seems to do occasionally, that, how-

ever philosophically weighted *The Ring* may be, it was always to
its composer, first and last, a music-drama; and that musical and
dramatic considerations were Wagner's unvarying preoccupation,
his passion as well as his profession, while political philosophy was
first a passionately pursued hobby and later a source of something
like despair. No doubt the Wagner who began the poem of *The
Ring* in 1848 was a different man from the Wagner who completed
that poem in 1852 and a very different man from the Wagner who
completed the music of *Götterdämmerung* in 1874.

The original *dénouement* of the whole poem was an optimistic
one – the gods' wrong-doing was atoned for by Siegfried's vicarious
acceptance of their guilt, Wotan was re-established in Valhalla and
joined there by Siegfried as a 'transfigured hero'. Even in 1853,
after the publishing of the text of *The Ring* poem, Wagner could
not give any logical explanation of why, once the gold is returned
to the Rhinemaidens, the gods need perish. Whether we ascribe it
to political disenchantment, to the influence of Schopenhauer or
simply to the instinct of the dramatist and the musician in Wagner,
the decision to give his poem a tragic ending was a matter of the
composer's feelings which, as he admitted, Schopenhauer helped
him to rationalise after the event. He made a further sketch for the
ending of *Götterdämmerung* in 1856 and appended a note to the
1872 edition of the poem, which shows that he was still uneasy
about the effect of the *dénouement* on the spectator. He had told
Röckel that he 'arrived at a clear understanding of his own works
of art through the help of another, who provided him with the
reasoned conceptions corresponding to his intuitive principles' and
it was undoubtedly Schopenhauer who, he felt, had provided him
with the key to his own instinctive actions, a kind of rough psycho-
analysis which gave Wagner much satisfaction.

Shaw, as we have seen, dismisses Wagner's vision of 'the world
going down in utter ruin yet somehow taken up into the arms of
redeeming love' as so much metaphysics and grand opera. But he
makes something more than a point of wit when he compares *The
Ring* with another revolutionary classic very nearly its contemporary. 'Although *The Ring*', he writes, 'may, like the *Communist
Manifesto*, be an inspired guess at the historical laws and pre-
destined end of our capitalistic and theocratic epoch, yet Wagner,

like Marx, was too inexperienced in technical government and administration and too melodramatic in his hero-contra-villain conception of the class-struggle, to foresee the actual process by which his generalisations would work out or the part to be played by the classes involved'.

In fact, Wagner was an artist and not a politician or even a political philosopher; and the story of *The Ring* is the story of Wagner's progressive surrender to the imperious instincts and deeply felt intuitions of his artistic nature.

9 Wagner as Christian Prophet or Jungian Adept

Until the disturbingly novel Bayreuth presentations divided the musical world into two camps, it was possible to dismiss Wagner's works as a nineteenth-century experiment in a new type of opera; successful perhaps in themselves but without any permanent value except *as* opera. Wagner's own insistence on their being something more, and something different, could be regarded as a symptom of his megalomania, his philosophising as a characteristically German form of intellectualisation. Wieland and Wolfgang Wagner have compelled us to reconsider the composer's apparently extravagant claims, and they have achieved this by doing conscious violence to his express wishes and removing his music-dramas from their late-nineteenth-century theatrical framework. Stripped of realistic details and comfortable stage upholstery *The Ring, Tristan* and *Parsifal* begin to emerge, one feels, as Wagner himself, however vaguely, conceived them – not as merely individual dramas but as symbolical musical and dramatic poems about fundamental and general truths of human psychology and philosophy.

Wagner was surprisingly aware of his inability to understand completely the significance of his own work. In a letter to August Röckel he speaks of the artist 'standing in front of his own work as before an enigma about which he may fall into just the same errors as others'. The error, common in the past, against which Bayreuth now ensures the spectator is that of believing that Wagner used Teutonic myth and mediaeval legend simply as a vehicle for crude theories of German nationalism or erotic fantasies based simply on the ebb and flow of his own sexual potency. If Wagner's grandsons have done nothing else, they have established the universal validity and the spiritual significance of his work, which till recently has been obscured behind a misleading theatrical façade.

What in fact is the spiritual significance of Wagner's work, so easy to talk about and so hard to define? Can there be said to be any longer an 'official' Bayreuth 'interpretation', a Bayreuth orthodoxy? I think not; and it may well be that Wieland and Wolfgang Wagner as men of the theatre, are content to present their grandfather's works with all the resources which modern German stagecraft puts at their disposal. They appear content to universalise and generalise their interpretation without committing themselves any further intellectually. Two essays published in recent Bayreuth programmes – one on *The Ring* and the other on *Parsifal* – suggest that a variety of approach is now encouraged where formerly there existed a strict dogmatic orthodoxy.

One of the essays, on *The Ring*, is by Dr Yolanda Jacobi, who expounds the myth and Wagner's use of it in the light of Jung's theory of archetypes. Brünnhilde is the key-figure, the *anima* or feminine personality of Wotan, the spiritual mother as well as the beloved of Siegfried. Siegfried's short, triumphal career in which he vanquishes the opposition of Wotan and attains full manhood through his experience of woman is, according to Jung, the pattern of all sun-god myths; and the incest theme symbolises a return, or turning inward, to the power already inherent in the self, the same process as that which lies at the root of artistic creation.

Siegfried stands between two opposing mother-images: the beneficent, spiritual maternity of Brünnhilde and the hostile, negative, stepmotherly parody of maternity in Mime. The search for his mother leads him to Brünnhilde, in whom he finds mother, sister, and wife; and here the dialogue in the final act of *Siegfried* seems to indicate that this was in Wagner's mind. Siegfried's first reaction on discovering the identity of the sleeping Brünnhilde is to invoke his mother: 'Mother! Mother! Remember me!' he cries, 'Remember thy brave child! A woman lies sleeping . . . *she* has taught me fear.'

Jung – to do him justice – is perfectly clear that no work of art can be exhaustively explained by psychological methods or by merely identifying universal mythological patterns. He is content to point to the existence of unconscious psychological truth and to the presence of a universal mythological symbolism in *The Ring*; for he knows how insuperably difficult it is to give a strictly logical account of any heroic myth. No passage, as he says, can be given any single, exclusive meaning and all the characters are, in a sense (as Jung himself puts it, 'with a grain of salt') interchangeable. I found this at first an almost comically disappointing conclusion, until I asked myself how it is that no amount of ridicule, no under-lining of its fantastic improbabilities can destroy *The Ring*. Sieg-fried may be in love with his step-aunt, who is also in some supra-sensible way his mother – and yet this does not seriously trouble us in the theatre. Why not? Why indeed does the whole fantasmagoria of *The Ring* make sense on some other level than the conscious, logical, intellectual?

The answer, which seems to bear out Jung's theory, is that we have all experienced just this sensation of profound ambiguity, of psychological truth revealed in impossibly illogical sequences of events in which characters change their roles and even have double identities. Where? In dreams, of course. It is the deep layers of dreams on which Wagner drew for *The Ring*; and the Bayreuth productions emphasise this dream, or nightmare, quality by omit-ting as far as possible all references to everyday reality and present-ing this dream-drama in a dream-light, with gauzes and curtains to filter and distort 'natural' effects and with stylised, exaggerated dress (though these are one of the least imaginative features) to depersonalise the characters.

I believe that Wagner might well have accepted Jung's views on artistic creation in general and *The Ring* in particular, and that he might have recognised that the attraction which he felt towards these myths and legends was founded on dream-experiences. But he would certainly have rejected, at least until the last years of his life, the explanation of his work suggested in the second of the two Bayreuth programme essays. This is called *The Blind Prophet* and is written by Anton Orel, with the imprimatur of the abbot pro-vincial of the Austrian congregation of the Augustinian Canons of St John Lateran. Wagner, we know, was willing to admit that he could not fully understand the nature of his own achievement; but if he was really, as Dr Orel makes out, an unwitting Christian prophet, then his understanding of his work was not merely incomplete but mistaken.

This does not worry Dr Orel. Nineteenth-century romanticism remains for him a nostalgia for the Church, even though it 'does not always lead to a happy home-coming'. In his view Wagner, in consciously rejecting Christianity and the Church, was rejecting the key to his own creation. Certainly the sense of mission, of being the instrument of a power that he did not understand, was strong when he wrote in 1859 to Mathilde Wesendonck:

> I let myself be guided without fear by my instinct. I am being used as the instrument for something higher than my own personality warrants. This knowledge is so native to me that I often hardly ask myself whether I will or do not will a thing. I am in the hands of the wonderful genius that I serve for my span of life and that intends me to complete what only I can achieve.

If Wagner's achievements were smaller, it would be easier to dismiss this certainty of being used by an unknown power as mere megalomaniac illusion. But even if we grant the superlative quality of Wagner's work, will it suffer a detailed, purely Christian interpretation like Dr Orel's? And should it not be related to a still deeper plane, one from which Christianity itself is only one of many emanations?

Dr Orel goes a long way with Jung in his acceptance of the mythological, and perhaps even the psychological, significance of Wagner's work. On the Thomist principle that all supernatural truth is mediated to humanity through nature, he accepts the mythology and would probably not reject Jung's psychological explanation of *The Ring*. But for Dr Orel, as for all Christians, the sun-myths and heroic legends of humanity's infancy are blind gropings towards a historical truth which was realised in Christ – who is thus the 'desire of all nations' as well as the Messiah foretold by the Jewish prophets. To Dr Orel the true Siegfried is Christ; Wotan and the giants are the forces of humanism and naturalism; while the Niebelungs represent materialism, both capitalistic and communistic. The Gibichungs, who bring about Siegfried's death, are the ageless trinity of avarice, lust, and pride – and so we have a picture of *The Ring* as a kind of fourteenth-century morality play.

Dr Orel, however, like Jung, insists on the existence of multiple meanings in this, as in every other myth. And so Siegfried, besides typifying Christ, is also the German nation, deflected from its true mission by the forces of naturalism and materialism. Wagner would have understood this; but he would surely have been astonished to read Dr Orel's definition of Germany's mission which is none other than 'to be Parsifal'. At first blush this seems to be carrying multiplicity of meaning to the verge of meaninglessness. Is there in fact any real connection between the figures of Siegfried and Parsifal, which to the ordinary Wagnerian appear antithetical? And was there any conscious connection between them in the composer's own mind? If we examine these two figures, we may be surprised to find how much they have in common.

Both are orphans in search of their mothers and both bring about the collapse of a paternal, authoritarian world of whose rottenness they are hardly even aware. Both come to spiritual maturity through their knowledge of woman – a woman in each case closely connected, and in some way identified with their own mothers. It is in the nature of these women that we find the true difference between Siegfried and Parsifal. The love into which Brünnhilde initiates Siegfried is the supreme affirmation of life in this world. But what Parsifal learns in Kundry's arms is the reality of guilt and sin, and when he leaves her it is to set out on the ascetic search for redemption from outside this world. Parsifal is, in fact, a kind of baptised Siegfried, and it is the reign of Love that he inaugurates at Montsalvat, with its mother symbol of the Dove. That alone can succeed to the old world of Authority whose twilight and final extinction we witness in *Götterdämmerung*. The spear which trembles harmlessly over Parsifal's head in Klingsor's magic garden is in this sense the same spear that broke in Wotan's hand when he tried to bar Siegfried's path to Brünnhilde's magic mountain.

I do not think there is any evidence that Wagner himself regarded *Parsifal* as a fulfilment or explanation of *The Ring*; but that is really beside the point, if we remember his own admission of not fully understanding the nature of his own work. Dr Orel does not suggest this, nor do the Bayreuth productions hint at any continuity of purpose. In fact the Bayreuth *Parsifal* has escaped from the old-fashioned 'Nazarene' presentation only to fall into a kind of fashionable grimness for the Montsalvat scenes and an equally fashionable near-triviality for Klingsor's garden.

In Germany itself there is almost certainly more consciousness of a national affinity with Siegfried, however played out this theme may be to many, than aspiration towards the role of Parsifal. I cannot think either that East Germans, whatever they may be thinking, are likely to be imagining themselves in the role of Parsifal. All we can say for certain is that up to now the German race has shown singularly little consciousness of any destiny to inaugurate the realm of self-less, spiritual love. Racial destinies, however, are foolish intellectual toys, all too easily snatched out of the hands of philosophers by politicians; and we shall do best to see *Parsifal*, as well as *The Ring*, as allegories of the individual rather than the race.

Whether we accept or reject either of the interpretations of Wagner's work elaborated in these two Bayreuth essays, we have to acknowledge that Wagner's significance is by no means exhausted. Indeed his attempts to understand the origins of man's emotional life and to renew the religious sense of existence are perhaps only now being understood and revealed. Whether or not the individual music-lover 'likes' Wagner's music is really irrelevant. Works of art of such richness and density of meaning, and showing such a perfect command of the medium, do not need to solicit an audience. In fact Wagner's instinct to act as the showman and promoter of his own works, even within the musical framework – something which has no parallel in any other music – easily repels the more fastidious. But then Wagner's works were only for a short time the preserve of the fastidious and the aesthetes who, as so often happens, missed their real significance, seeing the trees but missing the character of the wood in which they grew.

10 Nietzsche and Peter Gast

Nietzsche's place in the history of music is assured as a distinguished early Wagnerian convert and later as a spectacular renegade; but his devotion to the art was much deeper and of longer standing than his personal devotion to Wagner or his works. He was an amateur composer, a pianist maliciously praised as superior to Wagner himself and a speculator tireless in his discussion of the contemporary music of his day.

Lonely, prickly and suspicious after his break with Wagner in the mid-70's, he needed a more complaisant musical god whom he could alternately bully and worship, and so he created one out of a Bâle pupil, Johann Heinrich Köselitz. Ten years younger than Nietzsche, Köselitz had already spent three years at the Leipzig Conservatory when he arrived at Bâle in 1876, but although hailed by the philosopher as 'a new Mozart', none of his four operas, his orchestral or chamber music made any impression either on his contemporaries or anyone else beside Nietzsche. In Nietzsche he found his one-man public and it is not surprising that the rest of his life was virtually dedicated at first to the man and then, as director of the Nietzsche Archiv at Weimar and editor of his letters, to his memory.

'Peter Gast' was the name Köselitz used as a composer, and 'Pietro Gasti' Nietzsche called him in that enthusiasm for Italy and the Mediterranean which was one of his most German characteristics. The enterprising French publishing firm, Editions du

Rocher, has recently produced a French translation of Nietzsche's letters to Köselitz by Louise Servicen and a companion volume of introduction and notes by André Schaeffner (*Lettres à Peter Gast*, two vols). The letters start formally in May 1876, become steadily more frequent and familiar, and reach the number of 277 before the final pathetic telegram. This was dispatched from Turin on 4 January, 1889 as the shades of madness closed around Nietzsche, who signed himself 'The Crucified One'. Their tone is mostly one of fraternal warmth, and it seems unlikely that Köselitz ever seriously forgot his station or made it difficult for Nietzsche to admire his music by claiming equality as a human being. In fact the relationship was perhaps one of those rare and happy cases in which two mentally sick men discover that their neuroses are complementary. Much space is devoted to rather old-maidish discussions of the climate, temperatures and *pension* prices of small Italian and Swiss towns and villages, and to musical gossip. The letters were originally published in 1908 as Vol. IV in Nietzsche's *Collected Letters*.

Of far greater interest to music-lovers than the letters themselves, André Schaeffner's 200-page introduction is in fact a study of Nietzsche's whole attitude to music, the history of his tastes (including his enthusiasm for Wagner) and an estimation of his debt to French civilisation of which, like Schopenhauer and Bismarck, he was a great admirer.

Like all psychotically self-engrossed characters Nietzsche judged everything – his contemporaries, history, music, literature, philosophy – by standards which are hardly disguised compensations for his own weaknesses. Thus the physically delicate and unprepossessing German professor, sensitive and solitary, declares war on pity and charity and proclaims the handsome, ruthless Superman, at the same time rationalising his own inner loneliness as superiority to the common herd.

If the quarrel with Wagner has never been unambiguously explained, we can be fairly sure that jealousy and wounded self-esteem were at the root. What Nietzsche mocked was 'die ganze Wagnerei' – the hangers-on, the Bayreuth 'mystique' and the deterioration which these, he believed, had caused in Wagner himself. Only a year before he went mad he wrote that no composer counted with

him by the side of Wagner and that his enthusiasm for Bizet was
not to be taken seriously. It was, in fact, the typical manoeuvre of
a jealous person, this flaunted proclamation of a new god as unlike
as possible to the god who had refused to be his exclusive possession.

We can sympathise with Nietzsche's distaste for Wagner's ex-
patiations on the exquisite beauty of the sacrament of the Lord's
Supper, and sermons on chastity came oddly from his lips.
But there is something hysterical in Nietzsche's declaration, 'I
despise all those who do not consider *Parsifal* an offence against
morality.' Feelings of that kind are not engendered by intellectual
antagonisms but by personal pique, wounded vanity or an adoration spurned.

'Music as Circe! . . .', grumbled Nietzsche. '*Parsifal* will always
hold the chief place in the art of seduction, as its stroke of genius.
I admire that work; I should like to have composed it myself; not
having done so, I at least understand it.' And understand it he did,
not only its musical stature but its psychological import, which he
loathed because it penetrated his defensive armour. 'Someone
always wants to be saved in Wagner's works', he justly observed,
going on to complain of the 'neurotic decadence' of Wagner's
heroes and heroines, as though they were Tennessee Williams
characters.

Did he forget that Ajax and Orestes, Medea and Oedipus, Ham-
let and Lear, Phèdre, Faust and the Prince of Homburg deviate as
widely as possible from any conceivable norm of mental health?
Such 'sick souls' have furnished poets for more than three thousand
years with the subject-matter of their greatest works, and Wagner
was certainly not original in choosing unbalanced, redemption-
hungry characters as the protagonists of his music-dramas.

The generations which have grown up since Nietzsche have had
good reason to feel a need for redemption, and they have sought it
in a good many queer quarters that would have displeased him
perhaps even more than Christianity.

Today the commonest complaint against *Parsifal* is not its theme
of redemption through innocent suffering (which is close to the
chosen theme of Britten's operas, after all) but its inextricable confusion of sacred and profane love, religion and sex. This objection,
taken at its face value, is a strange one for an age which has just

begun to realise how inextricably confused are just these two vast regions which earlier generations regarded as mutually exclusive in the most absolute sense. *Parsifal* is in fact a pioneer work in a field in which psychologists and theologians are now working towards an astonishing measure of agreement. If *Parsifal* still arouses hostility, it can only be either among those whose conceptions of religion and of sex are incomplete – and these are probably the majority – or those who are repelled by the details of its presentation.

Wagner was certainly not free of blame in this. Lacking any personal experience of organised religious life and liturgy, he conceived of both as a kind of mediaeval pageant, and producers have exaggerated rather than corrected the theatricality of the Graal scenes. All too often the gait and gestures of the Knights have a self-conscious unctuousness which suggests a seminary of Tartuffes, and the illumination of the Grail is carried out in a manner worthy of some American West Coast sect. Wagner's own visual taste was, of course, that of mid-nineteenth-century Germany and therefore execrable. His own family at Bayreuth have been the first to recognise and try to correct this weakness, which is probably more nearly organic, and therefore incurable, in *Parsifal* than in any other of his works.

If Montsalvat presents difficulties, these are nothing compared with those of Klingsor's magic garden. Delibes, bored with the idea of a visit to Bayreuth, was cheered by the prospect of Act II of *Parsifal* where, he said, 'il y a toujours de petites femmes', and no production that I have ever seen has quite avoided the impression that Klingsor is in fact turning out 'les girls' in a kind of super floorshow.

Is it impossible, I have often wondered, to abolish the physical presence of the Flowermaidens entirely and to hear only their voices? Even if it were, we are faced with the crucial scene of the whole work, Kundry's attempt to seduce Parsifal.

This is crucial because, stripped of its fortuitous trappings, Kundry's predicament is that of every human being who has known and then lost his vision of holiness and spends a lifetime hankering for what is lost, while in fact plunging further and further away from it. If Kundry is made ludicrous – and Nietzsche's quip about Madame Bovary shows that this was the case, at least for some listeners, very early – *Parsifal* appears rotten at the core. The almost insuperable difficulty for producers throughout all this act lies in the fact that Wagner himself plainly conceived it in terms absolutely unacceptable to the modern opera-goer. What can be done with a scene which presents deep psychological and religious truth in terms borrowed from Sardou and the Paris Opéra under the Second Empire? Moreover, there is a further anomaly. Parsifal's realisation of guilt and Kundry's pleading are set to music whose chromaticism goes even further than that of *Tristan*. The tonal structure of this whole scene is so shifting and complex that it lies very close to Reger and early Schoenberg, while the huge leaps in the voice and the high-lighting of solo instruments complete the resemblance. So that the most subtly developed music is found accompanying the crudest of spectacles.

M. Schaeffner has some interesting speculations as to how much of Wagner's music Nietzsche knew and how well he knew it. Evidence is best for *Tristan* and *Die Meistersinger*, though for a long time he had only heard the Prelude of *Tristan* and knew the rest of the work from playing it through at the piano. His acquaintance with the *Ring* seems to have been sketchy and incomplete, and altogether we get the impression from M. Schaeffner that Nietzsche was one of those enthusiastic amateurs with very strong opinions of works which they do not actually know, though they have formed a very clear and often quite inaccurate idea of their general character. This impression is confirmed by his calling Offenbach 'a Voltairian spirit', very high praise from him but superficial as a judgment of either Voltaire or Offenbach. Nietzsche was no fool. Did he simply not know the works of either very well?

What would have been the course of Nietzsche's opinions, philosophical and musical, if France had won the war of 1870 and there had been no unification, no Reich? Was Wagner associated in his mind with triumphant militarism and was it the sheer successfulness of the new Germany, the crude mentality of the political 'nouveau riche', which sent this intellectual aristocrat scurrying from one humble Swiss or Italian pension to another? A bedraggled eagle, a cross between Bismarck and the Wandering Jew in appearance, he continues to fascinate even now that he has long ceased to shock.

11 Scriabin and the Russian Renaissance

The bubble reputations of an age often reveal its character more clearly than those which are formed more slowly, and prove in the event more durable. The mid-nineteenth century, for example, classed Meyerbeer with Beethoven and Michelangelo, and this, though it tells us little enough about Meyerbeer, tells us much about the mid-nineteenth century. Even great artists are often admired in their lifetimes for qualities which seem to later generations either non-existent or secondary. Their greatness, though felt instinctively by their contemporaries, is accounted for in terms of the fashionable philosophy of the day, which often proves inadequate.

Bubble reputations, on the other hand, attach to one of two classes of artist – those whose art merely satisfies the superficial fashionable taste of their age (Meyerbeer is the classical example) or those who appeal to a deeper, more enduring need but at a superficial level; and of those, Scriabin is almost a unique representative in musical history. Fifty years ago Scriabin's music was admired as that of a harmonic innovator and a new spiritual force. Today his harmonic 'innovations' appear as no more than the exploiting *ad nauseam* of a single chord, while his mystical beliefs are regarded as psychological fantasies of purely clinical interest. How are we to account for this complete reversal of opinion?

The generation in which Scriabin grew up was 'looking for a sign' – for some new extension of the language of music and some new revelation to take the place of Wagner's now familiar theodicy. Some found the new messiah in Debussy, some in Richard Strauss, a few in Mahler; but in Russia intellectual and artistic circumstances were so different from those in western Europe than none of these qualified for the messianic role. Pressure had been steadily accumulating throughout the second half of the nineteenth century behind the movement of political and social reform and intellectual emancipation, and by the 90's it had reached a strength and a density at which the smallest spark would, it seemed, cause an explosion. With all social and political activity denied them thinkers and artists turned with hysterical intensity to irrational, mystical, and unnaturally 'other-worldly' fields of interest.

Here the genuine was inextricably confused with a charlatanism which was often unconscious. Even as early as the late 70's, Dostoevsky, working on *The Brothers Karamazov*, had been deeply impressed by the writings of a certain Fyodorov who believed it to be the task of philosophy 'to raise the dead collectively, end childbearing and usher in the transfiguration of life here on earth'. Solovyov, a really distinguished religious thinker and poet on whom Dostoevsky modelled the character of Alyosha Karamazov, had apocalyptic dreams of the end of the world and was vouchsafed a vision of the Divine Wisdom in the reading-room of the British Museum. In fact this apocalyptic quality – this feeling that 'the end' was at hand – was the underlying characteristic of all Russian thought from the late 90's onward. Solovyov, who died in 1900, gave expression to this feeling in a much quoted line – 'the end is already near; the unexpected will soon be accomplished'. And other writers spoke of 'the feeling of sickness, alarm, catastrophe and disruption which lay heavy on the last generations of Russian thinkers before the revolution – the constant and wanton feeling of catastrophe evoked by an accumulation of indisputable facts' – 'the search for an integral way of life, for a single answer to all life's problems, some form of collective which would weld together the sundered fragments of Russian life'.

In this atmosphere the Messina earthquake of 1908 was seriously regarded by many as an apocalyptic portent. 'We know what the fragrant names of Calabria and Sicily mean,' wrote the poet Alexander Blok, 'but let us be silent and grow pale, knowing that if the ancient Scylla and Charybdis vanished from the earth, yet ahead of us and in the heart of the earth a more terrible Scylla and Charybdis await us. What can we do . . .? We can only put on mourning, celebrate our sorrow in the fact of the catastrophe. The battleship lowers its flag to half-mast – as though it were a sign that the flag has been lowered in our own hearts. In the face of the raging elements the haughty flag of culture is lowered.'

In this tense and nervous atmosphere, every kind of new religion and superstition proliferated: pantheism, theosophy, anthroposophy and the new semi-oriental gnostic philosophies of Gurdjiev and Uspensky, the erotic mysticism of Rozanov, Gorky's 'demotheism' and Merezhkovsky's belief in 'the secret three designed to be the nucleus of the new church of the Holy Spirit in which the mystery of the flesh awaited final manifestation' – a curious prototype of D. H. Lawrence's *mystique* of sensuality. There was much talk of 'the new religious consciousness' and the journal issued under Merezhkovsky's guidance was characteristically called first *The New Way* and later *Questions of Life*.

Perhaps the most characteristic of all was the equation of Christ and Dionysos, actually proclaimed in a book published in 1903 by the poet Vyacheslav Ivanov. The shadow of Nietzsche lay heavily over all these thinkers and poets who were united in their search of 'ecstasy for ecstasy's sake'. This was to be sought, according to Vyacheslav Ivanov, in 'symphonic culture' and non-acceptance of the world. In fact, the universal divorce between speculation and the reality implied in this 'non-acceptance of the world' reflected the tragic separation of culture from all practical, social, or political activity, and was eventually to infect the political world; so that even the political history of the years between the Russo-Japanese War and the 1917 revolution often shows the same unreality and dream-like hysterical quality as the symbolist plays and gnostic manifestos of the previous decade.

It was in these years and against this background that Scriabin grew up and made his reputation, for it was a Russian reputation in the first place. Music, as often before, lagged behind the other arts and was still suffering from Wagnerian fever when the Symbolists and the religious-literary sects had moved to a correspondingly later phase. At the end of a long life Rimsky-Korsakov, it is true, paid tribute to the prevailing 'spiritualism' of the day in his opera 'The Invisible City of Kitezh and the maiden Fevronia', a blend of naturistic pantheism with Orthodox symbolism. But Rachmaninov continued the Tchaikovskian tradition of romantic introspection, penetrated with the sense of impending doom and the nostalgia for a non-existent past, which was part of the very atmosphere that he breathed in Russia.

It was in the late 90's that Rimsky-Korsakov wrote of 'that star of the first magnitude newly arisen in Moscow – the somewhat warped, posing and self-opinionated Alexander Nikolaevich Scriabin'. Born in 1872, Scriabin was indeed exceptionally and precociously gifted but in many ways the characteristic product of a too exclusively feminine upbringing by the aunt and grandmother who took the place of the mother who died in his early childhood. He was a dandy in the aristocratic Cadet Corps before he entered the Moscow Conservatory to study composition with Taneiev and the piano with Safonov, winning a gold medal as a pianist in 1892. His earliest published compositions, dating from the late 80's, show a kinship with Chopin so marked and so all-pervading as to present a case of something like spiritual identification. They are miniatures of a 'salon' type, extremely elegant in form and *facture* but already distinguished by a heavy, disturbing and individual scent very different from the characteristically innocent and flowery scent of Chopin's smaller pieces.

The markedly 'indoor' character of the early music of Scriabin, with its literary and urban atmosphere, is never stronger than in the pieces of strongly erotic character, whose inspiration is plainly the boudoir rather than the salon. The erotic element, which remained one of the poles of Scriabin's art, already foreshadowed a kinship with Liszt that was to grow stronger as the composer grew increasingly discontented with the concept of music as a self-sufficient art and reached out vaguely towards a philosophical or religious meaning – or, in his own words, to 'the *being* of which every work of art is only a *becoming*'. The *Poème Satanique* of 1903 not only echoes Liszt's *Malediction* and *Mephisto* pieces but shows Scriabin committing himself to the 'magical' view of art which, as we have seen, prevailed in Russian intellectual circles of the day. He numbered among his friends Prince Sergei Trubetskoi, one of two philosopher brothers and the friend and protector of Solovyov: Merezhkovsky and his wife Zinaida Gippius: and Vyacheslav Ivanov at whose flat in St Petersburg – significantly called 'The Tower' – the young Berdyaev attended an apparently very mild attempt to revive the 'Dionysian mysteries'.

Already, in 1900, Scriabin's first symphony had shown a new taste for the grandiose and the religious. It is in six movements, the last of which is choral and consists of a Hymn to Art as a 'wonderful image of the Godhead'. With the fourth of the piano sonatas, written in 1903, he has begun to throw off the drawing-room elegance. Here we have already the fragmentation of melody, the caresses, sudden winged phrases and ecstatic trills that herald his mature manner.

Despite the manifest echoes of Wagner in that music Scriabin had already rejected the idea of an opera, on the grounds that it could only be the 'representation of a dramatic action, not the act itself'; and this idea of a musical performance as a magical rite, a liturgical incantation, the calling to life of hidden cosmic forces, completely dominated him from now onwards. It is explicit in the inscription over the visionary fifth piano sonata: 'I call you forth to life, hidden influences, sunk in the obscure depths of the Creative Spirit, timid germs of life, I bring you boldness!'

Hitherto Scriabin, for all his desultory reading in philosophy, had been a mystic without a theology. The movements of the third symphony, written in 1903-4, bore significant but still vague titles – 'Struggles', 'Delights' and 'The Divine Game' – this last an echo perhaps of Hegel's 'endless play of Love with itself'. By this time he had taken a positive and final dislike to the music of all other composers and was thus, both as artist and thinker, enclosed in a completely solipsistic world. The exact date of his first interest in theosophy seems to be uncertain, but he first became acquainted with the writings of Blavatsky and Annie Besant during a visit to Paris in 1907, and it was then that he developed something approximating to a philosophy of art. From now onwards he saw himself as the messiah, destined, as he believed, to bring about the Final Act by which Spirit was to redeem Matter, and a great liturgical rite, in which all the arts were to play a part, was to usher in a new era. We can find in his own writings as clear a statement as such beliefs permit – 'an ocean of cosmic love encloses the world', he writes, 'and in the intoxicated waves of this ocean of bliss is felt the approach of the Final Act – the act of union between the Male-Creator and the Woman-World'.

This sexual imagery always persisted and even so late a work as the seventh piano sonata, written in 1911-12 and particularly valued by the composer, contains – according to Leonid Sabaneiev, the composer's close friend and disciple – a naïve and rather crude erotic 'programme'. Unlike the vast majority of mystical thinkers, Scriabin always allots himself the male role in the mystic marriages and acts of union, of which he writes. 'Oh! I would I could possess the world as I possess a woman', he exclaimed, and his mystical cosmology is constructed round his own creative personality. In the first process of creation Spirit and Matter were one. They separate only in order to create the world and then unite once again.

Scriabin spoke of this first phrase of creation as 'creative agony' or 'lust for life', and it is followed by a second phase, the process of dematerialisation. 'The world glitters with the imprint of the Creator Spirit's beauty,' he wrote, 'but at the same time it moves further and further away from the Creator, diffusing itself in innumerable protean phenomena.' The desire of the world to be freed from the bonds of matter – and we are immediately reminded of St Paul's 'the whole creation groaneth and travaileth' – could only, he believed, be fulfilled by means of art, or a synthesis of the arts, in the hands of a messiah. Like many of his contemporaries in Russia, he attached particular importance to India, the home of 'ancient esoteric knowledge', and even planned to buy a site there for the temple in which the Final Mystery was to be accomplished. All his later works he regarded as sketches for this 'Preliminary Act', fragments of whose literary text were among the papers found at his death in 1915.

The nearest he approached to his ideal was probably the 'poem of fire' or *Prometheus* for orchestra, piano and *clavier à lumières*. This 'light-machine' was a first attempt to achieve a synthesis of the arts and a 'counterpoint of the senses' which Scriabin believed essential to his composite form. He dreamed of 'a musical phrase ending in a scent, a chord that resolved into a colour, a melodic line whose climax becomes a caress'. And he undoubtedly saw himself

as Prometheus (an extension of his Satanic fancies), the Free Redeemer rescuing the world of matter by the power of spirituality
and 'ecstasy'. The music itself makes a hypnotic effect by its repeated insistence on small cell-like phrases, harmonies built on
superimposed fourths and the profusion of trills. The French marks
of expression are a further guide – dark, threatening, strange,
charmed, limpid, defiant, stormy, bellicose, like a winged caress,
with an intense desire, like a shout, glittering, ecstatic, are a few
of them.

Listening to this unfolding of an *idée fixe*, it is easy to understand
that its appeal was largely to those who already felt the attraction
of Scriabin's personality and were moved by the strength of his
personal conviction, and most of all to those Russian audiences to
whom the spiritual background of the music, so completely alien
today, was already familiar. The nearest parallel at all familiar today
is to be found in the gnostic writings of Gurdjiev. Like Scriabin
planning his Final Act, Gurdjiev spent years on the plans for a vast
mystical ballet, believed in the possibility of a world-language and
in the magical, theurgic power of art. Scriabin compared his last
two piano sonatas to magic rites, the ninth a black mass and the
tenth 'white' or beneficent magic, and in both the fragmentation of
musical material reaches nearly the same point as Schoenberg was
reaching at the same time in his opus II piano pieces. We can see
the final point reached by Scriabin in the ninth sonata, written in
1912-13.

What are we to make of Scriabin? It is easy to dismiss him as a
spoiled talent, the composer of the youthful piano pieces in which
the spirit of Chopin is wonderfully revived and continued, but
later spoiled by crazy mystical notions and an obsession which
brought him to the verge of lunacy. In fact Scriabin's later piano
sonatas, however esoteric their musical content, remain interesting
from the purely pianistic point of view; and *Prometheus* and the
Poem of Ecstasy will retain their place in the history of the orchestra
– a place with, say, Schoenberg's *Pelleas und Melisande* and
Strauss's Domestic Symphony. But today Scriabin's career is chiefly
interesting as a warning, a kind of cautionary tale of the man who
lost his ability to distinguish between dream and reality because
he lost contact with humanity.

This, as we have seen, was the great weakness of the Russian artistic and intellectual 'renaissance' at the opening of the present century and its explanation lies in the political, social, and religious life of Russia. The revolution shattered the dream and blew up the ivory towers; but it has hitherto imposed on its artists a view of 'reality' almost as one-sided as that of the aesthetes and mystics. For the artist cannot restrict his human interests and sympathies to any social class or imagined category. Even the exclusive concern of the French classical dramatists with royal or princely personages is less restricting in fact than the Russian artist's obligatory concern with proletarian characters. It is an unimportant convention that Racine's Phèdre is a queen, for she is first and foremost a human being, whereas the creations of Soviet artists too often conceal beneath their party or proletarian status not so much a human personality as an ideological blueprint.

12 Scriabin's Mystical Beliefs

In the twenty years which preceded the revolution of 1917 the Russian religious sense, following the curve of political and social movements, developed a form of hysteria which lies, perhaps, never far beneath the surface in all religious natures. The mystical is a sense with which the Russians, as a nation, are particularly gifted: but it is a sense capable of many perversions, and in the last years of the Tsarist régime a wave of strange religious feeling passed over the educated world. It was not merely a court clique, led by the Tsaritsa, deeply impressed by the religious pretentions of the ambiguous Rasputin. Russian society, influenced by artists and intellectuals, developed a prophetic, apocalyptic sense, dimly foreseeing the near end of the world it knew and the birth of some new era of which social reform and a universal heightening of spirituality were the only two clearly distinguished traits. The chief guide and inspirer of this movement was the mystic and philosopher Solovyov; its greatest exponents in the arts were the poet Alexander Alexandrovich Blok and the composer Alexander Nikolaevich Scriabin. Suvchinsky, in his preface to Blok's poem of 'The Twelve', tells how only a few of the Russian intellectuals who had foreseen the coming of the revolution actually recognised and accepted it when it came. Blok was one of the few. Scriabin had died the year before, but he had seen in the Great War an Armageddon, the end of an old order out of which a new must rise, and in the Russian revolution he could hardly have failed to see the fulfilment of his dream – different, no doubt, from all his expectations, but without question the new world.

There are two types of mystical experience, speaking broadly; and it was to the less common type of the two that Scriabin belonged. His mysticism was primarily a mysticism of the will, and only secondarily of the emotions; so that although, in common with many other mystics, he makes use of the language of eroticism in order to describe his mystical experiences, yet, unlike the great majority, he speaks of himself as the lover and creator, the active and not the passive force. 'I am nothing: I am only that which I create,' he writes. 'The fate of the universe is decided. I will to live. I love life. I am God. I am nothing. I wish to be everything. I have engendered that which is opposite to me – time, space, and number. I myself am that which is opposite to me, because I am only that which I engender. . . . I will to be God. . . . The world seeks after God, I seek after myself. The world is an impulse towards God, I am an impulse towards myself. I am the world, I am the search for God, because I am only that which I seek. My search begins, and my return: the history of human knowledge begins.' Blok, too, occasionally breaks into language of this kind –

> Oh I would live madly!
> Eternalise all that exists,
> Humanise the impersonal,
> Embody the failing and weak.
>
> (From *Yambi*, February 1914)

– though he never goes the length of Scriabin, who cries out in one place: 'Oh! I would I could possess the world as I possess a woman!'

Of the other great mystics, Jacob Boehme alone uses this language of activity. Among the rest, the far commoner imagery is that which places the object of mystical experience – Christ, in the case of Christian mysticism – in the place of the lover, while the soul of the mystic is compared to the bride, waiting and longing passionately for her lover's coming, hardly existing except in the warmth of his presence. This is the language of Eckhardt, Suso, Teresa, John of the Cross, and Mme Guyon –

> Amado con Amada,
> Amada en el Amado transformada!

– and it is the opposite pole to the possessive ecstasies of Scriabin.

Again, although his conception of the universe was dualistic, it was not so in the conventional sense. Good and Evil he saw merely as two complementary exhibitions of energy. The two polarities for him were the principles of Activity and Passivity, the one creative and the other receptive, the one centripetal and the other centrifugal – Male and Female. The first principle of this universe he calls indifferently Creator, God, Death or New Life; but under these names lies the fundamental idea of spirituality as creating, and working through, the world of material phenomena. In the first process of creation these two poles were mystically united; and they separate only in order that they may create the world and then unite once again. This first phase of creation was spoken of by Scriabin as 'creative agony', 'lust for life'; and after it followed the second phase, the process of dematerialisation. 'This world glitters with the imprint of the Creator Spirit's beauty: but at the same time it moves further and further away from the Creator, diffusing itself in protean phenomena without number.' And of the desire of the world to be freed from the bonds of matter he writes ' . . . the tortured universe awaits a miracle, awaits the last great Act of Fulfilment, the act of union between the male Creator-Spirit and the Woman-World'. This union, he believed, could only be accomplished by means of Art, or rather a synthesis of all the arts, in the hands of a messiah. 'The messiah of the union must realise the final synthesis of all the arts', he writes. And he was convinced that this messiah was himself. He believed, in the language of biology, that ontogeny recapitulates phylogeny, seeing his music as a whole world in the small, himself as a creator-god, and his own creative processes as microcosms of the processes of world-creation. It is clear that Art, thus conceived as a religious factor, can have two aspects. As a rite of evocation its magic may be either black or white, cathartic and theurgic or ecstatic and satanistic. It was, in fact, into these two categories that Scriabin divided his own works. And since he was a pianist as well as a composer he came to look upon the performance of a work too, and not only its creation, as a rite whose object is the attainment of a new spiritual illumination, an initiation into the life of the spirit.

Scriabin evolved this mystical aesthetic between the years 1895-1905, at a time when the Symbolist Movement was starting in Russian literature; and in his later years when he was preparing his music for the Mystery – the final rite which, he believed, would play out the old world and usher in the new – his chief friends and confidants were the poets Vyacheslav-Ivanov, Baltrushaitis, and Balmont. These three men had all come under the influence of Solovyov who, like Scriabin, was convinced of the near end of the world. One of his poems ends thus, for example:

> And a voice keeps crying in the silence, crying unreprovingly,
> 'Already the end is near; the unexpected shall soon be
>   accomplished.'

Blok, too, was obsessed with the same idea. In one of the poems in *Strashni Mir*, a collection of verses written between 1909-16, a *Voice from the chorus* cries:

> Blacker and blacker shall grow the terrible world,
> Madder and madder the reeling dance of the planets,
>   For centuries, aye! centuries.
> And the last day, more awful than them all,
> We shall behold, both you and I.
> A hideous sin shall hide the heavens,
> The smile congeal on every mouth,
> Misery of non-existence. . . . !
> You will wait for the spring, my child –
> And the spring shall deceive you.
> You will call the sun into the heavens –
> And the sun shall not rise.
> And the shriek, when you begin to shriek,
> Will fall, like a stone. . . .

And again we find the same thought in a poem dated 8 September, 1914 –

> Ash-sprinkled years!
> Is your message a message of madness, a message of hope?

> From days of war, from days of freedom,
> A bloody reflection shines in men's faces.
>
> Dumbness all around – the jangling bells
> Have silenced men's lips from speaking.
> On hearts once fired with ecstasy
> A fated emptiness descends.
>
> High above our last resting-place
> Let the crows swoop with a cry –
> O God! God! grant that the worthy
> May look on Thy kingdom!

– an apocalyptic vision raised to the level of the highest poetry. Although Blok was unquestionably a far greater poet than Vyacheslav-Ivanov, he wrote of him in humble admiration. One of the poems of the *Razniye Stikhotvoreniya*, dated April 1912, is dedicated to him. It describes the sudden appearance of Vyacheslav Ivanov at a ball –

> There was a moment – an unknown force
> Tore at the heart in ecstasy,
> Deafening with its silver tone,
> Blinding with its cutting snow,
> Changing our path with its bliss!

And the poem ends in deepest humility –

> But I – sad, needy, and brutish –
> Have seen the dawn succeed the night
> And now at the dusty crossroads
> I gaze upon your regal procession.

In view of his interest in the literature of his time it is strange that the various trends of contemporary music interested Scriabin so little. They had no significance for him because they were more concerned with technique than with emotion. Scriabin's whole system was both irrational and amoral. Apocalyptic beliefs have naturally enough excited perhaps more ridicule than any other class of beliefs in the whole history of thought; and Scriabin earned more than his share of this ridicule, and even of open abuse, by his unshakable belief in his messiahship. His indifference to music other than his own was misconstrued into an artist's conceit; whereas it was due simply and solely to his feeling of being the first to realise fully the high place of music in the cosmic scheme – a position dimly apprehended by Wagner, but far beyond the vision of most musicians. He liked to apply to himself the line of Balmont –

Before me all other poets were but forerunners.

– and it is a fact that a large number of composers have been cobblers who have stuck rather over-conscientiously to their lasts, and have had small lives, or no life at all, outside the practice of their craft. Both Schubert and Brahms were such men: and it will always be a matter of personal opinion how far their narrowness of vision affected the purely musical quality of their works. To regard Art as the Way of Knowledge, as Scriabin did, is a high ideal. Only it is too often windy even on the heights of the spirit, and Scriabin, like many other idealists, was occasionally guilty of a bombastic rhetoric which leads even the warmest admirers of his music to mistrust a little his apparently sincere utterances as unconscious fraud. From a moralist's point of view, Scriabin was a weak man and his grasp on life small, in the sense that he came to lose all power to distinguish his dream-world of apocalyptic visions from the world of actual fact. With all his passion for the initiation of the whole world into the secrets of which he felt himself the appointed mystagogue, he never learned to wait nor to prepare himself consciously for his mission. Highly strung to the verge of a perpetual neuroticism, he became the victim of an *idée fixe* which he could not afford, in the end, to renounce, for he had staked so much upon it. But in spite of weakness and febrility, his character and his music – the one a perfect reflection of the other – stand out in the world of artistic personality and achievement as almost solitary examples of a winged, Dionysiac spirituality of vision and a uniquely lyrical mysticism.

Lines from a poem written by Blok in the September of 1909 sum up the essence of his ideals and Scriabin's. They are a call to desert the facile pleasures and successes of this world for the higher and more spiritual satisfactions, the illumination of another –

Launch forth thy boat, plunge to the distant pole
'Mid walls of ice – and slowly forget
How there below men fought and loved and perished,
And forget too the old past world of passions.

And 'mid the shudderings of the slow-moving cold
Teach thy tired heart to learn this lesson –
How here below her needs are all but nothing,
When from beyond the rays come streaming through.

(Arphi i Skripki)

13 Sergei Prokofiev

According to many western critics Prokofiev's career was a slow degeneration from the brilliant and ruthless young musical anarchist of pre-revolutionary days, through a period as 'playboy of the western world' during the 1920's, to the respectability of the Soviet laureateship and the unconscious philistinism of his latter years. The official Russian portrait, on the other hand, is of a musical 'prodigal' who left the fatherland to go whoring after the strange gods of the West and returned in middle life to his duty, to die in the odour of Soviet sanctity.

I believe that we may hope to understand Prokofiev if we compare him with his contemporary, compatriot, but absolute antithesis – Stravinsky. Stravinsky and Prokofiev have pursued diametrically opposite paths of development as artists, yet both have travelled the same psychological 'inner circle' – Stravinsky travelling, as it were, from east to west and Prokofiev from west to east. The differences that divided them were by no means merely temperamental, though those were certainly great. Entering the Russian musical world ten years later than Stravinsky, Prokofiev found that an impasse had been reached – a point at which established composers had exhausted the traditional language but still feared to embark on new experiments.

Prokofiev's hostility to the Russian musical establishment of his youth had the character of an instinctive recoil, immediate and prompted by no intellectual reasoning. In his recent 'Conversations' Stravinsky describes Prokofiev as 'the contrary of a musical thinker', and goes on to make fun of his commonplace mind and poor general culture. This is of course the perennial jibe of the intellectual musician against the musical 'natural'. It was Prokofiev's musician's instinct, not any conscious intellectual choice, that drew him from the very beginning towards Western music. Indeed the seeds of neo-classicism were perhaps first sown during one of those evenings in December 1906 when Max Reger visited St Petersburg and gave a concert of his own works. Prokofiev was then a boy of fifteen, and the impression that Reger's music made on him can be seen clearly in the 'Ten Pieces' for piano that he wrote during the next eight years.

If we consider such music against the background of Rachmaninov or Scriabin, its full originality appears. Here are fresh air, a clean palette, and no more souls or symbols, but also no theories of regenerating music by a return to the past, no intellectual justifications or *raffinement*. Prokofiev was indeed a self-conscious 'barbarian' in those days, and almost at the same time as the Regerish neo-classical pieces he wrote the Toccata whose persistent drumming rhythm and thick, graceless harmonic chunks must have sounded crude indeed in 1913.

The two chief centres of musical modernism in Russia during the years immediately before the revolution were the 'Contemporary Music Evenings' in St Petersburg and the Moscow magazine *Muzyka*. Both these institutions gave the young Prokofiev their fullest support and brought him into contact with the world of Diaghilev's magazine *Mir Iskusstva*, 'The World of Art'. This represented the reaction against what was then the Tolstoyan, and is more familiar to us as the Soviet, view of the artist as a moral agent with grave social responsibilities. When Diaghilev proclaimed that 'the only way to ensure progress and effectively to combat routine in the arts is to follow contemporary movements in Western Europe', he was declaring himself the last of the maximalist 'Westernisers'. How seriously Prokofiev was affected by any theories is doubtful (he always hated theorising), but there is no doubt that he felt the influence of Diaghilev's trump-composer, Stravinsky, and showed it clearly in his *Scythian Suite*, close to the *Sacre* in conception and often in sonority, and in the ballet *Chut*. Moreover, although he always remained on the outskirts of Diaghilev's personal circle, which regarded him as embarrassingly 'uncultured', what we may call a 'World of Art' strain persisted in his choice of subjects until the late 20's. We can see it in his preference for the poet Balmont, who provided him with the texts of a number of songs and the cantata *Seven of Them*; for Bryusov's *Flaming Angel*, with its magic and its religious mania; in the brittle, fantastic world of Gozzi's *Love of Three Oranges* and the sophisticated, 'abstract', and 'modernistic' ballet *Pas d'Acier*.

Prokofiev's initial attitude to the revolution was seemingly one of incomprehensible indifference. Music was in fact his sole interest, and he shared the common belief that a revolution which aimed at clearing the ground for a new society must automatically favour artistic innovation. When in 1918 he was disappointed in this belief, he left Russia without hard feelings and without cutting the ties that bound him to his past. For the next fourteen years he led the life of a travelling virtuoso pianist, with intervals dedicated exclusively to composition.

A list of the works completed or composed during these years reflects Prokofiev's instinctive preferences while he was under no sense of obligation, concerned only with satisfying his own creative impulses and making a living. In the first place we have three operas: *The Gambler*, *The Love of Three Oranges*, and *The Flaming Angel*, and four ballets: *Chut*, *Le Pas d'Acier*, *The Prodigal Son*, and *Sur le Borysthène*. Closely related to these are the third and fourth symphonies, based respectively on material of *The Flaming Angel* (never performed at the time) and *The Prodigal Son*. Since Prokofiev was making his livelihood as a pianist, it is strange that he wrote only one piano sonata and one concerto during these years. A handful of chamber works completes the list. None of this music brought Prokofiev any real and lasting success.

He was not, in fact, a lovable personality; and his music aroused in the Western European and North American public an unsatisfactory blend of admiration and even repulsion – 'the football pianist', they called him. Prokofiev himself declared that his chief interest at this period was 'the search for novelty and the breaking of tradition', and it does not need a Soviet aesthetician to find this a negative and incomplete ambition for a mature artist. The first sign of an approaching crisis in Prokofiev's artistic development was a falling-off, not so much in the quality as in the quantity of his work. Like all musical 'naturals', he had always written with extreme facility and seemed never at a loss for a musical idea; but during the latter part of the 1920's we find him repeatedly rewriting or arranging unsuccessful works rather than composing new ones. So that by the time he decided to return to Russia his output was in fact reduced to a trickle. His music was not wanted in Western Europe, and he needed the stimulus of performance, needed to put his gifts at the service of some welcoming and approving body. His thoughts returned to what was now a new public, his own people. In 1930 he was approaching forty and found himself at an age and in a position which send many 'prodigal sons' back to their fathers, or their fatherlands. In 1933 he tried to explain to Serge Moreux what was now a firm decision to return to live in Russia:

> I must see a real winter and a real spring again, I must hear Russian spoken round me and talk to people who are close to me . . . whose songs are my songs. Here I am restless and I'm in danger of becoming an academic.

This was a strange word and one that he used perhaps already in the Soviet sense of 'rootless' and 'formalistic'.

Was his return what Stravinsky calls it, 'simply a sacrifice to the bitch goddess', a confession of failure and a desperate attempt to win success by a recantation? It was not as simple as that, though I believe that Stravinsky's religious metaphor is apt, and that Prokofiev's return to Russia was in a sense a religious act, an act of faith and an attempt to 'save his soul', which he felt parched and withered in the fashionable avant-garde musical circles of western Europe. Certainly his fertility returned immediately and never left him again, though we can find evidence of his filling periods of diminished creative power by copious arrangements of his own music. In the twenty years of working life that were left to him – the whole of the second half of his life as a composer – Prokofiev wrote two-thirds of his whole output. Much of this music consists in frank trivialities, but there was also much serious and, in a new way, characteristic music.

'My lyrical gift', he once explained, 'was slow to develop because it was so little appreciated', and it is true that he was accepted in Western Europe as the extrovert, sarcastic, irreverent playboy of the 'contemporary' movement, the monkey whose tricks, as he got older, gradually ceased to amuse. Now, back in Russia, he was asked to develop his lyrical gift, and according to a formula that he had in the past repeatedly mocked – broad, immediately intelligible (that is to say traditional) melody of a 'life-enhancing' type modelled either on Russian folk-song or the Russian popular classics – which meant Glinka, Rimsky-Korsakov, Mussorgsky (though with reservations), and Tchaikovsky. The mature Prokofiev was incapable of imitation or pastiche of any kind. He was absolutely without Stravinsky's strong historical sense, the feeling for 'style' and 'period'. Although a self-borrower and arranger on a scale which outdid even Handel, he had none of the sophisticated musician's interest in recomposing other men's music or in recreating any past style.

The lyrical vein, which had lain for the most part dormant in him hitherto and was now consciously developed, was genuinely popular and unmistakably 'national', as we can see from two works composed before he was thirty. The first of these was a setting for voice and piano of Hans Andersen's 'Ugly Duckling'. This was written in 1913, at the height of his ruthless and brilliant youth when he was generally supposed to be devoid of all 'humanity'. It was a favourite with Gorky, who used to say that Prokofiev himself was the ugly duckling, pecked by critics and older musicians and spurned by the public but, in fact, a swan. Prokofiev's graphic music for the duckling's rearing, education, and first acquaintance with unhappiness vividly recalls Mussorgsky, with its brusque changes of rhythm and tempo and its folk-ish air, just as it clearly foreshadows the duck of *Peter and the Wolf*.

The other work in which we can find clear evidence of the simple, popular lyrical style that Prokofiev developed so assiduously during the last twenty years of his life is a collection of four piano pieces written in 1918 and bearing the significant title *Tales of an Old Grandmother*. This popular traditional lyrical style was developed by Prokofiev after his return to Russia in an enormous number of songs and small instrumental pieces. The success of his large works, too, with public and critics, seems to have been in exact proportion to their national and traditional lyrical content. In these works Prokofiev either silenced his sarcastic wit and his musician's instinct to explore new fields, or he skilfully discovered some external dramatic reason for indulging them – as in the *Alexander Nevsky* cantata, where the enemies of Russia are depicted in music that would not otherwise have won official approval.

On the other hand there were works in which the composer imposed less restraint on his imagination and showed that the old violent, bitter-tongued, mocking Prokofiev was by no means dead: these included the sixth symphony, the first cello concerto in its original form, and the seventh piano sonata. These were apparently unanimously declared 'negative' and regarded as unfortunate lapses into the bad habits acquired during the years of expatriation and Western contamination.

It would be false, I believe, to suppose that Prokofiev took refuge in some elaborate system of 'double think' – a kind of self-induced musical schizophrenia. The whole interest of his life was composition and he was fundamentally indifferent to doctrinaires of all kinds, the musical doctrinaires of the West and the politicians in Russia. He discovered, though, that he could satisfy the politicians without offending any deep conviction of his own, and thereby win a position in which he could be sure of having all his works performed and at the same time raise the level of Soviet music.

I should not expect Prokofiev to be remembered by the works such as the *Scythian Suite* or *Chut*, in which he was competing with Stravinsky or, on the other hand, by *War and Peace* or *Semyon Kotko*, in which he was merely doing more successfully what other Soviet composers were also doing – composing to a formula accepted for other than musical reasons. *The Love of Three Oranges* and *The Flaming Angel*, and possibly *The Betrothal in the Monastery*, are, on the other hand, unique both in conception and execution. As a symphonist Prokofiev showed a characteristically Russian inclination to confect 'symphonic suites' rather than symphonies originally conceived as such; and he is more likely to be remembered by his ballet music and his concertos, a form far better suited to his extrovert temperament, while the nine sonatas and more than 120 pieces that he wrote for the piano constitute a body of keyboard music unique in the twentieth century.

There is a considerable amount of repetition in his music: rhythmic figures, harmonic progressions and melodic shapes recur from work to work with only slight variation. But at his best his music has a character unmistakably its own. In judging the man and his work many people have been inclined to use criteria which do not apply to his psychological and aesthetic type, quarrelling (as it were) with a Siberian crab-apple for not producing peaches. Prokofiev remains one of the first half-dozen composers of the twentieth century, and until Benjamin Britten he was almost alone in demonstrating that the gap between the consciously 'contemporary' composer and the general public was not unbridgeable.

14 Gounod's Influence on French Music

Charles Gounod has probably succeeded Mendelssohn in the mind of the semi-educated musical world as the representative of all that twentieth-century music does *not* stand for. The younger generation may or may not, in its heart of hearts, care for *Faust*; but *Faust* is the only work of Gounod's which it knows, and it is not difficult to find material for contemptuous jokes in the libretto and the music. (It never has been difficult. In the 80's of last century, when *Faust* was a little more than twenty years old, Saint-Saëns and Chabrier used to do a party performance of the church scene, Saint-Saëns singing the part of Marguerite.) An older generation in England remembers the days when *The Redemption* stood almost on an equal footing with *Messiah* and *Elijah*; and it is impossible for anyone who has ever been a regular attendant at Anglican services not to have something of Gounod's religious idiom so deeply engrained in his musical consciousness as to be almost second nature. Gounod's evil reputation reposes, in fact, on a vast ignorance – on a shamefaced affection, often hotly denied, for *Faust*; on a healthy dislike of the mental and emotional furniture of his weaker disciples, Sir John Stainer and John Bacchus Dykes ('Our blest Redeemer, ere He breathed', 'Holy! holy! holy!') and on a rather exaggerated horror of the 'Ave Maria' arranged by Gounod as a descant to the first prelude of Bach's Forty-Eight Preludes and Fugues. Probably not one in a hundred English music-lovers realises that Gounod was in his day a revolutionary, a stern protestant

against the debased musical taste of his age, a fanatical admirer of
Bach and Palestrina and one of the heralds of the French musical
renaissance which flowered so quickly and so abundantly in the
years after the Franco-Prussian war of 1870.

Born in 1818, Gounod grew up in the years of clerical and mon-
archist reaction which followed the defeat of Napoleon, the end of
the First Empire and the restoration of the Bourbons; and the
atmosphere of those early years combined with Gounod's naturally
emotional and idealistic temperament to make religion one of the
most persistent and one of the deepest sources of inspiration
throughout his life. At the Conservatoire he was accepted as a pupil
as young as seven years old, studying with Lesueur, Reicha and
Halévy, who were probably the finest masters any young musician
of the day could have found in Europe. Lesueur was the solitary
representative of the old Gluck tradition in France, which had
borne a single fruit in Spontini and then almost disappeared except
in the mind of this single old eccentric, with his passion for the
vast, 'antique' musical canvases of the Revolution, his interest in
Greek, Roman and Hebrew music, and his inflexibly high principles, which he succeeded in handing on to another favourite
pupil, Hector Berlioz. Reicha was an immensely learned contra-
puntist, who had moved in Viennese musical circles, had known
Beethoven personally and cherished a vast admiration for his works,
which were still virtually unknown in France. Halévy was a brilliant
and gifted theatrical composer, who himself produced at least one
fine opera (*La Juive*, 1835) and trained a whole generation of French
composers, including Georges Bizet.

The combined influence of these three men had a permanent
effect on Gounod's musical ideals to the end of his life; and when,
in 1839, he won the Prix de Rome, it was as a fervent idealist and a
determined opponent of the fashionable worship of Rossini, Doni-
zetti and Meyerbeer that he set out for the Villa Medici. In Rome
he came under other formative influences which further moulded
his outlook. Ingres was then head of the Villa Medici and his
passion for music naturally inclined him to take a special interest
in the musicians in his charge: Gounod had charm and enthusiasm
and it was not long before he had become a personal friend of the
director. Musically the most important of his Roman experiences

were his friendships with two women, Pauline Viardot and Fanny
Hensel, the one a great singer and the other a fine pianist. Pauline
Garcia had some of both the charm and the artistic ability of her
more famous sister, 'La Malibran', the romantic ideal of a tragedi-
enne, who inspired the whole of the literary *Jeune France* by her
voice, her personality and her tragically early death. The influence
of Fanny Mendelssohn was entirely different. She was a cultured
German woman who introduced Gounod to the works of Bach,
Beethoven and her own brother, to the classics of German literature
and especially to Goethe, laying the foundation for that fine workmanship, that thoroughness and competence which were to distinguish all Gounod's compositions, even the most trivial. Finally,
in that other sphere which he always felt instinctively to be the
basis and foundation of his whole life and work, Gounod fell completely under the spell of the great Dominican preacher, Père
Lacordaire, whose sermons caused a sensation in Rome between
1838-41. These three personalities – the two women, so utterly
unlike yet both devoted to music, and the Dominican preacher –
represent the three fundamental elements in Gounod's character,
the three passions of his life: music, love and, transcending both,
religion.

In 1842 Gounod decided to move on from Rome to Vienna, where
he was to begin the German portion of his Prix de Rome years. He
stayed there a year, hearing a great deal of music (including the
works of Beethoven) and having two masses of his own performed;
and then moved on to Berlin, where he saw the Hensels, and finally
to Leipzig, where he spent happy days with Mendelssohn himself
and was introduced to the magnificent Gewandhaus orchestra,
which was probably the best in Europe during the 40's of last
century.

It was 1845 before Gounod was back in Paris, and he had been
six years away from France. His first action was to ensure a livelihood by accepting the post of organist to the fathers of the Missions
Etrangères in the Rue du Bac, where he shocked many of the
congregation by introducing the works of Bach and Palestrina in
place of the accepted theatrical vulgarities which passed as church
music in the 40's. But a decision was gradually being thrust on
him, a choice which could not be indefinitely postponed. Lacor-

daire's preaching had fallen on fruitful ground, and the daily familiarity with the heroism and piety of the fathers in the Rue du Bac had its inevitable result. In 1847 Gounod decided to start reading for the priesthood and entered the seminary of Saint-Sulpice. He was not there long. Either the call of music and the world was too strong or, as he is said to have admitted himself, he feared the emotional intimacy which he did not feel himself strong enough to prevent arising between himself and the women who might bring their secrets and their troubles to him in the confessional. Whatever the exact reason may have been, Gounod renounced the idea of the priesthood and left Saint-Sulpice.

In 1851 his renewed friendship with Madame Viardot, led to the composition of *Sapho*, his first opera; and in the same year his *Messe solennelle* was performed in London. His career as a composer had started; but it was by no means all roses. *Sapho* was praised by Berlioz, who nevertheless found it too fierce – 'il faut avant tout qu'un musicien fasse de la musique', he wrote, reversing (as modern eyes see it) the roles of lion and lamb. One penetrating critic discovered the real inspiration of the music, which was the operatic ideal of Gluck, as Gounod must have come to know it from Lesueur. *Sapho* is truly dramatic music, firmly but finely drawn, with a charm and discretion, an absence of over-emphasis and a clarity of style which are among the greatest qualities of the French artistic genius. The incidental music to Emile Augier's *Ulysse*, which appeared the following year (1852), was as apt, as charming and as little successful with the general public as *Sapho*; and in despair Gounod, who had married in the meanwhile a daughter of the musician Zimmermann, turned to a more popular genre. In 1854 his *Nonne sanglante* was produced at the Opéra. If Gounod had hoped for a repetition of the success of Meyerbeer's *Robert le Diable*, he was disappointed; for although his score was praised by both Berlioz and Théophile Gautier, it is inferior to *Sapho* and *Ulysse*, and certainly to the works of his own which were to follow in the immediate future. But he was making his mark. In 1855 Berlioz wrote of the musical life of Paris: 'à part . . . C. Saint-Saëns, un autre grand musicien de 19 ans, et Gounod, qui vient de produire une très belle messe, je ne vois s'agiter que des ephémères au dessus de ce puant marais qui s'appelle Paris.'

In 1857 Gounod succumbed to a nervous breakdown, in which it was feared that he would lose his reason; but he recovered quickly and so completely that during the next three years, 1858-60, he wrote three of his finest works: *Le Médecin malgré lui*, *Faust* and *Philémon et Baucis*. The Théâtre Lyrique was the least conservative of the three theatres in Paris where a young French composer could hope to have his works performed, and it was there that *Faust* and *Philémon et Baucis* were given. *Le Médecin malgré lui* was a brilliant restatement of Molière's comedy, witty, quick-moving and alive; but both this and *Philémon et Baucis* were inevitably swamped in the glory of *Faust* and its more showy successors, *La Reine de Saba* (1862) and *Roméo et Juliette* (1867); nor were they fully appreciated until they were rediscovered and performed after the First War. Both are what might be called 'chamber' operas which lose a great deal of their charm and point if they are performed on too large a scale; both are thoroughly individual and thoroughly national in a way that *Faust*, *Reine de Saba* and *Roméo et Juliette*, with their frequent overlay of Meyerbeerian glitter, could never be.

It is impossible to discuss *Faust* in detail here, but it is essential to realise, especially in this context, that the charm and the greatness of *Faust* to Gounod's contemporaries lay precisely in those qualities in which we now find it most lacking – in naturalness, simplicity, sincerity and directness of emotional appeal. This can only really be understood if one compares *Faust* with either *Les Huguenots* or *Guillaume Tell*, both of them indisputably great works in their way but so over-burdened with spectacular ballets, ingenious stagecraft, brilliant and pompous orchestration and theatricality of emotion that it is easy to contrast the appeal – I will not say of Gretchen, for she can hardly be said to appear – but even of the rather insipid Marguerite. Despite her false flowers and her falser jewels she has a simple heart, and after the heroism and devilry of Meyerbeer and Rossini a simple heart was very engaging.

It was criticisms such as that published by Scudo on *Philémon et Baucis* in the *Revue des Deux Mondes* which deflected Gounod from his natural path and sent him whoring after the strange gods of Meyerbeer. 'Les détails de la forme', wrote Scudo, 'les ciselures de l'instrumentation, les mièvreries du style ne suffisent point pour

IM L

faire vivre une composition dramatique où la passion, les idées franches et la variété des couleurs ne brillent que par leur absence.' This was a direct challenge to give up his own careful, sober, discreet and only faintly saccharine style for the tumult and the shouting, the captains and the kings of 'grand' opera. Gounod's answer was *La Reine de Saba* and *Roméo et Juliette*, in which his own personality is overlaid, if not completely absent, and every possible concession is made to the Scudos. But his capitulation was not final or complete. After a visit to Italy and Provence in 1863 he produced an enchanting *Mireille*, with music as fresh, winning and unsophisticated as its heroine, certainly one of his finest works, if not his finest, which still lives in France but seems quite unaccountably forgotten elsewhere. The scale is larger than that of the 'chamber' operas, but the freshness of inspiration and (to use a contemporary term) 'melodiousness' is, if anything, greater.

When the Franco-Prussian war broke out in the July of 1870, Gounod was a man of fifty-two. *Faust* (1859), after a not very successful start, had swept Europe and made him an international figure, giving him a reputation which *Roméo et Juliette* maintained even if it did not enhance. In France, with Berlioz dying in 1869 and Saint-Saëns still known only for his early orchestral works and that by a small minority only, his position was unchallenged. In September 1870 he fled across the channel to England, from which he did not finally return until 1874. In those four years he developed a new side of his personality but lost his position as leader of French music. His admiration for Mendelssohn and the whole attitude to music which he had learnt from Fanny Hensel seemed to revive in England, where he found a taste for choral and religious music – and especially that of Mendelssohn – such as he had never met before. There was a demand for semi-religious drawing-room ballads which he could and did supply, and for oratorio to which he soon began to turn his attention. He produced an elegiac cantata, *Gallia*, inspired by the plight of France and, in 1873, a patriotic *Jeanne d'Arc*. But when he returned, he found that new forces had been mobilised in the French musical world while he had been absent and that his position, at any rate as leader of the younger generation, was gone. The foundation of the Société Nationale in 1871 was the beginning of that national renaissance in French music which soon began to bear such copious and remarkable fruit. Saint-Saëns was at its head and the original 150 members included Bizet, Massenet, Lalo, Dubois, Bourgault-Ducoudray, Castillon, Franck and Widor. These were the men who were to produce the important works of the 70's and 80's, and Gounod's was not the decisive influence in their musical development.

Of the three operas written before he devoted himself finally to oratorio *Cinq Mars* (1877) is already a step removed from the purely operatic, *Polyeucte* (1878) a conscious attempt to unite opera and oratorio, while *Le Tribut de Zamora* (1881) is a completely unsuccessful attempt to recapture the old melodrama beloved of the fifties. Gounod was in a state of transition. Saint-Saëns has stated very well in his 'Portraits et souvenirs' the general qualities of Gounod's music and the particular ideals towards which he was developing during the 70's.

> The achievement of expressiveness was always Gounod's main preoccupation: that is why there are so few notes in his music . . . each note 'sings'. For the same reason instrumental music, *pure music*, was never his forte. . . . His great desire was to discover a beautiful colour on the orchestral palette and, in his search for this he refused to follow the ready-made processes of the acknowledged masters, but carried on his experiments directly, studying the various timbres, inventing new combinations and shades of colour to suit his brush. 'Sonority', as he once said to me, 'is still an unexplored country.'

These were always Gounod's chief traits, and the transition period of the 70's was really little more than a period of groping towards a new way of realising what were fundamentally the same ideals.

> He was anxious to reduce the number of modulations to a minimum, with the idea that the composer should not make light use of such a powerful means of expression. . . . [His ideal was] to obtain the maximum effect with the minimum apparent effort, to reduce the representation of effects to mere indications and to concentrate all the interest on the expression of feeling. . . .

Admirable principles, deriving plainly from the enthusiasm for Gluck inculcated by his old master Lesueur and perhaps from his talks with Pauline Viardot; and yet what were the results? In *The Redemption* (1882) and *Mors et Vita* (1884), where Gounod felt that he had at last achieved the style at which he was aiming, the effect – the total effect, that is – is one of bland and tender platitude. In the words of Blaze de Bury, 'Il s'écoute phraser'. This strain of self-consciousness was not new. While he was engaged on the composition of *Roméo et Juliette* Gounod wrote to a friend: 'Au milieu de ce silence il me semble que j'entends me parler en dedans quelque chose de très grand, de très clair, de très simple et de très enfant à la fois.' This consciously 'childlike' simplicity is always suspect in an artist, for it almost invariably conceals an element of pomposity and insincerity which tends to grow with age, and even more with success, until it finally rots the sounder elements in an artistic nature. And in fact as he grew older Gounod did suffer from what might be described as the same *cher grand maître* complex as infected Hugo and Tennyson. Not content with being artists, these eminent Victorians were inclined to pose as prophets and, in proportion as their 'message' – the actual content of their works – became thinner, the manner in which they stated it became more and more sublime, more portentous and more hollow-sounding. Gounod after 1870 might well have echoed Tennyson's despairing cry that he was the greatest master of English living and had nothing to say. This bromidic, self-consciously oracular state of mind is revealed in many of the stories which are told of Gounod's old age. 'Les enfants', he is said to have remarked to a friend, 'ce sont les roses du jardin de la vie.' And to a woman who had accompanied him to the performance of some new work and asked his opinion: 'Qu'en pensez-vous, cher maître?' 'C'est rhomboïdal', which called forth the immediate and deserved reply: 'Ah! cher maître, j'allais le dire.'

In 1893 Gounod died; and although for the last thirty years of his life he had been outside the main stream of French musical life, his death meant the disappearance of one of the great figures of nineteenth-century French music. For he was more than an individual composer: he was the voice of a deep and permanent strain in the French character. Actual pupils he had none; but a whole range of emotion, which had been voiceless before, had found in him its ideal expression, and his influence will perhaps never quite disappear for that reason. A few years before his own death Bizet complained that he was unable to hold his own against Gounod's influence; and in *Les Pêcheurs de perles* and *La Jolie Fille de Perth* this influence is again and again noticeable. Even in *Carmen* it is not absent: Micaela is a pure Gounod character and her duet with José in Act I and her 'J'ai dit que rien ne m'épouvante' in Act III could never have been written if Gounod had not found her emotion a voice. In Massenet the strain of Gounod's influence is still strong, though so exclusively concentrated on the tender and the erotic that he was given the apt sobriquet of 'la fille de Gounod'. In his earliest works – the cantatas *Marie Magdeleine* (1873) and *Eve* (1875) – he expressed just that same half mystical, half erotic emotion which d'Indy was to flay as 'l'érotisme discret et quasi religieux'. *Hérodiade*, *Manon*, *Werther* and *Thaïs* are the works of a man in whom an unbridled desire to please has conquered almost every other consideration and certainly removed Massenet from the fresher and more idealistic side of the Gounod tradition; yet in many turns of phrase, the charm and the *tendresse* of the melody there is no denying the influence of that tradition. It was this element of his great talent which Massenet transmitted to his many pupils, this rather than his own personal weakness; and so in the music of the many composers who came under Massenet's influence at the Conservatoire between 1878-96, Gounod's spirit was perpetuated. Romain Rolland in 'La Foire sur la place' (*Jean-Christophe*, V) makes his young German musician complain of the moments in Debussy's *Pelléas* when 'the Massenet slumbering in the heart of every Frenchman awoke and waxed lyrical'; and it is a reasonable complaint. But Massenet would never have caught and perhaps immortalised that peculiarly French emotional mood which is summed up in the music of Manon's Des Grieux, for instance, if Gounod had not first given it a purer and less popular expression in *Faust* and *Mireille*.

If Massenet represents a degradation of the Gounod tradition, Fauré represents that tradition refined, ennobled and rarefied. Saint-Saëns noticed the bourgeois strain in Gounod and assessed its value and its danger:

... Son écriture, d'une élégance impeccable, couvre parfois un certain fonds de vulgarité ... c'est comme un fonds de sang plebéien, mettant des muscles en contrepoids à l'élément nerveux dont la prédominance pourrait devenir un danger ... c'est l'antidote de la mièvrerie.

In the music of Fauré it is not the 'élément nerveux' which predominates, but a kind of classical refinement, a sobriety and a quiet distinction, that 'fantaisie dans la sensibilité' which was the hall-mark of the French musical genius in the eyes of Debussy. Gounod's music was out of the direct line of the French musical tradition inasmuch as the primary appeal of at any rate his most popular works – *Faust, Reine de Saba, Mireille, Roméo et Juliette* as opposed to *Le Médecin malgré lui* or *Philémon et Baucis* – was 'obviously emotional rather than intellectual and imaginative'. Fauré reversed this and by so doing garnered the harvest which Gounod had sown into the storehouse of the national art. We have seen Gounod finding inspiration in the German classics, musical and literary, in Mendelssohn and even, indirectly, in the German romantics. His individual style bears traces of all these foreign origins, French as it unmistakably is. Fauré, the most innately French of all French composers, assimilated this style, foreign elements and national alike, purified it of the emotional over-emphasis which was due partly to Gounod's temperament and partly to the romantic era in which he grew up, and produced the classical French style of modern times. Yet Gounod's best songs and orchestral music were unearthed again after 1918 by 'Les Six' and proclaimed as valid French models.

Gounod himself was more than vaguely aware of the new forces at work beneath the surface of French music before his death – aware and by no means hostile. He begged for a reasoned and sober attitude – 'ni Wagnerophobie ni Wageromanie' – towards the music of Wagner, of whose greatness he was certainly aware, though he deplored the excesses to which his admirers and his detractors were equally prone to go.

La France est essentiellement le pays de la netteté [he wrote] de la concision, du goût, c'est à dire l'opposé de l'excès, de l'enflure, de la disproportion, de la prolixité. La préoccupation –

j'allais dire, la duperie – du transcendental peut, à force de persistance, arriver à nous donner le change, je veux dire à nous faire prendre le gros pour le grand, le pesant pour le solide, l'obscur pour le profond, le brouillard pour le sublime. . . .

Here, on the one hand, is the charter of Gabriel Fauré's music. On the other we find Gounod writing to Charles Bordes in 1893, the year of his own death, after attending the first 'Semaine Sainte de Saint-Gervais' at which the great polyphonic classics of the sixteenth and seventeenth centuries were performed:

Il est temps que le drapeau de l'art liturgique remplace dans nos églises celui de la cantilène profane et que la *fresque musicale* proscrive toutes les guimauves de la romance et toutes les sucreries de la piété qui ont trop longtemps gâté nos estomacs. Palestrina et Bach ont fait l'art musical, en sont pour nous les Pères de l'Église: il importe que nous restions leurs fils et je vous remercie de nous y aider.

There spoke the young enthusiast who, nearly fifty years before, had shocked the congregations and puzzled the good fathers of the Missions Etrangères in the Rue du Bac. Unlike so many 'great' men, Gounod remained to the end true to his first enthusiasms, and he saw in the new schools which were arising in his old age – even in the first revolutionary flutterings of Claude Debussy – legitimate developments of just those principles which had inspired him, principles which he could with justice claim to have reintroduced into the French musical consciousness.

Part III

Songs and Singers

1 Schumann's Songs

'Do you, I wonder, feel as I do?' wrote Schumann to Hermann Hirschbach in June 1839. 'All my life I have thought vocal music inferior to instrumental and have never considered it to be great art.' Only eight months later, in February 1840, he wrote of 'composing nothing but songs' and in a letter to Clara, 'Since yesterday morning I have written nearly 27 pages of music – something new, of which I will only say that I laughed and wept for joy as I wrote. . . . Oh! Clara, what a joy it is to write for the voice, a joy I have lacked too long.' That is the typical Schumann, a theorist whose theories are always apt to be contradicted by the mood of the moment, emotional and unpredictable and glorying in the quick succession of extremes of feeling, the sun chasing the clouds, laughter and tears at one and the same moment, creating in his music the rainbow effects which he so much admired in the prose of his beloved Jean Paul Richter. Up to thirty the piano had been virtually his only confidant – for that is exactly what Schumann's piano music represents, confidences – but with the final blooming of his love for Clara Wieck he felt the need of a still more personal and intimate form of expression. Of Schumann's 250-odd songs very nearly half were written in the year of his marriage (1840) and that half contains almost all the best songs he was ever to write.

In spite of his letter to Hirschbach, Schumann had already tried his hand at song-writing before 1840. His Op. 11 originally consisted of eleven songs dedicated to his three sisters-in-law. Three

of these were published by Brahms in the supplementary volume
of the Collected Edition; six by Geiringer in 1933, and one – a
setting of Goethe's *Der Fischer* – as a supplement to the *Zeitschrift
für Musik*, also in 1933.[1] But Schumann was not satisfied with them
as songs and used three of them in his piano-works of the 30's.
'An Anna II' (composed 31 July, 1828) appeared as the Aria in the
G sharp minor piano sonata; 'Im Herbste', as the andantino of the
F minor piano sonata; 'Der Hirtenknabe' (composed August 1828)
in the Intermezzo, Op. 4, No. 4. In fact the new lyrical impulse
which Schumann brought to his piano-writing made the distinction
between instrumental and vocal music more blurred than it had
ever been before; and made him, too, the ideal link between
Schubert and the next generation of song-writers, for whom voice
and instrument were of equal importance. His literary taste and
affinities gave him a feeling for prosody and a sensitiveness to the
atmosphere of a poem such as no previous song-writer had ever
had. A glance at the list of poets set by the mature Schumann gives
an idea of his literary taste. Heine easily heads the list, with 42
poems. Then come Rückert (27), Goethe (19), Eichendorff (16),
Justinus Kerner (14), Chamisso (11), Lenau (10), Burns (9), Geibel,
Mary Queen of Scots, and Hans Andersen (5 each), Mörike and
Hoffmann von Fallersleben (4 each), Schiller (3), and Tom Moore
(2). Of nonentities he hardly ever set more than a single poem,
except in the case of the young poetess Elisabeth Kulmann, whose
romantic life and early death at the age of seventeen led Schumann
into mistaking her for a genius. 'Wilfred von der Neun' (whose real
name was Toepff) was no more than a talented amateur, but his
poems at least provided Schumann with the larger and vaguer
background that he needed in 1850, and they are certainly superior
to the pretty platitudes of Elisabeth Kulmann.

Heine was the ideal poet for Schumann not only because a
certain spiritual affinity existed between them, showing itself in the
deliberate cultivation of sharply contrasted emotional moods within
a single lyric; but also because of the conciseness and point of his
style. Schumann, with his admiration for Jean Paul, was quite
happy dreaming his way through the most circumstantial and
flowery writing, pursuing the most far-fetched metaphors to their

[1] The eleventh, Jacobi's 'Klage', was apparently never finished.

logical and ludicrous conclusions, savouring the extremes of comedy and sensibility on the same page and quite oblivious of the absence of plot or formal arrangement.[1] Heine's poetry served him as an unconscious discipline, curbing his natural tendency to divagation and forcing him to come to the point, to condense his emotions to their sweetest and their bitterest. When, in July 1828, Schumann sent his first songs to Gottlob Wiedebein, the Brunswick *Kapellmeister*, the advice he received was to 'look to truth above all. Truth of melody, of harmony, of expression – in a word, poetic truth.' It was really Heine who enabled Schumann to follow that advice.

Thirty-seven of the forty-two Heine settings were composed in the year 1840. Heine's ballad 'Belshazzar' was one of the first poems he set, on 7 February of that year (although it only appeared six years later, as his Op. 57) while the first of the opus numbers consisting of songs was the Op. 24, the *Liederkreis* of Heine poems, dedicated to Pauline Viardot. His Opp. 25, 27, 30, 31, 35, 36, 37, 39, 40, 42, 45, 48, 49, 53, 57 were all written the same year and a study of these songs alone would give a complete idea of Schumann as a song-writer. In the next twelve years he never wrote anything better and only occasionally anything nearly as good as appeared in this sudden enormous spate; and as he grew older his literary instinct seems to have faltered. How important this was to the quality of his music he was himself perfectly aware. 'Parallel to the development of poetry, the Franz Schubert epoch has been followed by a new one which has utilised the improvements of the accompanying instrument, the piano', he wrote in his *Observations on Composers and Composition*. 'The voice alone cannot reproduce everything or produce every effect; together with the expression of the whole, the finer details of the poem should also be emphasised. All is well as long as the vocal line is not sacrificed.' It is not sur-

[1] In case the reader may tire of reading the name of Jean Paul repeatedly or may suspect that modern denigration of his style is unjust, I choose at random one of his high-flown metaphorical passages. This is taken from the *Flegeljahre* and Vult is speaking. 'O reiner, starker Freund, die Poesie ist ja doch ein Paar Schlittschuh, womit man auf dem glatten, reinen, krystallnen Boden des Ideals leicht fliegt, aber miserabel forthumpelt auf gemeiner Gasse.' ('My pure, strong friend, poetry when all is said and done is a pair of skates, on which one can skim lightly over the smooth, clean crystal surface of the Ideal, while in the ordinary street they make one's progress a wretched hobbling.')

prising to find the piano playing a more prominent part in the
songs of 1840 than in the later ones, for Schumann was still first
and foremost a pianist at that point. What is more surprising is that
no single one of these early songs is a piano solo with obbligato
voice. (In fact it is possible to detect, on internal evidence alone, the
authorship of No. 2 of Op. 37, one of the three songs contributed
by Clara to the twelve settings of poems from Rückert's *Liebesfrühling*. 'I have no talent at all for composition', sighed poor Clara
and certainly 'Er ist gekommen' is simply a piano solo with a voice
part added, just the song one would expect a piano virtuoso to
write.) The preludes and postludes, generally considered to be typical of Schumann's song writing as a whole, most frequently occur in
the 1840 songs and are nowhere so prominent as in the *Dichterliebe*
and *Frauenliebe und -leben* series. Another feature which is strongly
characteristic of the 1840 songs and hardly appears afterwards is
the turn. This appears in 'Widmung', 'Lied der Suleika' (Ex. 1),
'Aus den östlichen Rosen', 'Er, der Herrlichste von allen' and 'Helft
mir, ihr Schwestern' but on the rare occasions when Schumann
uses it in his later songs ('Himmel und Erde', Op. 96, No. 5, for
example) it strikes a false note and seems out of style. Whether the

Ex. 1.

turn is to be considered as fundamentally a pianistic trait – a habit of the fingers in a composer much given to improvising – or to be related to Schumann's unconscious imitation of the operatic style, it remains a distinct mark of the year 1840.

The fingers obviously suggested another trait which is common throughout the whole range of Schumann's songs but particularly so in those of 1840. This is the anticipation of the voice by the piano or vice versa, such as we find in 'Es treibt mich hin', 'Intermezzo' and 'Aus den hebräischen Gesängen' (Ex. 2) in one form and in 'Stille Liebe' in the other. Occasionally this device of syncopation, which became almost a mannerism in Schumann's

Ex. 2.

piano works, is used with programmatic effect, as in 'Lieb' Liebchen' where it represents the beating of the lover's heart and gives rise to the subtly dramatic ending of each quatrain, where the words 'Totensarg' (coffin) and 'schlafen kann' (can sleep) are left hanging in the air by an accompaniment which has come to an end a bar earlier. These illustrations or programmatic devices are rare in Schumann's songs, but when he attempts them they are almost always carried out with the finest musical sensitiveness and never exaggerated. The fall of the rose petals in 'Der Hidalgo' and the rippling of the waves in 'Aufträge' are effective because of their simplicity and their musical unpretentiousness; but Schumann is at his happiest when he is suggesting another musical instrument. The Romantic predilection for the horn and its associations with hunting, with the life of the forest and knightly adventure, finds expression in innumerable songs of which 'Waldesgespräch', 'Der Knabe mit dem Wunderhorn' and the late 'Der Gärtner' are only typical examples among many others. The organ-like piano part of 'Stirb' Lieb' und Freud'' suggests the cathedral setting of the poem, and the harp-player's broken chords are discreetly suggested in 'Wer nie sein Brot mit Tränen ass' and 'Wer sich der Einsamkeit ergibt'. In a more humorous vein are the suggestion of the military band in 'Husarenabzug', the brilliant imitation of a wheezy concertina in the first of the 'Der arme Peter' songs and the guitar in 'Der Contrabandiste'. Occasionally Schumann writes a whole dance movement where the poem demands it, as in 'Es ist ein Flöten und Geigen' (No. 9 of the *Dichterliebe*) and 'Der Spielmann', but even here the voice is never overridden.

If we had not his own word for his dislike of Spohr's chromaticism, we might be surprised by the very sparing use of chromatic melody or even strongly chromatic harmony which we find in Schumann's songs. A considerable number suffer from a tendency to the opposite extreme, unrelieved diatonic harmony only too often combined with a square march rhythm, also unrelieved. This can generally be traced to Schumann's desire to write something in either ballad or folk-song style (e.g. 'Sonntags am Rhein') or else to an attempt to recapture the carefree, youthful atmosphere of the *Knaben Wunderhorn* ('Freisinn', 'Frühlingsfahrt' or the 6/8 swinging march of 'Wanderung' and 'Der Knabe mit dem Wunderhorn'). This rhythmic monotony was already a noticeable trait of some of the longer movements of the piano works (the last of the *Etudes symphoniques* for example) and a tendency to square-cut rhythm remained with Schumann throughout his life. His rare use of chromatic sequences and harmony in the songs is often dictated by the text and he obviously felt very strongly the atmosphere of extreme melancholy, even verging on despair, which such passages produced. In this he was still a child of the eighteenth century. On the other hand his love of quick transitions of mood made him on the whole avoid complete songs in what he felt to be this exaggeratedly melancholy manner. 'Aus den hebräischen Gesängen' and 'Einsamkeit', with their strongly chromatic, melancholy opening sections, both have comparatively diatonic middle sections in the major key; and only 'Zwielicht', which is considerably shorter, is allowed to remain in the mood of unrelieved, chromatically coloured gloom throughout. This sparing use of what he plainly felt to be an extreme atmospheric effect makes it all the more effective, and on the very few occasions on which Schumann falls into a strongly chromatic manner in order to express anything but melancholy the result is unpleasantly saccharine and reminiscent of the worse hymn-tunes of John Bacchus Dykes. This resemblance is strongest perhaps, in 'Wehmut' where both tempo and rhythm suggest the hymn-tune; but 'Nur ein lächeinder Blick', where the chromatic alterations in the melody are combined with a slow 6/8 rhythm and an abysmally vapid poem, may be considered the parent of count-less Victorian drawing-room songs which delighted our grand-parents but arouse nothing but distaste in us.

The quality which is most typical of Schumann's songs, his most individual contribution to the development of the German *Lied*, is really a noble variety of this sentimentality, the lily which festering in 'Nur ein lächelnder Blick' smells more rank than any weed. The German word for it is 'Innigkeit' and it is virtually untranslatable by any single English word. 'Innigkeit' is a variety of warm, inti-mate and meditative emotion, essentially self-conscious and there-fore dangerously closely allied to sentimentality but saved, at least in its nobler manifestations, by a genuinely childlike simplicity. When this simplicity is also self-conscious, its childlike language becomes something like baby-talk and 'Innigkeit' is then indistin-guishable from archness and sentimentality. It is remarkable how many of Schumann songs bear the superscription 'Innig' ('Nur ein lächelnder Blick' among them) and how typical, for good and for evil, these songs are in almost every case – 'Widmung', 'Schöne Fremde', 'Was will die einsame Träne' for example on the credit side and 'Frage', 'O ihr Herren', 'Liebesbotschaft' and 'Er, der Herrlichste von allen' on the debit, among many others of both complexions. On the whole it is the 'innig' side of Schumann that dates his music most noticeably, just as it was this which endeared him to our grandparents. The circumstances in which the 1840 songs were written – on the eve, or immediately in the wake, of an extremely happy marriage – sometimes give their lyricism a dom-estic, conjugal quality which may strike the modern listener as a little complacent. Certainly the humble adoration of the chosen male that breathes from the poems of Chamisso chosen by Schu-mann for his *Frauenliebe und -leben* wakes very little echo in a modern listener. It reflects rather the feelings that the nearly forty-year-old Chamisso was delighted to find in his eighteen-year-old bride. But to a modern taste there is something supremely unattractive in the poet making his bride speak of herself as a 'nied're Magd' (lowly maiden) who only asks to gaze on her husband in all humility ('nur in Demut ihn betrachten') and is blinded by the beauty and amazed at the condescension of so superior a being. We feel that to be false, possibly quite unjustly; but if not false, then at any rate the prelude to a 'Frauenleben' bounded by the 3 ks – 'Kirche, Kinder und Küche'. It is perhaps significant that the second song of the cycle ('Er, der Herrlichste von allen') is not only the most abject in sentiment but also the least successful musically, with its square dotted rhythms and hammered accompanying chords extending uninterruptedly over four pages. Rückert's two poems in a similar vein ('Lied der Braut', Nos. 1 and 2) show the girl torn between her love for her mother and her husband. Here again a modern reader of the poems might divine a certain gloating over the situation, comparable with the excessive interest shown by elderly spinsters in the details of a wedding-day programme or the exact disposition of bedroom furniture in the household of a newly-married couple. But Schumann extracts the last ounce of sentiment from the poems, down to the sighing 'lass' mich' with which No. 2 closes, without self-consciousness and therefore without offence.

Nevertheless, it is a very welcome change to move on to the quite unmatrimonial sentiments of Heine, to find for a change the male sunk in hopeless adoration and to savour the caddish and venomous revenge reserved for the last line or couplet of a poem that seems to start in tremulous humility. Not that Schumann ever achieves real venomousness; to see how far he falls short of the possibilities we have only to compare his setting of 'Anfangs wollt' ich fast verzagen', a solemn and resigned chorale, with Liszt's wonderful dramatic miniature. Nor did Schumann attempt to set 'Vergiftet sind meine Lieder', which is perhaps Liszt's masterpiece; the venomous quatrain in the style of Martial could hardly have appealed to the composer of *Frauenliebe und -leben*. Even so, the lyricism of the *Dichterliebe* is a far lighter, more mercurial, more *musical* lyricism than anything that Chamisso ever achieved, for all his French blood. Of the nine songs of the Heine *Liederkreis* (Op. 24) only two come up to the level reached by all sixteen of the *Dichterliebe*. The two sets are virtually contemporary, the *Liederkreis* songs composed between 1-9 May and the *Dichterliebe* begun on 24 May and finished on 1 June; so that the difference in quality can only be connected with the choice of poems. 'Ich wandelte unter den Bäumen' and 'Lieb' Liebchen' (Nos. 3 and 4 of the *Liederkreis*) would not be out of place in the *Dichterliebe* any more than the four songs which originally belonged to the set but were only published at the very end of Schumann's life or posthumously. These are 'Dein Angesicht' (Op. 127, No. 2), 'Es leuchtet meine Liebe' (Op. 127, No. 3), 'Lehn' deine Wang' ' (Op. 142, No. 2) and 'Mein Wagen rollt langsam' (Op. 142, No. 4, wrongly said by Dr Ernest Walker to be Schumann's last song: it was actually composed on 29-30 May 1840).

What distinguishes all these Heine settings from the remainder of the *Liederkreis*, and from all but a few isolated songs spread over the rest of 1840 and the rest of Schumann's life, is not only their intensity of feeling but their economy of expression. Already in 'Ich wandelte unter den Bäumen' we meet for the first time that astonishing blend between the simplest folk-song manner and the most subtle and highly organised psychological suggestion, which

Ex. 3.

is the distinguishing note of the *Dichterliebe*. Schumann begins the voice part with a perfectly simple diatonic melody, rhythmically devoid of any subtlety whatever; the accompaniment follows the voice exactly. But after two lines, 'da kam das alte Träumen, Und schlich mir ins Herz hinein', the 4/4 rhythm is interrupted by an inimitable triplet phrase which is twice echoed in the piano part (Ex. 3). The second quatrain repeats this pattern and then, with a sudden change – not really a modulation in spite of the dominant minor ninth – the key shifts from G major to E flat major and the

triplet rhythm returns, though at a slower tempo, as the birds offer
to tell the poet the magic word they have overheard, the secret of
his love. But he will not be robbed of his grief and the folk-song
melody returns, only to dissolve into a kind of arioso recitative at
the twice repeated 'ich aber niemanden trau' which dies away in a
whisper. The eeriness of the whole poem arises from the suggestion
of the 'secret' which the poet refuses to be told, although it would
lighten his grief. It is this which gives the neurotic, 'psycho-
analytical' atmosphere to so many of Heine's poems, the suggestion
of a split personality and a self-torturing, masochistic rapture beneath the conventional roses and nightingales. Here, in 'Ich wandelte unter den Bäumen', Schumann juxtaposes but does not mingle
the two personalities. In the *Dichterliebe* his method is far more
subtle, for he makes the two 'persons' speak at the same time.
Heine plainly enjoyed the torments of unrequited love – 'Liebesleid
und Weh' – quite as much as the pleasures of mutual passion, which
were the only thing that interested Chamisso. (How profoundly
disturbed Chamisso was by any less conventionally happy amorous
situation is shown by his pathetic poem 'Was soll ich sagen?', which
Schumann seems to have set without really understanding its
significance. Chamisso remained Frenchman enough to be mortally
embarrassed by an amorous, as opposed to a specifically erotic,
relationship between an old man and young girl.)

Schumann, with instinctively right judgment, chose miniature
poems of Heine, almost all of them in the extremely simple style of
the folk-song. Only one – 'Die Rose, die Lilie' – is as simple in
matter as it is in manner and Schumann's setting is as natural and
unclouded as the poem. In all the other poems Heine's simplicity
of manner is deceptive and what begins apparently as a straightforward lyric assumes before the end the complexion of an enigma
or a satirical epigram. 'Wenn ich in deinen Augen seh' ', for example, starts like a folk-song and continues conventionally enough
until the last couplet. Then, instead of the lover's happiness being
full when the girl confesses her love for him, we find the exact
opposite, tears: 'Doch wenn du sprichst: ich liebe dich! so muss ich
weinen bitterlich.' Schumann starts in a straightforward G major,
modulating to the subdominant by means of supertonic minor
harmony (which we shall see later to be typical). The first hint of

some strange fly in the ointment is the chord of the diminished seventh on the word 'sprichst' but, by a stroke of genius, the actual words 'weinen bitterlich' are in no way underlined harmonically and only the piano postlude gives the hint of something mysterious and uncompleted, by converting the tonic of G major immediately into the dominant seventh of C major so that the tonality of the whole postlude hangs ambiguously between the two keys of C and G.

Sometimes the piano part alone suggests the mystery beneath the poem's surface from the very beginning. The chord of the German sixth with which 'Am leuchtenden Sommermorgen' opens and the syncopated accents throughout the piano part mentally prepare the listener for the wonderful modulation to the key of G major and the close, once again on the German sixth, which Schumann discovered for the gentle, enigmatic entreaty of the flowers: 'Sei unsrer Schwester nicht böse, du trauriger, blasser Mann.' Finally, in the postlude, the picture of the garden is completed, and over the slowly rippling arpeggios another voice rises, this time the piano's, answering with wordless consolation the unspoken complaint of the poet. I personally should place this one song among the very greatest miniatures in the whole of music, a faultless dramatic lyric (with the lyricism unbroken on the surface and the drama implicit), the *locus classicus* of 'Innigkeit' at its very best.

The two dream poems of the *Dichterliebe* – in which we should naturally expect the strange and pathological element to predominate – are in marked contrast to each other. 'Ich hab' im Traum geweinet' owes a large part of its effectiveness to the long pauses, the unaccompanied phrases of the voice and the sinister dotted quaver figure in the piano part which punctuates the lines of the poem (cf. Duparc's 'Le Manoir de Rosamonde'). Once again we find extreme agony of mind expressed in the chromatic harmony of the accompaniment to the last couplet, where the voice part ends on a chord of the dominant and out of key (dominant of A flat in the key of E flat minor). The dream is precise, bitterly clear in every detail. 'Allnächtlich im Traume' with its short, gasping phrases and sudden changes of rhythm is the dream which remains clear only as a general impression, all the details being blurred. Schumann's setting has the breathlessness of Heine's poem, the sudden, childish spurts of confidence, ending with the pathetic, frustrated confession, 'und das Wort hab' ich vergessen': the whole point of the dream has eluded him. Singers are apt to take the song too slowly and to make it an expression of bliss, when the sense of both words and music demand an atmosphere of restlessness and anxiety. Schumann never modulates properly to the key of the dominant, either in this song or in 'Ich grolle nicht'. If he reaches the dominant he moves away from it at once, after a single beat, preferring subdominant harmony or, in 'Ich grolle nicht', a maximum of variety without actually leaving the tonic key at all. This is the only one of the *Dichterliebe* cycle with a repeated-chord accompaniment, which is justified by the shortness of the song and the urgent, persistence of the words, the quick mounting to a thunderous climax (where, by the way, the alternative, higher voice part was added by the composer only as an afterthought when the song was in proof). Hardly less of a dream is the last song but one of the set, 'Aus alten Märchen', one of the most successful of Schumann's 6/8 march songs, with the persistent rhythm mitigated by considerably greater harmonic variety and changes in the weight of the accompaniment than in other songs of the same kind. The augmented version of the melody in the last verse, marked 'mit innigster Empfindung,' concentrates the whole weight of the song in the close and makes the sudden evaporation of the whole vision in a series of diminished sevenths both more unexpected and more effective. 'Die alten, bösen Lieder,' which ends the set, opens with a dramatic flourish that is very rare in Schumann's songs, and the piano part – with its marked resemblance to No. 4 of Chopin's *Études*, Op. 10, which had appeared in 1831 – bears the main burden of the musical interest until the, by now familiar, concentration of energy and intensification of emotion which herald the final quatrain. The weighty, mounting octaves in the bass of the piano part recall a similar passage in the first movement of the *Eroica* (probably intentionally), but when the voice has finished the octave portamento rise on the C sharp, the whole mood of the music changes in a moment from brutal violence to tremulous self-pity. This is the reverse of the usual Heine process; the sting is not in the tail of the poem, for once. Instead of a savage or enigmatic close Schumann has dramatic justification for one of his most cherished effects – the sun suddenly bursting through the clouds, a wave of tenderness bursting in upon harsh sarcasm. He achieves this by an enharmonic modulation pivoting on the C sharp, which is suddenly treated as the leading note in the key of D instead of the dominant of F sharp. This lasts only two bars and the voice part dies away over a dominant harmony in the original key of C sharp minor. Then the consoling voice of the piano rises – exactly as in the postlude to 'Am leuchtenden Sommermorgen' – only here the postlude is followed by a further instrumental passage in the nature of an improvisation which rounds off the whole cycle. A descending quaver passage in the right hand is developed sequentially and harmonised with rich chromatic harmony until it finally dies away in a thrice-repeated sigh.

No other poet provided Schumann with the concentrated intensity of feeling and the verbal terseness and economy that were the two things he most needed from a poem. Or if an occasional lyric (Mörike's 'Das verlassene Mägdelein' or Ulrich's 'Die Fensterscheibe', for example) has these qualities, we still miss the mysterious, charged atmosphere of the Heine settings. Nos. 11 and 12 of Op. 35, 'Wer machte dich so krank?' and 'Alte Laute', have something of the same quality; but Justinus Kerner, the poet, was a doctor and an occultist and the mystery behind the poems is objectively imagined rather than subjectively experienced. This accounts for the tame ending of 'Alte Laute', the introduction of the conventional figure of the angel and the correspondingly conventional cadence in the music, which had started so promisingly with the single, tense chord of G major modulating by a chromatic slip of the bass into the tonic, A flat major (Ex. 4). Far more typical of Schumann's general lyrical manner is No. 10 of the same Op. 35, 'Stille Tränen'. Kerner's poem is one of the innumerable lyrics inspired by the secret grief of the poet and the uncompre-

Ex 4.

Das du so krank ge - wor - den

hending attitude of the world, a Romantic commonplace which he treats no better and no worse than a hundred other minor poets have done. It lacks entirely the drive and bite that Heine's sense of humour and power of self-criticism give to even his most effusive poems; and Schumann's music, for all the beauty of the melody and the richness and subtlety of the modulations, is too discursive and rambling. His repetition of the last couplet, preceded and followed by an interlude and postlude of comparative lengthiness, represents a third of the whole song, which is thus artificially enlarged. There is no case of Schumann's treating a Heine poem in this way, though it becomes almost a mannerism in his settings of other poets. Even the beautiful No. 1 of Op. 39 (the Eichendorff *Liederkreis*) 'In der Fremde' repeats the last line simply for the sake of repeating the effective cadence (a G natural in the key of F sharp minor). The other song of the same name in the same set ('Ich hör' die Bächlein rauschen') repeats the last line of the poem three times without even the excuse of a harmonic or melodic *trouvaille*, and in a really poor song such as 'Liebesbotschaft' (Op. 36, No. 6) the general rambling and sectional character of the whole setting is enhanced by a spate of arch repetitions at the end.

Apart from five poems in the *Myrthen* of 1840, Schumann did not attempt to set any but incidental poems by Goethe until the nine songs from *Wilhelm Meister*, Op. 98a. Goethe's balance and serenity, philosophic depth, and dislike of romantic exaggeration all made him a quite unsympathetic figure to the young Schumann; and later Schumann's attempt to widen his horizon and to achieve a musical language capable of expressing Goethe's thought led him, at least as a song-writer, to go against all his natural instincts – or rather, since instinct generally gets the better of the artist, to give free rein to the most unfortunate of his natural tendencies, rambling and divagation. The lyrics from the *West-östliche Divan* in *Myrthen* are charming and effective even if only one of them, 'Lied der Suleika', really catches the spirit of Goethe; and even there the otiose repetitions are a serious blemish in the setting of such a formal master as Goethe. The ballad of 'Die wandelnde Glocke' is one of the better of Schumann's songs in this style. It attracted him from a literary and theoretical point of view but was in no way suited to his essentially lyrical and subjective temperament. The

Wilhelm Meister songs, on the other hand, are among Schumann's most conspicuous failures as a song-writer. Painfully oppressed by the philosophic significance of Mignon and the old harp-player, he rambles on in a portentous pseudo-symphonic style, with frequent modulations and unnatural vocal phrases, losing the thread of the poem and of his own musical design, and sometimes, as in No. 6, visibly at a loss how to continue (Ex. 5). Only Philine's 'Singet nicht in Trauertönen' is at least half successful, though here again the repetitions of the last line, and then again of the last phrase, are unforgivable.

Ex. 5.

In addition to settings in ballad style scattered all over his sets of songs, Schumann wrote four sets with the definite title of *Romances and Ballades*, Opp. 45, 49, and 53 in 1840, and Op. 64 in 1847. These contain sixteen songs in all, with texts by Heine, Eichendorff, Mörike, Seidl, Lorenz and von Fröhlich. In the same category are Heine's 'Belshazzar', Op. 57 (though actually one of the first of the February 1840 songs), Schiller's 'Der Handschuh', Op. 87, and the melodramas or ballads for declamation – Hebbel's 'Schön' Hedwig', Op. 106, and 'Ballade vom Haideknaben', Op. 122, No. 1, and Shelley's 'Die Flüchtlinge' ('The Fugitives'), Op. 122, No. 2. Of the three poems by Chamisso, Op. 31, two are definite ballads, 'Die Löwenbraut' and 'Die rote Hanne', and the third, 'Die Kartenlegerin', is a romantic genre picture in much the same style. Two of the Heine settings are miniature dramas consisting of three poems each, 'Der arme Peter', Op. 53, No. 3 and 'Tragödie', Op. 64, No. 3. They are very unequal in quality and only one song from each triptych is comparable with Schumann's best settings of Heine. The concertina which accompanies Grete's dance with Hans, poor Peter's rival ('Der arme Peter' No. 1) turns the whole song into a slow country waltz or *Ländler*. Peter's misery finds no expression in the music; he is merely part of the picture, in the true ballad style. The second song in 'Tragödie', on the other hand, is lyrical in character and only successful in comparison with the fatuity of the first, and the sentimental banality of the third, parts. 'Belshazzar' starts rather unpromisingly like a piano solo – in fact the semiquaver figure in the piano part which dominates half the song is closely related to a passage in No. 5 of the *Fantasiestücke*, Op. 12 ('In der Nacht'). The great length of the poem, eleven verses of four lines each, made it extremely difficult to avoid monotony; but Schumann succeeded here as he seldom did in later ballad settings. This is chiefly owing to the way in which the piano part becomes increasingly simple and tends more and more to make way for the voice as the dramatic interest of the poem increases. The semiquavers, which are almost continuous in the first half of the poem, give way first to repeated quaver chords, with the accent off the beat, and then to isolated chords merely supporting the voice in the last two verses, where the tempo decreases and the chief point lies in the dramatic recitation of the text ('In langsamern Tempo, leise und deutlich zu recitiren'). The glaring fault of both 'Die Löwenbraut' and 'Blondels Lied', rhythmic monotony, was thus avoided in 'Belshazzar' as in the lyrical ballad of 'Die beiden Grenadiere'. In 'Die Löwenbraut' there are forty continuous bars of slow 3/2 time, unrelieved by any variation in the piano pattern, which follows the voice exactly. Similarly in the 124 bars of Blondels Lied' – 'nicht schnell' 4/4 – there are only twenty bars in which the piano part does not follow the voice exactly; often it is in octave unison or in the simplest diatonic harmony devoid of harmonic, melodic, or rhythmic interest. Schiller's 'Der Handschuh' is an exciting story told with the obvious and rather self-conscious dramatic effect we should expect. Schumann amuses himself by some equally naïve dramatic effects (major and minor ninth intervals in the voice when the lion roars and lashes his tail) and there is plenty of variation of key and rhythm, so much so in fact that musically the song does not really cohere at all. It is in fact a hybrid between a real ballad such as 'Belshazzar' and the declaimed melodramas, in which the actor plays the main role and the music is merely 'background'. Unfortunately this is a role that music obstinately refuses to play and the melodramas are complete failures, though the 'Ballade vom Haideknaben' is an exciting story and Schumann's illustrations are often apt enough.

At the opposite extreme to the ballads stand Schumann's salon pieces. They are not many, for the simple reason that Schumann was never by nature a frequenter of salons. Domestic, conjugal felicity, which speaks rather too smugly for modern taste from some of the songs, satisfied both his emotional nature and his demands for the society of his fellow creatures. Nevertheless, every middle-class drawing-room in the Germany of the 1840's and 50's had its cultural pretensions and was, indeed, a miniature salon, if only for the family circle. Albums, pressed flowers, needlework, water-colours, piano duets and, of course, singing all contributed to this specifically domestic form of culture; and though it was only in exceptional salons that these rose much above the status of genteel crafts or achieved that of arts, the demand on all artists to produce at least occasional pieces for home use was continuous and, as their works show, fairly continuously met. The works of even such a comparative misanthrope as Grillparzer contain innumerable *pièces d'occasion* 'for Miss X's album', 'on a water-colour by Miss Z', and the like, while a socially-inclined artist like Liszt must have had the greatest difficulty in refusing demands which, if satisfied, would have taken up all the time he had for composition. As it is, a large proportion (25 out of 57 in Kahnt's three volumes) of Liszt's songs are settings of elegant trifles written by friends, of both sexes, belonging to the *beau monde*. Schumann was probably less plagued than many artists because of his inclination to solitary brooding, his frequent 'absence' in social gatherings; but it would have been unnatural if there were not some salon pieces among his songs. Indeed, his gifts as a miniaturist and his lyricism, though rather intense and highly charged for the drawing-room, fitted him for this minor genre, and there are at least two models of the kind among the 1840 songs, Rückert's 'Jasminenstrauch' and Catherine Fanshawe's 'Rätsel' (the poem itself consisting of a parlour game and wrongly attributed to Byron). Far more typical of the general level of such works is the song 'Liebste, was kann denn uns scheiden', No. 6 of the poems from Rückert's 'Liebesfrühling' which Schumann and his wife collaborated in setting. The four verses of the poem, each starting with the question, 'Beloved, what can part us?', continued with verbal assonances on 'meiden' and 'scheiden', 'mein' and 'dein', and the obvious variations of an arch party-game. (It is worth comparing the song with Liszt's setting of Charlotte von Hagen's 'Dichter, was Liebe sei, mir nicht ver-

Ex. 6.

hehle', a more personal and dangerous variant of the same game.) The musical interest is virtually non-existent. Both 'Röselein, Röselein' and 'Schneeglöckchen' (Op. 96) are all more highly developed, more sophisticated salon pieces; and even 'Stille Liebe' and 'Aufträge' are not really much more. The arch 'question' in the piano part with which 'Stille Liebe' opens (Ex. 6), with its superscription 'innig', is comparable with the teasing triplets at the opening of Liszt's 'Dichter, was Liebe sei', though the emphasis is all on emotion in Schumann and on grace in Liszt. In the same way the rippling demisemiquavers that represent the wave in 'Aufträge' are a great artist's version of what is in origin no more than a parlour trick.

Among these amusements and accomplishments of the nineteenth century, drawing-room duet-singing had a place which was half artistic and half (shall we say?) social. Music, as Plato knew, is an excellent dissolver of inhibitions and barriers of all kinds and if Edward could persuade Bertha to learn a duet with him he could reckon on the power of both music and text (generally discreetly amorous), the appeal of his own charming tenor, and his exquisite tact and consideration in turning pages, modifying his tone so as not to drown her pretty soprano, the necessity of looking one's partner straight in the eyes so as to ensure a perfect entry of both voices together and a hundred and one delightful details which gave courtship all the excitement of an honourable adventure and a good many of the thrills of the chase. Nineteenth-century duets, then, are not to be judged on purely musical grounds. Like many Russian symphonies, they were strictly *Gebrauchsmusik* and, as such, the capabilities of the performers must not be rated too high by the composer. Of Schumann's thirty-four duets only a handful are of any interest musically. The majority are comparable in interest of design, as in original intention, with the small form of sofa called a *causeuse*, large enough for two people sitting very close together and making no violent movements. Typical of this sort of duet are 'Liebesgarten' (which looks like a banal sketch for 'Im Walde', though it was actually written later) and the duet numbers from Rückert's 'Liebesfrühling', including the duet version of 'Liebste, was kann denn uns scheiden?' 'Familiengemälde' with its sentimental comparison of the young couple and the old Darby and Joan, is a typical conversation-piece in Schumann's most bourgeois manner. The four duets, Op. 78 contain some much better music. The 'Tanzlied' is a charming drawing-room game, needing considerably more musical ability than anything of the kind that Schumann had written previously; but I suspect that the boldness of the text ('morgen, o Trauter, dein ganz') confined performances to professional singers in any case. This applies also to the two 'vergebliche Ständchen', 'Liebhabers Ständchen' and 'Unterm Fenster'. The setting of Goethe's 'Ich denke dein' keeps the voices singing mostly in thirds and sixths like all the salon pieces, but it has a pretty romantic sentimentality and must have been a powerful weapon in Edward's amorous arsenal. 'Wiegenlied' (Cradle-song for a sick child) has not the mawkish flavour we might expect and though the relation between the two voices is still very primitive and uninteresting, the contrast between triplets and plain four-in-a-bar quavers, the sudden modulations from E minor to C major and from C to E flat, and the exploitation of the passing note (A sharp in the E minor triad) makes the song unique among the simpler salon duets of Schumann. The duets in the *Liederalbum für die Jugend* and the settings of Elisabeth Kulmann (*Mädchenlieder*) are of no interest musically.

There remain the two sets of Spanish pieces, *Spanisches Lieder-spiel*, Op. 74 (five duet numbers), and the two duets in the *Spanische Liebeslieder*, Op. 138. Spanish pastiche attracted Schumann rather in the same way that Hungarian gipsy pastiche attracted Brahms. In neither case was there any attempt at understanding a different musical tradition, and the resemblance of the result to the original is only occasional and superficial. Nothing further was aimed at, of course, but even so Schumann's Op. 74 does contain some very extraordinary things. Of the duets 'Erste Begegnung' and 'Liebes-gram' have vaguely exotic rhythms, strongly dotted, that is to say, with occasional accents off the beat and some 'passionate' triplets, exactly like Brahms's so-called Hungarian pieces. 'Intermezzo' is a very German serenade, more like a cradle-song imitated from German folk-song, such as Brahms affected later. 'In der Nacht' again suggests Brahms's future style, in its most un-Spanish combination of Bach-like chromaticism (Ex. 7) and sweet, warm German sentiment. Finally 'Botschaft' opens with a direct quotation

Ex. 7.

from the middle section of Chopin's C sharp minor Polonaise, Op. 26, and makes considerable demands on the singers in the two really independent vocal lines which only come together for florid ornamentation with wide intervals (Ex. 8). This same tendency to wide intervals is found in one of the solo numbers of the 'Lieder-

Ex. 8.

spiel', 'Melancholie', a strange and violent little song, again with Bach-like characteristics (Ex. 9) and containing dramatic leaps of ninths, tenths and even in one place a fourteenth, which are most unusual in Schumann's vocal writing. 'Der Contrabandiste', with its guitar accompaniment, coloratura and triplets imitating a horse's

Ex. 9.

gallop, is really a parody and quite an amusing one. The guitar is suggested again in the 'Romanze' from the *Spanische Liebeslieder*, Op. 138, whose title and pianoforte duet accompaniment obviously gave Brahms the idea for his own *Liebeslieder*. None of these solos or duets bears the remotest resemblance to anything genuinely Spanish, and the general musical level of interest is below that of the earlier *Liederspiel*. Thus 'Bedeckt mit Blumen' is rather like the earlier 'Liebesgram', only less successful, and 'Blaue Augen hat das Mädchen' is a much less interesting essay in the German folk-song style than 'Intermezzo'. Of the solo songs 'O wie lieblich ist das Mädchen' and 'Hoch, hoch sind die Berge' are essays in much the same style and their chief distinction lies in the fact that, once again, Brahms (I suspect) had a passage from 'Hoch, hoch sind die Berge' (Ex. 10) in mind when he wrote 'Vergebliches Ständchen'.

Ex. 10.

In between the ballads and the salon pieces, and partaking of the nature of both, come first the *Liederalbum für die Jugend*, Op. 79, and the *Seven Songs*, Op. 104, settings by the child 'poet' Elisabeth Kulmann. Like the *Kinderscenen* for piano, these songs are written for children as they exist in the sentimental imagination of an adult rather than for children as they are. It is possible that in the nineteenth century children could be persuaded to adopt, at least in public and before their parents, some of the qualities attributed to them in the songs – extreme naïveté, love of nature, a sense of pity and at least nascent Sabbatarianism. But that any children, in any country, at any date, should really have been anything but complicated, indifferent to nature, pitiless and impious by nature, I cannot believe. Schumann, then, either writes for the 'Kunstkind', the product of intensive nursery training, or not for children at all.

'Schmetterling', 'Frühlingsgruss', 'Sonntag', 'Hinaus ins Freie',
'Weihnachtslied' and 'Kinderwacht' are all carefully simple musically, unctuous in tone and quite devoid of any interest. But spread
among these thirty-odd songs there are some exquisite miniatures.
The first of the two 'Zigeunerliedchen' (Ex. 11), for example, and
'Der Sandmann' have a lightness and aptness of touch, a sureness
of psychological instinct shown in minute detail, such as only Hugo
Wolf has equalled. They are neither folk-songs nor children's songs
but spring from a spontaneity of feeling and directness of expression
which Schumann at times possessed in common with 'primitive'
people and children. No child ever thought or felt in terms of
Hoffmann von Fallersleben's 'So sei gegrüsst viel tausendmal, hol-

Ex. 11.

Un - ter die Sol - da - ten ist ein Zi - geu - ner bub' ge - gan - gen

der, holder Frühling' but any child might prick up its ear at a story
which began 'Unter die Soldaten ist ein Zigeunerbub' gegangen'.
'Des Sennen Abschied' from Schiller's *William Tell* might be taken
as a companion piece to Lenau's 'Die Sennin' (Op. 90, No. 4) as
both depict the descent in the autumn from the high mountain
pastures of the Alps. Schiller's poem is the shepherd's own song
and Schumann's accompaniment suggests a primitive pipe-tune
which gradually dies away in the distance. Lenau's is a German
equivalent of Wordsworth's 'Highland Reaper', a deeply subjective
lyric full of Ruskin's pathetic fallacy (the mountains miss the girl
and remember her songs). The harmonic scheme is correspondingly
more rich and complicated, and whereas 'Des Sennen Abschied'
only modulates occasionally to the dominant or the relative minor
of its tonic C major, the voice part of 'Die Sennin' ends on a chord
of the dominant, while the piano part dies slowly away on a mediant
major chord (D sharp major in B major).
     The two Goethe settings which have somehow found their way
into the *Liederalbum für die Jugend* are quite out of keeping with the
rest of the contents. Lynceus' song from *Faust*, Part 2, is a mono-
tonous piece in the four-square dotted rhythm beloved by Schumann, the setting of 'Kennst du das Land' obviously belongs to the

IM N

other *Wilhelm Meister* songs in Op. 98a, where it also appears. It cannot compare with the setting, however faulty, by Liszt or the magnificent one by Hugo Wolf, but it is very much better than the rest of the *Wilhelm Meister* songs and interesting for Schumann's very rare insistence on the chord of the dominant minor ninth ('Was hat man dir, du armes Kind, getan?').

Schumann's admiration for the poems of Elisabeth Kulmann, which issued in his Op. 104 (1851) is explicable partly as the result of failing powers of judgment, perhaps, but partly also as one of those quite frequent lapses in taste which may occur to any artist of a deeply emotional character liable to be influenced by personal circumstances. Elisabeth Kulmann was born at St Petersburg in 1808 and lost her father and six of her seven brothers while she was a young child. She herself died of consumption in 1825, after living in poverty with her mother. Her poems show her to have been a sensitive and idealistic young woman, whose imagination was probably stimulated by the disease from which she suffered. She had a poetic facility which enabled her to imitate the lighter, occasional lyrics of the Romantic school with a certain elegance, and a spiritual quality which showed itself in the simplicity and resignation with which she faced death. Schumann was greatly struck by the unusual pathos of her story and, in an introduction which he printed to his settings of seven of her poems, he went so far as to prophesy her universal recognition as a great German poet and to speak of her poems as 'wisdom's highest teachings expressed with the poetic perfection worthy of a master'. It must be remembered that his literary taste was always very personal rather than aesthetically correct, and that to the end of his life he rated Jean Paul as the equal of Goethe and Shakespeare. The settings of Elisabeth Kulmann's songs witness to the soundness of his musical instinct, in any case, for the unpretentiousness of the music exactly matches the poems, with their maidenly lisping of swallows, greenfinches, dead flowers, clouds and the moon. They are of no intrinsic musical interest whatever.

It is an interesting fact, which says much for Schumann's understanding of the nature of vocal music, that the rhythmic complications, anomalies and puns which are such a marked feature of his pianoforte style seldom, if ever, appear in the voice parts of his songs; and hardly ever oppressively even in the piano parts. In fact, as we have already seen, a considerable proportion of the songs suffer from the opposite fault, monotony and jejuneness of rhythm. Schumann always tended to confine his rhythmic experiments to detail, often to inner parts, while the movement as a whole – whether it be orchestral, vocal or chamber music – progresses in uniform, scarcely disguised march time. His most completely successful pieces are generally miniatures and, in the songs at least, the subtlety and effectiveness of his rhythm is generally in inverse proportion to its complexity. Compare, for instance, 'Die Fensterscheibe' with 'Abendlied', both from Op. 107. Schumann very seldom changes the time signature in the course of a song. When he does – as in 'Allnächtlich im Traume' or 'Jemand' – it is for a quite definite dramatic purpose. In some of the most successful songs the piano continues the same rhythmic pattern from beginning to end ('Der Nussbaum', 'Mondnacht', 'Frühlingsnacht' and most of the *Dichterliebe* songs) and the voice has its own, perfectly distinct melody which is either completed or commented on by the piano ('Nussbaum') or leads an entirely separate existence ('Das ist ein Flöten und Geigen'). A note-by-note accompaniment, with the top note of the piano part permanently in unison with the voice, is sometimes skilfully masked by ornamentation, as in 'Und wüssten's die Blumen, die kleinen,' or broken up into brilliant fragments, as in 'Frühlingsnacht'. It is generally only left quite undisguised in the march songs in 'folk' or student style ('Frühlingsfahrt', 'Wanderlied' and the rest) and even then not for the whole song in the better examples. Hymns like 'Zum Schluss', 'Talismane', or 'Über allen Gipfeln' are of course derivatives of these march songs; but even in these Schumann generally breaks the plodding 4/4 by some device, the flowing quavers in the middle section of 'Talismane' and the festoons of crochet triplets at the words 'Warte nur!' in the Goethe poem. Occasionally Schumann overworks an idea which is good in itself but loses its initial point by repetition. The piano part of 'Muttertraum', with its wandering semiquavers and cross-bar suspensions, sounds like a two-part invention to which the voice part has been added afterwards and, though it makes an effective opening, it does not seem to correspond to two whole quatrains of Andersen's poem. In much the same way 'O Freund, mein Schirm, mein Schutz' (No. 6 of Rückert's *Minnespiel*, Op. 101) seems rather an essay in the style of Bach – perhaps suggested by Rückert's poem which addresses the earthly much as Bach's cantata arias address the heavenly lover – than a genuinely original inspiration. The exclusive use of passing-note harmony and the same angular rocking rhythm, as of a broken cradle, for nearly fifty bars without a single break is an extraordinary instance of lack of self-criticism in such a self-conscious artist as Schumann. Compare this with a song of much the same length (though admittedly much quicker tempo) like 'Ein Jüngling liebt ein Mädchen' where Schumann starts with the idea of a strong accent off the beat and indeed carries it right the way through the song but is careful not to emphasise the syncopated rhythm except in the piano solo passages, prelude, interlude and postlude.

This scrupulousness in his treatment of the poems which he set places Schumann, as we have seen, half way between the unscrupulously musical Schubert and the almost painfully literary Wolf. His two misquotations ('Blätter' for 'Äste' in Mosen's 'Der Nussbaum' and 'lieblichen' for 'guten' in Heine's 'Das ist ein Flöten und Geigen') are little more than misprints and the only serious criticism that his poets could make of Schumann's settings of their poems is that he tends, for purely musical effect, to repeat their last lines or last phrases. The examples of this are innumerable and I have referred to some already. Even Heine is occasionally mishandled in this way ('Berg und Burgen', 'Ich wandelte unter den Bäumen') though generally the construction of his poems makes it virtually impossible without giving the impression of repeating the end of a witty story to be sure that the audience has not missed the point. What led Schumann to offend against literary canons in this way was his desire to impart a dream-like, echo effect to a song, a heightening of emotion as the music dies away in the distance. Sometimes this effect is achieved by a simple repetition of the last phrase, differently harmonised but with no piano postlude, as in 'Im Walde'. Sometimes – and this is the more frequent method – the last line or phrase is repeated and a postlude added as well, as in 'Stille Tränen', 'Nur ein lächelnder Blick', 'Liebesbotschaft' and many others. But the same effect is achieved by purely musical means and without deforming the poem in all Schumann's best songs simply by the piano postlude taken in conjunction with the last line of the poem, as in 'Widmung', 'Der Nussbaum', 'Mondnacht', 'Frühlingsnacht', 'Am leuchtenden Sommermorgen', 'Jasminenstrauch', 'Auf das Trinkglas eines verstorbenen Freundes', 'Die beiden Grenadiere', 'Die Fensterscheibe' – to choose examples from every date and category. In these songs the musical and literary emphasis coincide, instead of Schumann coming to the end of his poem before the music has reached its natural climax, as in 'Stille Tränen' – the most flagrant example of all – where twenty-one bars out of a total seventy are tacked on after the poem has finished, in the form of interlude, repetition of the last couplet and long postlude.

As we have seen, Schumann was conservative in his use of chromaticism, but this does not mean that the songs are in any way poor harmonically. A few, as we have seen, are too rich and a considerable number suffer from a deliberate simplicity employed, often unsuccessfully but always deliberately, for a definite purpose – the creation of an imaginary 'folk', child or student atmosphere. None of Schumann's masterpieces come into either of these classes, the over rich or the artificially slimmed. In fact, the beauty of his most successful songs depends very largely on the perfect accord between poetical matter and harmonic manner. In setting a simple poem such as Mosen's 'Der Nussbaum', Schumann employs a very simple harmonic scheme which does not go beyond the tonalities of the mediant (minor), the subdominant, dominant and supertonic minor. Within these keys there are no further chromatic alterations and the ambiguous chords of the dominant seventh or chromatic alterations of the sixth are instinctively avoided. In an intensely emotional lyric such as Eichendorff's 'Mondnacht', on the other hand, Schumann deploys much more harmonic subtlety. The actual form of the song is simple almost to monotony: the voice part consists of the same eight-bar phrase repeated four times and followed by two four-bar phrases which lead to the fifth and last repetition of the original phrase slightly varied to make a full close. In 'Der Nussbaum', as in many other songs, Schumann tended to avoid the dominant, to shy off it by a harmonic side-slip (the only occasion where the dominant seventh is used) and to prefer the minor of the mediant or supertonic. In 'Mondnacht' the piano prelude modu-

lates to the dominant (B major) within two bars and seems to insist
on it until the voice enters and we find ourselves almost immediately in F sharp major, that is to say the key of the supertonic from
the point of view of E major (the tonic key) or the dominant from
the point of view of B major. This playing with ambiguities of
chords of the dominant reaches its climax at the beginning of the
last quatrain where, on the word 'spannte' ('spread') an inversion
of the dominant seventh in the tonic (E major) suddenly becomes
a dominant major ninth in the key of A, as the spreading of the
soul's wings is suggested by the wide interval and spreading semiquaver phrase in the piano part. Schumann even ends the voice
part on a chord of the dominant seventh, out of the key (A major
instead of E) and there are many instances of this, at that time
revolutionary, process throughout the songs. In the *Dichterliebe*
alone 'Im wunderschönen Monat Mai', 'Ich hab' im Traum
geweinet', 'Das ist ein Flöten und Geigen', and 'Am leuchtenden
Sommermorgen' end on chords of the dominant seventh out of
the tonic; and 'Aus meinen Tränen spriessen', 'Ich will meine
Seele tauchen', 'Im Rhein, im heiligen Strome', 'Allnächtlich im
Traume', 'Aus alten Märchen' and 'Die alten bösen Lieder' all
close either in the key of the dominant or else on a dominant seventh
in the tonic. This applies only to the voice parts, of course, and in
most cases Schumann makes the piano postlude come to a more or
less conventional cadence in the tonic. Not always, however. In
'Die Nonne', for example, both voice and piano part close on a
dramatic dominant seventh and in 'Die Sennin' the voice ends on
a dominant seventh of the tonic and the piano part unmistakably
in the key of the mediant. Occasionally Schumann opens a song
with a chord of the dominant or diminished seventh ('An meinem
Herzen, an meiner Brust' from *Frauenliebe und -leben*; 'Flügel!
Flügel! um zu fliegen', 'Was will die einsame Träne?' 'Die Tochter
Jephtas') and even more frequently whole passages in the course of
a song are built up on sequences of dominant sevenths. Among the
most obvious examples is the quiet middle section of 'Widmung'
and the magnificent chain of dominant sevenths which leads up
to the climax in 'Aus alten Märchen' ('und laute Quellen brechen'
to the twice repeated 'Ach!'). We have already seen a more sophisticated version of the same thing in 'Mondnacht' and there are two

other noticeable examples in the Eichendorff *Liederkreis:* 'Schöne Fremde' and 'Frühlingsnacht'. All these nocturnes or night pieces are in extreme sharp keys, as though Schumann felt that this blend of richness and ambiguity were his own way of expressing the Romantic adoration of the night – Novalis's 'herrlicher Fremdling mit den sinnvollen Augen, dem schwebenden Gange und den zartgeschlossenen, tonreichen Lippen'. More rarely a comparatively diatonic song will close with a postlude which consists almost entirely of a chain of dominant sevenths ('Schöne Wiege meiner Leiden', Ex. 12, and 'Rose, Meer und Sonne').

Ex 12.

There was nothing unusual in Schumann's use of the dominant seventh; that is to say, there was nothing unusual in the fact that he used it. A far more unmistakable harmonic finger-print of Schumann's is his predilection for – almost his obsession with – supertonic minor harmony (especially, it seems, in the key of A major, where passages in B minor almost always appear sooner or later). The opening phrases of 'Was will die einsame Träne' (Ex. 13) and 'Lied der Suleika' (Ex. 1) are typical instances, but examples are spread thickly throughout songs of every period. It is dramatically crucial in some of the *Dichterliebe* songs, at 'da ist in meinem Herzen die Liebe aufgegangen' in 'Im wunderschönen Monat Mai' and at 'ich liebe dich' in 'Wenn ich in deine Augen seh'. Again in 'Was soll ich sagen?' we find the same harmony at the dramatic climax, 'du heissest mich reden'. Sometimes it is reached through the subdominant, as in 'Stille Tränen' (C major), where the D

Ex. 13.

minor ('ob allen Landen') is reached through the dominant seventh of F major, the subdominant of the tonic key; or by means of the dominant, as in 'Aufträge'. Sometimes it is a mere passing effect, almost always emotional, as in 'Heimliches Verschwinden' or

Ex. 14.

'Meine Rose' (Ex. 14); or it is used as an ornament to give dramatic emphasis to a phrase, as in the last bars of the voice part of 'Ihre Stimme' (Ex. 15).

Ex. 15.

Another favourite and very effective device of Schumann's, which he uses with great care and never wastes, is enharmonic modulation. The roots of almost all his harmonic experiments can be found in Schubert, including the technique of jumping from dominant to dominant which we have just seen, and the turning to the key of the mediant where more conventional composers would have modulated to the dominant ('Zwischendominanten' and 'Mediantenrückung', as the Germans call these devices). The pivoting on a single note we have already met in the last bars of 'Die alten bösen Lieder', where Schumann used it to express the sudden change in the poet's mood. In 'Die Lotosblume', 'Stille Tränen', and 'Alte Laute' there is no dramatic literary reason and Schumann is guided by purely musical instinct. The effect is certainly breathtaking when the A flat major breaks in on the C major at 'Der Mond, der ist ihr Buhle' in 'Die Lotosblume' and at 'So lang du ohne Sorgen' in 'Stille Tränen': and hardly less when the simple, sequential phrases of 'Alte Laute' are suddenly transferred from the dominant (E flat) to G flat major, i.e. the key whose tonic is the third note in the minor of the dominant (Ex. 16). This is a sophisticated form of the tendency to mediant harmony which we have already noticed (in 'Der Nussbaum', for example). Although there is no immediate dramatic reason for these enharmonic changes

Ex. 16.

Schumann nearly always uses them in songs whose general sense and atmosphere have something eerie or uncanny; and this is obviously in accordance with his general feelings, already noticed, of the extreme power and effectiveness of chromaticism in any shape or form. We have already noticed the enharmonic modulations in two songs from Op. 35, both poems by Justinus Kerner, the doctor and occultist. A third of his poems, No. 6 of Op. 35, 'Auf das Trinkglas eines verstorbenen Freundes', is an unusual combination of Schumann's extremely rigid, four-square, dotted rhythm – a cross between the march and a prayer like 'Zum Schluss' – with harmonic experimentation which alone suggests to the listener the mystery of the poem. The piano follows the voice part note by note for three quatrains, without ornament of any kind apart from the harmonic colour. At the end of the first quatrain the music has reached what is presumably the dominant of B flat major (the song being in the key of E flat). This unison F Schumann now chooses to regard as the mediant of D flat major and a four-bar phrase, repeating exactly the rhythm of the first two couplets, now follows in that key. This in its turn ends on a chord of D flat major with the mediant uppermost and is followed by a four-bar phrase identical with what has gone before but in the key of F minor (the supertonic minor of the original E flat, for which Schumann always hankers). The next quatrain is based entirely on a punning use of the chord on the flattened sixth of the scale, alternating with the dominant seventh first in the key of B flat, then of E flat (Ex. 17),

Ex. 17.

and this, significantly, is the heart of the poem's mystery, which lies in the words 'was ich erschau' in deinem Grund ist nicht Gewöhnlichen zu nennen' ('what I descry in your bowl is not to be spoken of before the common herd'). After this the last quatrain is devoted to depicting the slow movement of the moonlight down the valley and the solemn tolling of midnight. This passage is another example of Schumann's chains of dominant sevenths and very effective it is here, with the voice released at last from its note-by-note bondage to the piano and even varying slightly the

♩ | ♩. ♪♪ ♩ | ♩. ♪♪ rhythm which Schumann pursues inexorably throughout the whole song.

Schumann himself was quite aware of the novelty and originality of many things in his songs. On 31 May 1840 he wrote to Clara that 'it often seems to me as though I were treading quite new paths in music' ('als käme ich auf ganz neue Wege in der Musik') and a year later we find him writing to Kossmaly, author of an essay on 'The Song', with proper consciousness of his own originality:

> It vexed me rather that you put me in the second class. I did not expect to be included in the first class, but I believe I can claim a place of my own and least of all am I pleased to be ranked with Reissiger, Curschmann, &c. I know that my endeavours and my means far exceed theirs, and I hope you will remember that and not call me vain, which I am far from being.

He was generous in proclaiming the influence of Clara on the compositions of 1840. 'When I was composing them', he writes to her, 'I was entirely taken up with you. It is not possible to write such music without a bride such as you – and I mean that as high praise of you.' But the desirability of Clara's influence on the final versions of some of the songs has been questioned. Not her personal influence on Schumann, who told the same Kossmaly that his music had always been 'the expression of himself both as human being and as musician', with no cleavage or hostility between the two. But Clara Wieck was first and foremost a pianist formed in the classical and neo-classical school, with none of the instinctive leanings to Romanticism which her husband had always felt. Her musical taste leaned towards Mendelssohn quite as much as towards Schumann and there is, to say the least of it, a strong tradition (traceable directly to Theodor Kirchner, a disciple and friend of Schumann) that she persuaded Schumann to make various alterations in the text of his songs, always in the interest of academic 'correctness'. Schumann, in his aphorisms, expressed himself quite unambiguously on the subject of revisions:

> Two different readings of the same work are often equally good. (*Eusebius.*)
>
> The original one is generally the better. (*Raro.*)

And in point of fact the alterations that we can trace from his notebooks are seldom of great importance and more often than not aim at perfecting the prosody of a song rather than any specifically musical improvement.

It was Schumann's practice to go on making alterations, which were often continued to the last moment, when the music was in proof. It will only be possible here to give a few typical examples of Schumann's revisions, as any more thorough study would necessitate a prohibitive amount of quotation. Most interesting of all is to see[1] how in many cases the songs which seem the most spontaneous and 'inevitable' were actually those on which Schumann took the longest time to make up his mind. Thus there exist three versions of 'Mondnacht' (Schumann gave his mother-in-law a manuscript copy which differs from both the original and the corrected, published version), in which the composer seems chiefly concerned with giving the text and his illustrations more perfect expressiveness, though the musical character of the song receives hardly any alteration at all. On the other hand 'Frühlingsnacht' has a major alteration of the text of bars 15-17, as important as some of the major operations to which Beethoven's sketch-books bear witness. Compare the simplicity and expressiveness, the apparent 'inevitability' of the published version with the fussiness and ineffectiveness of the original (Ex. 18), in which the word 'herein' is repeated for no reason.

On the other hand, was Clara responsible for the 'toning down'

---

[1] Viktor Ernst Wolff: *R. Schumanns Lieder in ersten und späteren Fassungen* (Leipzig, 1914). Wolff's 'first' versions, however, are themselves fair copies, not initial sketches.

Ex. 18

of bars 69–76 of 'Das ist ein Flöten und Geigen', in which the chords of the original three-bar version (Ex. 19) seem to suggest either the climax of the festivity or the dagger-thrusts in the

Ex. 19.

unfortunate lover's heart – or, knowing Schumann, both? Certainly the contradictory spirit of Jean Paul hangs over the whole song (Schumann probably had the last scene of the 'Flegeljahre' in mind, the ball and its extraordinary results for Walt, Vult, and Wina), for over bars 75–8, which show the lover moving slowly away from the scene of his misery, Schumann wrote 'Vivat hoch' which, presumably on reflection, he enclosed in brackets. Dr Wolff sagely remarks that this outburst is a 'memorial of Schumann's

Janus-like temperament. In the heat of creation Florestan was led by his dramatic visions to make such annotations, which Eusebius later bracketed in a moment of cooler reflection.'

The manuscripts of the *Dichterliebe* are particularly heavily scored with revisions. Here again the most apparently spontaneous songs – 'Die Rose, die Lilie' and 'Hör' ich ein Liedchen klingen' – are shown to be the fruit of considerable reflection, if only on points of prosody, while 'Am leuchtenden Sommermorgen' appears as a minutely calculated work of art, each of whose effects is carefully planned and either subtly prepared or deliberately surprising (e.g. the inclusion of two bars in the piano part between the first two lines of the poem, bars 6 and 7, in which the harmonic effect of bars 8-9 is cunningly prepared). Schumann did not immediately make up his mind on the dramatic enharmonic modulation at the end of 'Die alten, bösen Lieder', where (bar 49) the effect of the dissonance was originally intensified by two quavers (E natural followed by C sharp) on the 'und', later replaced by the less violent single crochet C sharp. Was this Clara's handiwork? Certainly I should suspect her influence in the change (bars 59-60) from the unconventional quintuplets in the manner of Chopin to the conventional gruppetti before the sixth beat in each bar.

Sometimes Schumann's second thoughts seem to have been definitely disimprovements. Why, for example, did he alter the opening bars of 'Liebesbotschaft', in which the original version opens canonically, with one bar of piano solo (bar 1 of the final version) and the voice following with the same melody one bar later? Clara cannot have objected to anything so academically respectable as a canonic imitation. Internal evidence provided by Schumann's very rare use of canon in a few other songs would suggest that he regarded this device – as we have seen that he regarded chromaticism – as producing a definite effect (presumably of ancient, semi-ecclesiastical venerableness, as in 'Auf einer Burg') and this was certainly out of place in setting the amorous platitudes of Reinick's 'Liebesbotschaft', though from the purely musical point of view the song loses interest in the final version. Schumann would perhaps reply that what concerned him first and foremost was old Wiedebein's advice, to 'look to truth above all'.

Liszt praised Schumann for choosing as texts for his songs poems

'whose beauty of form proceeded from a feeling capable of a still
higher expression than words could give'. Actually the form of the
poem was the only thing about it which Schumann tended to
treat with little respect, repeating to his heart's content if he felt
musically inclined, as we have seen. But Liszt was right in praising
Schumann's sense of musical possibilities in a poem. There are
very few instances of his setting to music poems complete in themselves and lacking in the atmospheric suggestion which was the
first necessity in Schumann's case. The five poems by Mary, Queen
of Scots (Op. 135) are certainly one example. In translation they
lose the pathos of their sincerity and verbal simplicity (especially
No. 5, 'Gebet', whose whole charm lies in its tripping Latin assonances); and it was probably the glamour of the author, unwittingly
transferred to her poems by Schumann (as in the case of Elisabeth
Kulmann), which made him choose such completely un-romantic
words. But in general we have to go forward to Hugo Wolf before
we find another German song-writer with such a fine instinct in
choosing and setting his poems. Brahms was a more perfect craftsman than Schumann, with a more genuine understanding and less
sentimentality in his approach to German folk-song. He was rhythmically far more adventurous, but at the same time he knew when
the listener would have had enough of a good thing and he could
never have written a whole song, like Schumann's 'Abendlied', with
cross-rhythms persisting throughout. On the other hand his North
German tendency to sentimental brooding led him to choose poems
such as Klaus Groth's 'O wüsst' ich doch den Weg zurück',
Daumer's 'Wir wandelten' and Almers' 'Feldeinsamkeit' for some
of what proved to be his most successful songs; and the quality of
the poetry had a definite influence on the quality of the music.
Schubert might have set such poems with impunity; and Schumann
might have conceivably chosen them, though they would have
become poor songs in the second or third rank of his output.
Brahms's masterpieces – for masterpieces they are, in their way –
are founded on banal literary material and emotion, which they
faithfully reproduce with great charm. Whereas the great songs of
Schumann are a joint triumph for Schumann and Heine or Eichendorff, many of the great songs of Brahms are a triumph (sometimes
Pyrrhic) for Brahms alone. It is only in the folk-song pastiche,

where Schumann generally failed so signally, that Brahms is consistently his superior. We have only to compare the older man's 'Liebhabers Ständchen' or 'Unterm Fenster' with his successor's 'Vergebliches Ständchen', 'Lied eines Schmiedes' with 'Der Schmied', 'Sonntags am Rhein' with 'Sonntag' (and the list could be prolonged) to see Brahms's unquestioned superiority in this vein.

Schumann's influence on Liszt as a song-writer was, I rather think, unfortunate. In his settings of Heine, Liszt owes nothing to Schumann; he was a dramatic miniaturist, as we have seen, and a lyrical poem like 'Du bist wie eine Blume' appears as an exception. How differently the two men treated even the same poems of Heine's can be seen by comparing their settings of 'Anfangs wollt' ich fast verzagen' and 'Im Rhein, im heiligen Strome', where Liszt paints and dramatises phrase by phrase, bar by bar, and Schumann lays down a solid rhythmic pattern which is pursued almost owlishly from beginning to end. It was in his settings of Goethe that I suspect Liszt of following the bad example of Schumann, in wandering from section to section and hammering together what often amounts to four sides, a lid and a bottom all belonging to different boxes. The chronology of Liszt's songs is uncertain, even such a trifle as 'Dichter, was Liebe sei' appearing in three different versions dating from 1844, 1855, and 1878. But the majority were written in the 40's, after Liszt settled at Weimar (1842). And certainly a big blowsy song like 'Ich möchte hingehn' or the sprawling settings of 'Wer nie sein Brot mit Tränen ass' (1845 and 1860) were written with a full knowledge of Schumann's songs, good and bad. That Liszt did not always distinguish the one from the other is shown in his choice for piano transcription. Thus by the side of 'Widmung' and 'Frühlingsnacht' stand thoroughly second-rate songs such as 'An den Sonnenschein' and (significantly) 'An die Türen will ich schleichen' and the rather colourless numbers from the *Liederalbum für die Jugend*. Perhaps the truth is that both Liszt and Schumann suffered, especially as they grew older, from the same, typically Romantic failing – a passion for the vague, large and high-sounding which led both men in their different ways to a form of musical meandering among windy generalities.

Hugo Wolf, who owed much to Schumann, instinctively turned to songs of an entirely different kind. A dramatic miniaturist like

Liszt, he developed and made explicit the drama which is often only hinted at by Schumann. The two men's settings of Mörike's 'Er ist's' and 'Das verlassene Mägdelein' provide typical examples of their different methods. Schumann's setting of 'Er ist's' is included in the *Liederalbum für die Jugend* and it has the self-conscious simplicity which, as we have seen, Schumann associated with children. It is marked 'innig', whereas Wolf's mood is clearly shown by 'sehr lebhaft, jubelnd' ('very lively, with jubilation'). Both songs open with two bars for the piano, Schumann's based on a descending scale passage with dotted rhythm, bringing in the voice on his favourite dominant seventh in the key of the dominant (dominant seventh of E in the key of A major) (cf. 'Loreley' and 'Schöne Fremde'). Wolf merely sets in motion a vigorous rhythmic figure which is to dominate the whole song, a broken tonic triad (G major) over which the voice enters with an opening phrase spread over the notes of the triad. At the end of the first quatrain, where Schumann has modulated through the minor of the mediant (C

Ex. 20.

a) Schumann

Etwas zurückhaltend

Veil - chen träu - men schon

wol - len bal - de kom - men   Horch!

b) **Wolf**

Veil - chen traü - men schon

wol - len bal - de kom - men

Horch!

sharp) to a conventional close in the key of the dominant in the
interlude for the piano, Wolf has quickly reached the remote key
of C sharp major. A comparison of the two settings of the next two
lines, with exactly the same rhythm in the vocal parts (Ex. 20, *a*
and *b*) will show how completely differently two composers can
envisage the same poem. The piano part is of primary importance
in each case, of course. Schumann's is actually the more independent, Wolf's more in the nature of an accompaniment. Both composers instinctively aim at expressing the atmosphere of expectancy,
which is the note of the poem, by a series of generally unresolved
dominant sevenths, Schumann's naturally far less sophisticated
than Wolf's. Both emphasise the 'Horch!' by a harped dominant
seventh right out of the key of the preceding bars: but Schumann

continues the shy, hesitant ('etwas zurückhaltend') manner and the rather self-conscious, Dresden-china prettiness already suggested by the mordents in the piano part, whereas Wolf quickly works up to his climax and gives final vent to his excitement in a long piano postlude (twenty-one bars in a song of under sixty). The last lines of the poem read in Wolf's version:

> Frühling, ja, du bist's! (twice)
> Dich hab' ich vernommen!
> Ja, du bist's!

This already has two unwarranted repetitions. Schumann, in a happy haze, 'innig' rather than 'jubelnd', murmurs the words again and again:

> Frühling, ja, du bist's! ja, du bist's, du bist's!
> Dich hab' ich vernommen, ja, du bist's!
> Dich hab' ich vernommen,
> Frühling, ja, du bist's! ja, du bist's!
> Ja, du bist's, du bist's, du bist's,
> Dich hab' ich vernommen,
> Ja, du bist's!

There is only the shortest postlude (in which the 'pretty' mordents recur). These are the dangers of 'Innigkeit' and too much Jean Paul, the dreaming aloud and the soulfulness which is not so simple and unselfconscious as it would like to seem, but pins on some arch little ornaments and is not above an occasional simper.

Between the two settings of 'Das verlassene Mägdelein' the resemblance is so marked that it is impossible that Wolf had not got Schumann's in mind when he wrote his own.[1] But Schumann's is a *cri du cœur* whereas Wolf's is a picture. Schumann cares nothing for the suggestion of early morning cold and desolation which Wolf

---

[1] Since writing this passage and what follows I have found confirmation of this in Ernest Newman's *Hugo Wolf*, p. 182, note 3, where he says that in a letter to Eckstein dated 27 March 1888, Wolf wrote that he greatly admired Schumann's setting of 'Das verlassene Mägdelein' and had no intention of setting the poem himself: but that being deeply affected by the poem the music came to him almost against his will. The comparison of the two settings which follows was written without knowledge of Mr Newman's (p. 190), with which I am in general, but not complete, agreement, as comparisons will show.

gives in his piano prelude, still less for the sparks which Wolf strikes
as the girl lights the fire, interrupting the heavy tread of the rhythm
♩ ♫♩ ♫ , an exaggeration of Schumann's, which is alleviated
by the movement of the inner parts. Schumann places his two-bar
piano interlude between the two lines of the poem where the girl
lights the fire and then sits gazing miserably into it. Wolf, with a
better literary and dramatic instinct, puts his four bars of interlude
after the lines and makes them depict the girl's misery, so that his
'plötzlich, da kommt es mir' sounds like a real, sudden memory.
He paints the ecstasy of the girl's dream of her lover in three
repeated phrases, ritardando, and ending on a pause before the
tears start falling hopelessly. Schumann, aware only of the girl's
misery, carries straight on from the dream to the tears with an
accentuation of the harmonic clash (dominant minor ninth, Ex. 21;

Ex. 21.

cf. 'Mignons Lied') which is a characteristic feature of the whole
song. Wolf, in an era of greater harmonic sophistication, when
minor ninths had become small beer, chooses a subtler chord as the
symbol of the girl's grief, the augmented triad or 'whole-tone'
chord in its various positions. Again Wolf's postlude, with its bare
open fifths, suggests the misery and desolation of the opening,
whereas Schumann has no postlude at all but comes to rest on a
rather inept 'tierce de Picardie', the tonic triad with the major third
instead of the minor. The unusually chromatic harmony in Schumann's setting (in accordance with his regular association of
chromacitism with extreme grief) becomes with Wolf simply a

pianissimo dying-away of open fifths, which accords well with
the simple emotion of Mörike's poem and suggests the girl's deso-
late hopelessness. Not that a comparison of the two songs need result in a judgment value between them; it is merely instructive to
see how differently the two composers work on a given poem which
admits (unlike 'Er ist's') of only one emotional approach, from
what different angles they approach it and what are the alterations
Wolf makes in what is almost certainly an (unconscious) 'rethinking'
of Schumann's music as well as Mörike's verses.

There are other songs by Wolf which often seem to be sophisticated rethinkings of Schumann's material. The two 'Zigeunerliedchen' from the *Liederalbum für die Jugend* have already been
mentioned on pp. 177 and a comparison between the first of
them ('Unter die Soldaten', Ex. 11 with, say, the opening of Wolf's
'Schweig einmal still' (*Italienisches Liederbuch*, Vol. 3, No. 43) will
give an idea of what I mean. Wolf's soldier songs, also, seems to
hark back to Schumann's (compare, for example, Schumann's 'Die
Soldatenbraut' with Wolf's 'Der Tambour') though again the later
songs have a variety, both rhythmic and harmonic, and a dramatic
sophistication which often make the earlier seem homely and naïve
in comparison.

In Schumann's special domains he is supreme and need fear no
comparison: the romantic night-pieces like 'Der Nussbaum', 'Frühlingsnacht', 'Mondnacht', 'Schöne Fremde' or what may for want
of a better title be called psychological, rather than dramatic, lyrics
as those of the *Dichterliebe*, 'Wer machte dich so krank?', 'Die
Fensterscheibe'. In the night-pieces he found musical expression
for a specifically new, romantic emotion. (New to music, that is to
say; Novalis's 'Hymnen an die Nacht' were nearly fifty years old
in 1840, while Edward Young, whose 'Night Thoughts' originated
the cult, had died as long ago as 1765.) In Schubert's 'Nacht und
Träume' there still remains something of the eighteenth century, a
marmoreal serenity and an absence of the 'Orphic' or 'Dionysian'
quality which begins to appear in Schumann's night-pieces ('In
der Nacht', from the *Fantasiestücke* for piano, for example, as well
as the songs) and found its fullest expression in that 'vast nocturne',
Act II of *Tristan*. It is a specifically German quality, quite unlike
the elegant melancholy of Chopin's Nocturnes or Tom Moore's

'At the mid hour of night', no less beautiful for being tributes to a literary fashion but only incidentally night-pieces, whereas Schumann's music really suggests another world of feeling, solemn and mysterious, peopled with poetic imaginations which would fade in the light of common day, and foreshadow Tristan's 'göttlich ew'ges Urvergessen'.

To speak of Schumann as merely a miniaturist is a by now dangerous platitude; but it is certainly true of Schumann as a songwriter. He managed his larger songs worse than any of the great German song-writers, Schubert, Brahms or Wolf; but in return he showed himself a master of pregnancy and compression in the psychological lyric, a genre which is virtually his invention. He was not a dramatist like Wolf; we have seen how differently the two men reacted to the same poem. But Schumann's literary background and his reading had given him an instinctive understanding, a psychological acumen, which combined with his lyrical gift and his own intensely emotional character to create something like a new form. While much of Schumann's music, including a considerable proportion of his songs, bears the traces of the naïvely emotional and complacent background which determined the composer's mentality, there remains an irreducible minimum of works which have that ageless quality which is the only certain hall-mark of genius. At the very centre of that core are the great songs, so that if future generations remember Schumann for nothing else, he can hardly fail to be counted among the very greatest of the German song-writers.

2 Claire Croiza

In 1924 France celebrated the four hundredth anniversary of the poet Ronsard's birth and during those celebrations Paul Valéry heard a voice, a speaking voice, that was new to him and impressed him profoundly. The voice was Claire Croiza's and Valéry in his enthusiasm spoke of it as 'the most expressive voice' (*la voix la plus sensible*) 'of our generation'. No poet, perhaps, could claim to possess a more expert understanding or a more exquisite natural sense of words than Valéry – their colour, texture, shape, association and the vast variety of their mutual relationships, musical and intellectual. If it was the voice of a singer rather than an actor that won Valéry's supreme approval, this is much less strange in France than it would be in England. A correct and beautiful pronunciation and enunciation of the French language is an important part of the French singer's art. Much of the greatest French vocal music has been a kind of heightened declamation and the relationship between words and music has been closer in France than in any other European country. Thus Paris ousted Italian and insisted on truly French opera, with a French text, a hundred years before any other country; and the architect of that French opera, Lully, advised his singers to model their singing on the declamation of a famous actress of the day, La Champmeslé.

This strong literary affinity was at the base of Claire Croiza's art as a singer, and her mastery of the spoken word was the foundation of that understanding and mastery of *verbal* beauty on which Croiza's whole art as a singer was built.

It is therefore doubly surprising to find that neither of her parents was French. Her father was an Irishman and her mother an Italian, and her real name was Conelly. She was born in 1882, studied with Revello and had a few lessons with Jean de Reszke; and her first engagement was at the Nancy Opera House in 1905. She made her first appearance in Paris the following year, when she sang the Angel in *Gerontius* – somehow an improbable part but one which made her immediately remarked upon. Her first great successes came to her between 1908 and 1912, when she was at the Brussels opera. Her mezzo-soprano voice belongs to a category which has not been very generously treated by composers of opera. However, in those Brussels years she sang the part of Dido in Berlioz's *Troyens*, the title roles in Massenet's *Thérèse* and *Ariane* and Charlotte in *Werther*, Saint-Saëns's *Delilah* and Bréville's *Eros Vainqueur*. Most important of all, in 1909 she sang Gluck for the first time – *Orfeo* and the part of Clytaemnestra in *Iphigénie en Aulide*. After the War her appearances in opera became increasingly rare. Instead she devoted herself increasingly to concert-singing and particularly to the performance of French songs.

That she was now at the height of her powers, is shown by Valéry's praise. It was during these years, too, that she first consciously developed the literary side of her art, arranging with Jacques Copeau a series of concerts under the title 'Poésie et Musique'. In these programmes Croiza recited and sang a group of poems chosen either from a period or from the works of a single poet – the Romantics, for instance, or Verlaine. She had long been an admired friend of the older generation of French composers, including Fauré, d'Indy, Saint-Saëns and Debussy. Now she made personal friends among the musicians of a later generation, Caplet and Honegger, or those whose names were then less well known to the public – Florent Schmitt, Déodat de Séverac, Albert Roussel and Pierre de Bréville. Her championship of these composers' songs, along with the already 'classical' songs of Fauré, Duparc, Debussy, Chausson and Ravel, did more than any other form of publicity to make them widely known.

Croiza's voice was the perfect instrument for the interpretation of French song. The mezzo-soprano has neither the brilliance of the soprano nor the often dangerous richness of the contralto. It is the viola among voices, impressing by its distinctive colouring and by art rather than by nature. Croiza's tone was firm but never rich. There is a certain spareness which enhances the beauty of her vocal line, a sobriety of colouring and an instinctive avoidance of dynamic extremes, all of which are characteristically French and allow the listener to become aware of her perfect enunciation and the subtlety with which she characterises each phrase.

There was nothing that Croiza disliked more than false pathos. She was fond of Debussy's description of French music as 'quelque chose comme la fantaisie dans la sensibilité', but deplored the fact that she found among her pupils so much sensibility and so little fantasy. Gaiety, wit, fantasy, irony were the characteristics of her art as of her conversation, and she deplored the rather mawkish melancholy particularly common, and perhaps secretly cultivated, among her women pupils. 'If there is a moment, even a second, in a song when the sense allows you to smile, smile for heaven's sake', she once said. She had excellent advice for those who were studying a song such as Duparc's 'Chanson Triste' which can easily be sentimentalised. First, complete sincerity – 'the singer must strip to the soul, as the artist's model strips to the skin. It's not easy the first time, but it must be done at all costs – give everything and then one's interpretation gains life and one's tone emotional depth.' Secondly, physical vitality, which will ensure the singer against sagging rhythms and flabbily emotional phrasing. 'Vous avez une belle voix, madame', she said to a surprised pupil who had sung 'Chanson Triste', 'chaleurisez-la par votre chaleur animale, par votre force animale.'

The first secret of interpretation according to Croiza was self-forgetfulness. This, as she knew, is an art in itself and one which needs long practice to achieve. 'Your expression', she would say, 'will only be good if you do not try to be "expressive". Never give anything more importance than it has by right, or you will ruin everything' – this speaking of Poulenc's 'Bestiaire', her own singing of which is a perfect example of her verbal as well as her vocal skill. 'In singing,' she added, 'one may prefer either the sound or the word. No sound however beautiful will ever give me personally the joy that I get from a beautifully enunciated vowel.'

She was a fully formed artist and no longer a young woman when she started singing the music of Milhaud, Honegger, Schmitt and Roussel, and she found some of it hard on her voice and almost impossible to carry off with the poise that she considered essential to all singing. 'It's as though someone said to you: "Throw yourself from a fourth floor window and mind you fall gracefully",' she observed of one of Schmitt's works.

Although Croiza did not generally discuss songs in technical detail, she was a fanatical observer of the composer's intentions, a stickler for the exact observance of note-values and rests and above all of a strict and steady rhythm. After her performance in Fauré's *Pénélope* the composer is said to have remarked: 'How nice for once to hear my music as I wrote it.' If you follow her recording of Debussy's 'Il pleure dans mon cœur' from the *Ariettes oubliées*, for example, you will find that she takes no liberties whatever. And yet her performance seems to be perfectly spontaneous. Croiza knew her songs so intimately and so accurately that a textually flawless performance came to her naturally.

During the last twenty-five years of her life Croiza did an enormous amount of teaching, but at heart she remained a woman of the theatre. She felt very strongly about operatic production and once said that, if she had the money, she would like to tour the world producing four operas – *Carmen*, *Louise*, *Pelléas* and *Pénélope*. Even in the concert-hall she insisted on the importance of stance, *tenue* (she herself always sang in a hat) and above all of facial expression. Too many gestures and movements she considered a mistake, but the face could and should aid and increase the expression of the voice.

She had the instinctive French fineness of perception, distinguishing nicely between categories. Of the Villon-Debussy 'Ballade' for instance, she insisted that it was a prayer, not a poem; and that no prayer must ever sound sad. 'A sad prayer, I think, must bore le Bon Dieu' – and her own recording – one of the last she made – is characterised by a delightfully matter-of-fact tone of voice, which yet contrives to increase the impression of sincerity and urgency.

Claire Croiza died in May 1946 of a cerebral tumour. She had continued her teaching in Paris during the War and, with few foreign pupils and no foreign tours, her life was a hard one. There is no truth in the story at one time current that she in any way 'collaborated' with the occupying Germans. When she was suspended from teaching at the Conservatoire during the first hysterical days of witch-hunting after the liberation of Paris, a group of writers and musicians signed a document asserting her innocence and recalling her lifelong work for French music at home and abroad. The signatures included those of Valéry, Marcel, Lacretelle, Désormière, Auric, Bréville, Poulenc, Honegger and Munch. Her name was cleared, but nothing could replace the loss caused by her death which followed soon after. The extraordinary haunting quality of her voice, the somehow fragile and essentially feminine nobility of her musical nature, the aristocratic reserve allied with a deeply human pathos and simplicity, the gleaming wit and the dash of irony – these made up a unique artistic character.

Part IV

Poets and Poetry

1 Music in the German *Novelle*

'Once my father took us to a feast . . . and bade me enjoy the delicious dishes; but I could not, whereupon my father became angry and banished me from his sight. . . . My heart full of infinite love for those who disdained it, I wandered into far-off regions and for long years I felt torn between the greatest grief and the greatest love. . . . And so the news of my mother's death reached me and I hastened home. . . . We followed her body in sorrow and the coffin sank into the ground. From that time on I again remained at home. Then my father took me again to his favourite garden and he asked me whether I liked it, but the garden wholly repelled me, and I dared not say so. Reddening, he asked me again, – did the garden please me? I said "no", trembling, and my father struck me and I fled, turning away a second time and wandering far, with a heart filled with endless love for those who scorned me. For many a year I sang songs, but whenever I tried to sing of love, it turned to pain, and when I tried to sing of pain, it turned to love. Thus were love and pain divided in me.' This allegorical tale, generally known as 'Schubert's Dream' and dated 1822 may or may not have been written by the composer among whose papers it was found – in either case it reflects very clearly the style and the ideas of Novalis, the poet and mystic who died even younger than Schubert in 1801, leaving behind him an extraordinary wealth of poems, essays, philosophical reflections and two *novellen* – long short stories, one finished and the other fragmentary – in which he foreshadowed many of the ideas and images that were to obsess the German romantic writers. An enthusiastic Christian, Novalis dreamed of *Totalwissenschaft*, or syncretism of beliefs, that should combine the world of mediaeval religious thought with the findings of natural science, the pietism of the Moravian or Herrenhüter sect (to which he belonged) with the erotic idealism and the belief in the primary creative power of art that are central in his vision of the world. In his unfinished *novelle The Disciples at Sais* Novalis interpolates an allegory or fairy story – a kind of Platonic myth, in fact – whose hero is Orpheus, a seer who could penetrate the secret unity behind the multiplicity of phenomena:

He looked for analogies in all things, conjunctures, correspondences, till he could no longer see anything in isolation. All the perceptions of his senses crowd into great variegated images: he heard, saw, touched and thought at the same moment ... Now men were stars to him, now stars men, stones were animals, clouds were plants; he played with powers and phenomena, he knew exactly where and how to find this shape and the other, to make them appear; and thus he himself drew sounds and melodies from the strings.

Although Novalis speaks little of music as an individual art, his writings are full of musical metaphors. His great Night Hymns find an echo in the love-duet of *Tristan* and his theory of correspondences between the senses prompted not only Wagner's ideal of the *Gesamtkunstwerk*, but many passages in writers as far apart as E. T. A. Hoffmann and Baudelaire, through whom he was to influence first the Symbolists and, at a greater remove, the Surrealists.

The *Märchen*, or fairy-story allegory, was regarded by Novalis as the highest of literary forms because it was nearest to the dream – the state in which human imagination has freest play and can most easily transcend the limitations of the intellect. Little wonder, then, that music – the least earth-bound and most mysterious of the arts – recurs again and again in the stories, the verbal imagery and the mythology of the German poets and prose-writers of the next generation. Goethe had already created a precedent for the insertion of lyrical poems or songs in a prose narrative; and the

figures of Mignon and the Harfenspieler in *Wilhelm Meister* represent the classical ideal of music as a heightened, purified, transfigured means of expression – the fine flower, as it were, on the
plant of prose, something different not in kind but in function.
With the romantic writers music is something entirely different –
a form of magic, an intoxication of the senses, a secret language of
the emotions, and a symbol of imaginative freedom and power.
In Brentano's fairy-stories the songs which frequently interrupt
the prose-narrative are spells often rooted in folk-lore and couched
in a kind of hypnotic, semi-nonsense language half way between
nursery-rhyme and *Alice in Wonderland* (the 'dream-novelle' in
its purest form):

> 'Schnarch', Karrasper, scharche!
> Schnarassel schnarcht im Sarge'

In Heine's *Florentinische Nächte* we find this sense of music as a
magic power diffused throughout. The stories are told to a girl
dying of consumption. She lies on the borderland between sleep
and waking and Heine's brisk Voltairean prose moves, as it were,
in and out of her dreams. Woven among his factual, journalistic
anecdotes of Bellini and Paganini, Heine conjures up the figure of
the devil prompting and guiding Paganini's performance in a kind
of 'automatic writing' and the unnamed painter for whom 'musical
sounds themselves are an invisible sign-language (*Signatur*) in
which colours and shapes can be heard'. In the second story the
dog, the dwarf, the drummer and the dancer performing on an
embankment of the Thames conjure up a vision that Stravinsky was
to embody in *Petrushka*, and the description of the dancer's mime
as 'getanzte Privatgeschichte' looks forward to the aesthetics of
Expressionism:

> It was a dance that did not attempt to amuse the onlooker by
> exterior movements, steps or gestures. These seemed rather to
> be the words of a special language which tried to make a specific
> communication . . . while the trivial accompaniment of drum
> and triangle seemed deliberately to mislead me and set me on a
> false trail.

In fact music to the German romantic writers was before all

else a mystery, its power immediate in effect as that of a natural phenomenon. This is nowhere more strikingly expressed than in Kleist's *Legend of Saint Cecilia*, which has as its subtitle *The Power of Music*. The scene is laid in the Netherlands during the Reformation period. Three brothers collect a band of reforming zealots and go to a convent chapel on the feast of Corpus Christi with the intention of creating an uproar during the celebration of Mass and wrecking the church. The nuns hear of their plan but fail to forestall them. The organist nun is at death's door but surprises them by appearing at the last moment and directing the music – described as 'an old masterpiece of the Italian school' – which has such an immediate and overwhelming effect on the brothers that they are not only converted on the spot but spend the rest of their lives in the madhouse, praying and singing. Was the sick nun replaced by St Cecilia the patron saint of music? Kleist never says so in so many words, and his description of the office is confused; but the miraculous nature of the whole incident becomes increasingly clear when it is revealed that the organist nun never left her bed on the morning in question and died the same evening.

Magic, mystery, miracle – it is the same even for those writers who – unlike Novalis, Brentano, Heine and Kleist – had some technical knowledge of music, like E. T. A. Hoffmann, or personal knowledge of a great composer, as Grillparzer had of Beethoven. For all of them the intellectual element in music, and even more the mastery of a musical craft, is not simply indifferent but something hostile to the essential nature of the art. For Hoffmann and for Grillparzer the true musician is a simpleton, an innocent, a kind of 'holy idiot', like Dostoievsky's Myshkin or Alyosha Karamazov – selfless, chaste, humble, unworldly, hopelessly clumsy and unpractical not only in everyday affairs but even in the practice of his art.

Der arme Spielmann (1848) is Grillparzer's tale of a rich man's son whose love of music has brought him to pauperdom. He hated the violin when he was made to learn as a boy, but turned to it for consolation when rejected by his family and unhappy, through no fault but innocence, in love. In the streets he plays the simplest popular airs and collects a bare livelihood, but his evenings are given over to 'fantasieren' – improvising – which

is his dearest delight. The narrator visits him in his attic and
finds to his astonishment that this 'improvising' is the most
pathetic, primitive and clumsy form of music-making – the passionate savouring of a single note and the simplest intervals – third,
fourth, fifth and sixth. In his playing the Spielmann is concerned
only with the purest consonance:

> . . . instead of emphasising the sense and rhythm of a piece he
> would dwell on the notes and intervals that delighted his ears,
> even repeating them with a kind of ecstasy.

and his description of the chord of the diminished seventh suggests
a kind of aural addiction, an intoxication with the musical sound
in itself, quite divorced from melody, harmony and rhythm:

> the neverfailing bounty and grace of a single note, the musical
> sound in itself: miraculous satisfying of the thirsting, languish-
> ing ear.

For the sound-addict words are a profanation of music and there
is no question of rhythm, harmony or even the simplest melodic
shapes.

Where did Grillparzer find the model for such a figure? Some
of the Spielmann's experiences are drawn from the writer's own
experience. But is it possible that a friend of Beethoven's (and one
whom the composer wanted as a collaborator) possessed so primitive a musical organism as this? No, it seems much more probable
that Grillparzer was here embodying a common romantic conception of the musician or was, consciously or no, influenced by
another fictional musical character – the 'Johannes Kreisler' of
E. T. A. Hoffmann. Kreisler the bohemian Kapellmeister, introverted and psychologically unstable, the mockery of his musical
friends, first appears in Hoffmann's novel *Kater Murr*, where his
adventures at a small German court are 'doubled' and interwoven
with the autobiography of a professor's cat which has learned to
read and write. The *Kreisleriana*, which prompted a set of piano
pieces from Schumann who recognised a kindred spirit in Hoffmann's imaginary musician, are supposed jottings from his diary
and personal papers. In them Kreisler makes a mystery of his birth
and describes himself as 'a new kind of being', one in whose consti-

tution 'too little of the phlegmatic element has been included'. He burns whatever he composes and his chief delight is improvisation. But, like Grillparzer's street-musician, he has absolutely no natural technical facility and his lack of this, coupled with his hatred of virtuosos and their music, earns him the name of *Musikfeind*, music-hater. Only his aunt understands him and his obsession with the beauty of pure isolated musical sounds. 'She spoke of feeling, while my father spoke of understanding music.' There is an account in the *Kreisleriana* of the meeting of a 'musical-poetical club', at which Kreisler improvises on a piano whose upper strings are broken. To a very simple progression of low-lying chords –

A flat major, A flat minor, E major, A minor,
F major, B flat major, E flat major, C minor,
C major –

with detailed dynamic gradations he declaims what one of the impatient club-members very justly describes as 'mad nonsense' – *tolle Schnickschnack* – and yet Hoffmann himself does not merely sympathise, he identifies himself with Kreisler. Although he was an ardent admirer of Beethoven's music during the composer's lifetime, the characters in his stories, like Grillparzer's street-musician, are chiefly interested in old music. One of them, the Baron von B, claims to be the only surviving representative of the old seventeenth-century Italian school of violin-playing. He speaks with enormous authority, dismissing all contemporary violinists except those who have studied with him. Finally, he offers the narrator of the story a lesson, tells him many interesting and useful hints about violin-playing and at length offers to demonstrate the production of the perfect violin-tone. The result is absolutely pathetic – 'like an old woman humming a song with a quavering voice' – but the Baron himself is entranced, in ecstasy. As his pupil leaves, he finds that he has been paid for coming; and yet once again Hoffmann insists that the Baron, far from being a charlatan, is more deeply a musician than the virtuoso 'with his leaps, trills, fast passages and decoration'.

This hatred of the virtuoso was of course an exaggerated reaction against the taste of the day which was all for 'brilliant execution' – the kind of thing which we today know at its very best in the emptiest keyboard music of Weber and Mendelssohn and the florid arias of Rossini. Even so, it is difficult to understand why any intelligent writer, however ignorant of the technique of music (and Hoffmann was by no means that) should identify the musical character with a kind of idiocy in all matters of the understanding and performance of music. It is almost as though the romantic writers regarded music not only as a secret language of the emotions, which it was profanation to speak with fluency and grace, but even as a kind of hieratic code of which the very syllables, the single notes, were sacred and should be enough for the devout worshipper. When the discontented club-member complained after Kreisler's improvisation that he would rather have heard 'a nice Allegro of Haydn's', the reader is plainly meant to shiver at such uncomprehending Philistinism, and Kreisler himself emphasises the abstract nature of music in unambiguously religious terms. 'Our kingdom is not of this world', he says, 'for where do we find in nature any prototype of our art, as the painter and the sculptor find for theirs', and he goes on to elaborate his favourite theory of 'correspondences' in the vein of Novalis.

It is no mere metaphor or allegory when the musician says that colours, scents and beams of light appear to him as sounds, and that he experiences their mingling as a miraculous concert ... the sudden promptings in a musician's mind, the birth of melodies, are the unconscious – or rather the verbally inexpressible – recognition and grasping of the secret music of Nature as the principle of all life and activity.

We are not very far here from the Platonic conception of an abstract 'music beyond music', that harmony of the spheres in which idealists have believed, from Saint Augustine to Bruno Walter in our own day, while a belated follower of Novalis, in his belief in the magical powers of music, might be found in Scriabin.

Those who are impatient with such metaphysical fancies might compare two of the most famous Mozart-stories of the German romantic era – Hoffmann's *Don Juan* and Mörike's *Mozart auf der Reise nach Prag* – and ask themselves which is the more revealing, in fact the truer of the two. Mörike's painstakingly and, it must be said, charmingly recreates the exteriors of the scene – the language,

the clothes, the social attitudes, even the composer's personal
mannerisms as he travels by coach from Vienna to Prague for the
performance of *Don Giovanni*. This is a skilful genre-piece, in
which factual accuracy is combined with historical imagination.
Hoffmann's story, on the other hand, is a penetrating, however
fantasmagorical account of a deep musical experience. The traveller
who finds himself attending the performance of *Don Giovanni* by
an Italian company in a small German town and receives a mysterious visit from the Donna Anna, is no ordinary music-lover.
Even if we divest the story of its literary form and its uncanny
atmosphere of mystery, the musical and psychological penetration
of Hoffmann's comments were unique in his own day and have
hardly been bettered since. No one has ever analysed more con-
vincingly the true character of Don Juan or the true tragedy of
Donna Anna. Such pages as these and Grillparzer's go a long way
to reconciling even the most hard-headed music-lover to these
mostly half-forgotten enthusiasts of another age and another
mental world.

2 E. T. A. Hoffmann

'The higher life of the spirit', exclaimed the Princess Hedwiga, 'is rooted in a dichotomy, in the tension between the most diverse emotions and the most incompatible sentiments!' She was speaking not only for herself but for her creator, giving expression to a deep-seated conviction which was Hoffmann's most personal contribution to the romantic canon. Duplicity and mystification, ambiguities and magical anatomies, animated puppets and philosophising animals – Hoffmann's concern was always with the shadows cast by human existence upon the screen of his imagination rather than with human existence itself. He is the poet of the *Doppelgänger*, who was haunted in his own life by a malicious double and wasted much of his energy in a vain attempt to harmonise his real with his imaginary existence. Most bitter of all was his search for a means of self-expression, the struggle to 'double' his life as a civil servant with the life of a practising musician, conductor and composer; and, when that struggle was eventually successful, the disillusion with his own musical powers which eventually led him quite late in life to writing.

He was the child of a marriage which came to grief two years after his birth and he was brought up by an uncle whose total lack of imagination only exaggerated the bohemian tendencies which he inherited from his father, a Koenigsberg lawyer. Many years later he put into the mouth of Johannes Kreisler, the most autobiographical of all the characters that he created, a fantastic story

whose classical Freudian imagery reveals something of the atmosphere in which Hoffmann grew up, an atmosphere of inhibition
from which he eascaped by constructing a dreamworld of his own.
'As a boy', says Kreisler, 'I was not allowed without my father's
permission into the wood, but the tree and the stone – a murdered
girl was buried beneath this stone – attracted me irresistibly. Whenever the little gate in the garden-wall was left open, I used to slip
out to my beloved stone and I never tired of gazing at the strange
patterns of mosses and plants which covered it. I often imagined
that I understood the meaning of these patterns, as though they
illustrated the stories told me by my mother; and as I gazed at the
stone, I thought involuntarily of the song my father sang almost
every day. . . .' It's not surprising perhaps that even as a young
man he was afflicted by forebodings of death and haunted by the
idea of a *Doppelgänger*, his imagination shaped by repeated reading
– 'perhaps thirty times', he says – of Rousseau's *Confessions*, the
handbook of romantic self-analysis. In a letter written on his
twentieth birthday he mentions 'Jean Paul', the writer who was to
have most effect not only on his style but on his aesthetic ideals;
for it was Jean Paul who cultivated what Hoffmann was later to
note in his diary as one of his most frequent moods – 'romantic and
capricious to excess, a state of exaltation bordering on madness'.
Madness, too, haunted Hoffmann's imagination, whether asleep
or awake; and he deliberately cultivated just that simultaneous
experiencing of the most diverse emotions which Schumann so
much admired in Jean Paul – a kind of amateur, self-induced
schizophrenia which had such fatal results in Schumann's case.
During his early love-affair with a married woman at Koenigsberg
Hoffmann wrote to his friend Hippel, 'every emotion that I feel
for Cora is immediately muted by some comical joke and my heart-
strings are so damped that the sounds they give are inaudible'.
Hoffmann's metaphors are already musical, but his career at first
was almost ludicrously prosaic. After leaving Koenigsberg in 1796,
he spent two years in the depth of provincial Silesia and a further
two in Berlin, before finally qualifying for the Prussian Civil Service. In 1800 he left for seven years state-service in Prussian Poland
– two years at Poznan, two at Plock and three in Warsaw. Already
in Warsaw composing and painting took up more of his time than

administration, and after a second short stay in Berlin he obtained his first musical appointment – that of 'theatre conductor' in Bamberg. The diary which he kept during his Bamberg years, between 1808 and 1813, is starred with butterflies, wine-glasses, which bear wings on occasions of special 'exaltation', private abbreviations and odd Polish and Italian phrases – all a system of (remarkably transparent) mystification enjoyed for its own sake but consciously employed to conceal from his wife the nocturnal exploits, both bacchic and erotic, in which he tried to forget the day's disappointments. For he was hysterically in love with a sixteen-year-old pupil, Julia Marc, and he was disappointed in his musical work, bringing himself slowly and painfully to face his own lack of originality as a composer.

None of the dichotomies in Hoffmann's life was more striking than that between his creative work as a musician and writer. He was a passionate (*schwärmerisch* is the appropriate word) student and admirer of the musical past – of the Italian seventeenth-century masters, of Gluck, Haydn and above all Mozart – and one of the earliest and most vocal admirers of the 'new music' of Beethoven. But this very admiration was his most serious handicap when he started to compose. The fantasy, the poetry and the wit, which were to make his name as a writer, never find expression in his music, which is in fact no more than a close and often clumsy imitation of his models. Even *Undine*, his single operatic success and praised by Weber, contains hardly a spark of that romantic imagination which had delighted the public in Fouqué's fairy tale, but was not to find musical expression until Weber produced his *Freischütz* five years later.

Nevertheless it was through music that Hoffmann came to writing. In 1809 his *Ritter Gluck* was accepted by Rochlitz for the Leipzig *Musikalische Zeitung*; and with this and his fantastic *Don Juan* story, Hoffmann satisfied both his impulse of ardent veneration for Gluck and Mozart and his need to express himself in writing. During his last years at Bamberg he wrote 'Fantastic pieces in the manner of Jacques Callot' and 'News of the latest adventures of the dog Berganza', a continuation of Cervantes' story.

Only when he visited Dresden and Leipzig in 1813 did Hoffmann's imagination suddenly blossom in unmistakably personal form. Here he found himself the involuntary spectator of a bitterly fought war, daily faced with the reality of 'those hacked and mutilated corpses that have always haunted my dreams'. It was in this atmosphere of violence and uncertainty that he wrote the most fantastic of all his tales, *The Golden Pot*; and finally in Berlin, where he was to spend the last eight years of his life, the spirit which, like some bottled homunculus, had been seeking in vain for escape in his music, finally burst loose and spread itself in a galaxy of tales, novels, night-pieces and fairy-stories. By the time his opera *Undine* was performed, he had already transferred his primary allegiance from music to literature, and it was among writers that he made his closest friends – Fouqué, his librettist, and Chamisso, by whose *Peter Schlemihl* – the story of the man who sold his own shadow – he had been so impressed.

   The Deed of Entail and *The Sandman*, translated during the 1820's, formed the text of a sermon on the evil of introducing the supernatural into fiction. Altogether Hoffmann's success in England was never great. The reason may have been that to a nation that with *The Castle of Otranto* had virtually invented the medium, Hoffmann offered nothing new. In France, however, according to Gautier, he was more popular than in Germany. That popularity was eventually, of course, to determine Offenbach's choice of Hoffmann's tales as the subject for his one serious opera; but it was also to colour the imagination of many of the French romantic artists. Hugo's Quasimodo, for instance, is a Hoffmannesque figure and, consciously or not, Berlioz's *idée fixe* and indeed the whole programme of the *Symphonie Fantastique* are pure Hoffmann. For composers who found nothing to learn from Hoffmann's music have almost up to the present day divined an element in his literary imagination that demands musical fulfilment. Perhaps it is that Hoffmann was the first, not to feel but to preach in words, music as the art *par excellence* of the 'misfit', of the morbidly emotional man or woman, the neurotic haunted by forebodings of 'death' and 'mutilated corpses', of those who share the feeling which he confided to his diary for 1811: 'Destruction is hanging over my head and I can do nothing to avoid it.' His own Kreisler and the Princess Hedwiga of *Kater Murr* are characteristic nineteenth-century musical types, introverted and psychologically unstable, who find it difficult or impossible to come to terms with everyday life and seek in music for an escape-world such as no other art offers. Later in the century such people became ardent Wagnerians, and many German courts could boast of a Kreisler and a Princess Hedwiga, their passions of resentment and frustration satisfied vicariously in *The Ring*, their longings for an impossible love immortalised in *Tristan* and their religious emotions exaggerated in *Parsifal*.

The first and most ardent Hoffmann-admirer among composers was Schumann, who found in Johannes Kreisler something that he recognised as a soul-portrait of himself, involved in mystery and contradictions, Byronic cynicism alternating with a tremulous emotional idealism *à la Jean Paul*. A whole world away from Schumann but bearing eloquent witness to the hold obtained by Hoffmann's peculiarly Germanic, even Gothic fantasy in neighbouring France and Russia, Delibes and Tchaikovsky based their ballets of *Coppelia* and *Nutcracker* on his stories. And in our own day Busoni and Hindemith have turned to the same source for their opera-books of *Die Brautwahl* and *Cardillac*. At a further remove Ravel's *Gaspard de la Nuit* – suggested by the writings of a French follower of Hoffmann, Aloysius Bertrand – can be claimed as belonging to the canon; and certainly *Scarbo* is a wholly Hoffmanesque vision.

By investing the horror-stories of Monk Lewis and Mrs Radcliffe with a wealth of Gothic ornament and fantasy, by deepening and enriching their psychological interest and hinting at philosophical, even metaphysical, implications Hoffmann added a new province to the imagination. It was a province soon to be claimed from across the Atlantic by Edgar Allan Poe, who exploited much of the wealth which had remained unrealised in Hoffmann's lifetime and was succeeded in his fortune by his French discoverer, Baudelaire. The indebtedness of Poe's *Tales of Mystery and Imagination* to Hoffmann is a common-place; but Poe learned more from Hoffmann than is to be found in his tales; and much of what Baudelaire actually learned at secondhand from Poe he might well have found at first hand in Hoffmann. Listen, for example, to Kreisler expounding what was to become Baudelaire's famous theory of the 'correspondences' between the arts:

It is no mere image or allegory when the musician says that colours, scents and light-rays appear to him as musical sounds, that their blending is to him a magnificent concert. An ingenious scientist has explained that hearing is a form of internal sight; and in the same way sight is to the musician a form of internal hearing, a means to the deepest consciousness of the music that streams from every object that presents itself to his eyes, and vibrates to the same rhythms as those of his spirit.

Or in a simpler, more concrete form:

The scent of dark-red carnations affects me with an extraordinary magical power. I sink involuntarily into a dream-like state and hear in the distance the deep, swelling and fading tones of the basset-horn.

This deliberate confusion of sense impressions is but one more example of Hoffmann's instinctive desire to 'double' every experience, to conceive of existence as on two simultaneous planes of which that which is conventionally considered the less real, the shadow- or imagination-plane, is the more intensely experienced. In what is probably his best long work – *Lebensansichten des Kater Murr* – Hoffmann carries this principle to its furthest extent and doubles the story of Kapellmeister Kreisler's adventures at a small German court with the autobiography of a professor's cat which learns to read and write and thus adds the splendours and miseries of authorship to the normal pleasures and pains of feline existence. This is the art of the gargoyle and the grinning Miserere-seat, which form in a Gothic cathedral the complement to the statues of heroic saints, crucified Christ or Virgin Mother. And, just as in the cathedral we sometimes turn with relief to the human-all-too-human revelations of the Miserere, there must be many readers of *Kater Murr* who tire of the noble and slightly fatuous Prince Irenaeus and his *exaltée* daughter, of the amiable Coppelius-like figure of Master Abraham and even of Kreisler himself, and turn with delight to the adventures of Murr, his friend Muzius and the poodle Ponto.

It would hardly be an exaggeration to say that all the specifically Hoffmannesque effects have been commercialised. The split personality is a commonplace of the cinema, Kater Murr has suffered the final disgrace of being reduced to Micky Mouse. Olympia and Master Abraham's invisible woman have been adopted by the new science of cybernetics, and the whole shadow-side of life – crime and its detection, insanity, abnormalities of body or spirit – is either treated dispassionately and clinically or exploited by writers for whom a mystery means a murder and imagination consists in the invention of some petty detail of circumstance instead of the elaboration of a new mode of feeling, as it meant for Hoffmann. Hoffmann's reputation is nevertheless ensured, a small reputation perhaps but as unique as the life with which his works are inextricably interwoven.

3 Joseph von Eichendorff

The general ignorance of German romanticism in this country is easily explained by the language-barrier, for lyric poetry is untranslatable. Its essence evaporates on being transferred, as it were, from one bottle to another, and it was as creators of a new lyric poetry that the German romantic writers excelled. Their only other distinctive literary genre, the *Märchen* or fairy-story, depends so much on the language for its artificial naïveté, its praeternatural, dream-like quality and many atmospheric effects that, though formally prose, it hardly survives translation any better.

The only medium in which the German romantic world has in fact become known to the non-German speaking world is that of music; and it would hardly be an exaggeration to say that the German *Lied* is as much a creation of the romantic poets as of the composers. Goethe was still wholly a man of the eighteenth century in his attitude to music. He regarded a song as a lyrical declamation with discreet musical accompaniment; and although there are scenes in the second part of *Faust* which can truly be called operatic, there is no instance in his poetry of the characteristically 'musicable' atmosphere of the true romantics – naïveté, mystery, nostalgia clothed in neo-mediaeval imagery or in symbols drawn from the mystical or metaphysical writers. Even a member of the older generation of romantics like Novalis remains rooted, as a poet, in the purely eighteenth-century world of Young's 'Night Thoughts' and intensely subjective, pietistic religion. But Novalis died before the appearance of the richest of all source-books of German romantic writing – the three volumes of German folk-poems and ballads published by Arnim and Brentano with the title of *Des Knaben Wunderhorn*, between 1805 and 1808. That the originals were in many cases faked or drastically 'restored' mattered not at all as far as their influence on poets went – and without this collection the poetry of Eichendorff and Mörike and much even of Heine is unthinkable.

There is very little mediaeval, 'folkish', *Wunderhorn* romanticism in the songs of Schubert, who chose his poems from minor and already old-fashioned Viennese poets, from the eighteenth century or the first generation of romantics. Of his six Heine settings, for instance, only *Der Doppelgänger* belongs unequivocally to the psychologically ambiguous night-world of romanticism. It is not until Schumann's songs of 1840, including most of his settings of Heine and Eichendorff, that we see the full impact of *Wunderhorn* romanticism on the song. From then onward, through Wolf and Mahler and in more obscure quarters almost up to the present day, this vein has persisted as one of the strongest in German song-writing.

Heine used folk-song forms and mediaeval imagery for his own purpose. They were a mask consciously adopted and sometimes derided, even parodied. But for Eichendorff this was the real world of poetry, in which he moved naturally, without self-consciousness or any hint of Heine's cynical *double entendre*.

His range as a poet may be comparatively small but his sincerity is absolute. Nature for him is friendly and harmonious, even in its mysteriousness. His Christian piety is not a neo-mediaeval stage-property, as it was for Sir Walter Scott and the editors of the *Wunderhorn*, for whom Catholicism was picturesque and 'old world'. Even the aristocratic ideal of the mediaeval knight was more of a reality to this son of a Silesian baronial family than to the urban and middle-class poets who exploited its historical charm.

Eichendorff's life followed the expected pattern of his age and class. He was born in 1788, attended the university first in Halle and then in Heidelberg, where he was on the edge of the Arnim-Brentano circle. He fought against Napoleon like a good patriot and then, in 1816, received a post in the Prussian Civil Service,

living chiefly in Breslau until his retirement in 1844. His first
Novellen date from 1812, the best known *Aus dem Leben eines Taugenichts* ('The life of a ne'er-do-well') from 1826, and he published
his collected poems in 1837. They were new to the public, in fact,
when Schumann set a dozen of them three years later. His favourite
subjects represent the greatest possible contrast to the life of a
Prussian Civil Servant: nostalgia for a youth spent in the country
and the free, untrammelled 'Bohemian' life that he can only have
known as a student and perhaps as a soldier. His countrysides are
Central European, with the forest as the image of mystery, romance
and danger – the role played by the sea in the poetry of maritime
countries.

> Mir aber gefällt doch nichts so sehr
> Als das deutsche Waldesrauschen

'But I love nothing so dearly as the whispering of a German forest'
Waldesrauschen and *Waldeinsamkeit* – the sound and loneliness of
the deep forest – were genuine experiences for Eichendorff, not
poetic conventions. Sometimes the loneliness is interrupted by a
fanciful mediaeval scene, as in 'Waldesgespräch' – a kind of Belle
Dame sans Merci with the hunting-horns sounding in the distance
and brought to life in Schumann's setting. Or 'knights in glittering
armour' appear as a vision which suddenly fades, leaving an overwhelming sense of terror as night falls – the true romantic *Schauer*
suggested in Schumann's setting of 'Im Walde'.

Night – the antithesis of the 'every day' – recurs again and again
in the poetry of Eichendorff, as in that of the other German romantics. 'The far distances of memory, the longings of youth, the
dreams of childhood, all the short joys and frustrated hopes of a
lifetime, crowd around us after sunset, in grey garments like the
evening mist', wrote Novalis. 'Must the day always dawn again?
Will the power of earthly things never end?' Mystery, secrecy,
spiritual renewal, the return to childhood innocence, the religion
of erotic consummation half veiled in metaphysical, archaeological
or even botanical symbols – we find them all in Eichendorff; and
this nocturnal element in his poetry was seized on avidly by the
composers. It is seen at its fullest and most magnificent in two of
Wolf's songs – 'Verschwiegene Liebe' and 'Nachtzauber'.

In 'Nachtzauber' all Eichendorff's favourite images are combined and each is suggested with wonderful skill by Wolf's music. We hear the murmur of the forest and the streams which run to feed the solitary woodland lakes, with their marble statues. Night descends, bringing the memory of old melodies heard in a dream. In the moonlight a flower stands – or is it a girl? The nightingale, wounded to death by love, sings of happy days long past. 'Come, come to that silent glade.'

There is something of the same spirit, though infinitely less intense and richly variegated, in Schumann's 'Schöne Fremde' with its characteristic couplet:

> Was sprichst du wirr, wie in Träumen,
> Zu mir, phantastische Nacht?

But as a rule Schumann instinctively chooses the more innocent, straightforward night-poems of Eichendorff, as in the amazing miniature of 'Frühlingsnacht'. Here the passionate excitement of the poet is communicated at once by the racing repeated chords in the piano accompaniment – a spring night in a garden, the first flower scents and the birds returning from the south, the poet half in tears, half laughing with incredulous ecstasy as the old miracle renews itself.

In another of Schumann's Eichendorff songs, 'Mondnacht', the beauty of the moonlit night prompts the same kind of religious emotions in the poet that we find in Tennyson's 'St Agnes Eve', with the soul 'spreading her wings to seek her true home in heaven' – once again no mere poetical fancy to the genuinely religious Eichendorff, whose complete sincerity communicates itself to Schumann's music. 'Zwielicht', on the other hand, is an unusually ambiguous, allegorical poem of anxiety. Its four verses are set strophically for the voice, though the piano part varies in complexity from a Bach-like chromatic style to simple accompaniment in the last verse, 'Twilight spreads its wings, the trees shiver; clouds gather like oppressive dreams. What does this uneasy moment mean? Have you a favourite hind? Do not let her graze alone. There are huntsmen in the woods. Have you a friend? Do not trust him at this hour. Those tired today are born again tomorrow. Much may be lost in a single night – take care.'

IM Q

The inhabitants of Eichendorff's poetical world are as remote
from those he met in his life as a Prussian civil servant as the
settings of his nature poems are remote from office life in Breslau,
Danzig or Königsberg. The ne'er-do-well hero of *Aus dem Leben
eines Taugenichts* is a kind of comic Parsifal, a 'pure fool' who
acknowledges no civic responsibilities or domestic ties, leaves
home to amuse himself and see the world, and gets involved in a
succession of picaresque adventures, including a romantic love for
a woman whose identity he mistakes. He is a musician – very much
the wandering, fiddling *Musikant* and not at all the studious *Musi-
cus* – and some of Eichendorff's most delightful lyrics are scattered
throughout the text (once again one thinks of Tennyson, this time
of *The Princess*). 'Der Musikant', for example, which Wolf set, says
– 'I love a wandering life, taking the luck of the road. Even if I
wanted to exert myself, I know that it would never do for me.' If
girls take a fancy to him, he warns them that marriage would kill
his music. This wandering musical tramp is plainly a descendant
of the old Harper in Goethe's *Wilhelm Meister*, but a descendant
who has shuffled himself free of the Harper's mysterious load of
guilt. The wandering scholar is another of Eichendorff's most
touching, instinctive expressions of patriotism – which meant a
love of German scenery, of Northern forest, river and mountain
with a warmth of feeling which no Northerner can help feeling
when he leaves the Latin South behind him and travels home over
the Alps. So bone-German is Eichendorff that the foreigners in his
stories are hardly more than pasteboard figures, like the Italian
painters in the *Taugenichts*, or thinly disguised Germans like the
peasants whom he meets on his Italian wanderings. But he would
not be the typical Romantic that he is, did he not attempt to portray
one of that race who, 150 years ago, had much the same fascination
for artists of every description as negroes have today – I mean the
gypsies. He succeeds with his genre-picture of the gypsy-girl waiting for her lover and shooting a cat to make him a fur cap. 'He must
be dark, with a Hungarian moustache and a gay heart for a wandering life' – Wolf turns the whole scene into a miniature drama in
his most characteristic manner in 'Die Zigeunerin'.

Eichendorff has attracted song-writers almost to the present day
by the musicality of his verse, its simple imagery, sincerity and

strange combination of wisdom and naïveté and frankness. Mendelssohn and Brahms each set a handful of his poems and more recently Pfitzner more than a dozen and a whole cantata. The Swiss composer Othmar Schoeck is alone in having based an opera as well as almost forty songs on Eichendorff texts. Schoeck's opera is based on *Das Schloss Dürande* but no composer has ever made a picaresque opera out of the *Taugenichts*. (This and Schnitzler's story *Casanovas Heimkehr* are surely gifts to the musician.) Pfitzner's cantata *Von deutscher Seele* dates in its original version from 1921 and consists of almost exactly the same cycle of poems as Schoeck set later in his *Wandersprüche* for voice, clarinet, horn, percussion and piano. And these poems, as Pfitzner divined, are part of the very essence of the *deutsche Seele* – the German soul. Their simplicity may often sound affected in translation, their imagery conventional and their sentiments alternately rarefied and naïve. But by his magic use of the German language Eichendorff silences criticism, and the simplicity and sincerity with which he uses what are mere conventions in lesser poets give his works an almost unique place in German literature. Mörike perhaps stands nearest to him, and the two of them played a double role in the later development of the German song, by which they will be remembered far beyond the borders of the German-speaking countries.

4 Eduard Mörike

'True to the kindred points of heaven and home' – it was tempting to transfer Wordsworth's own skylark image to the poet himself. The mid-Victorian public loved it; and it must be admitted that the poet had done everything, short of actively conniving, to propagate this image of his middle-aged and elderly self. The twentieth century has treated the poetic idols of the Victorian age much as it has treated Victorian furniture – which has been stripped of its heavy veneer – and Victorian buildings which it has cut down to their 'true' scale. Behind Tennyson the seer we have discovered the neurotic, doubt-racked nature-poet and Wordsworth's formidable Establishment façade is no longer allowed to conceal the nature-mystic and the man of passion. The process has been surgical and some of the surgeons needlessly ruthless; but the layers of convention concealing the true poet were perhaps thicker here than elsewhere. The very existence of a Swinburne or a Rossetti made it impossible for the nervous, hero-seeking public to admit a shadow-side to their accepted idols; and no lay person would have dared to write, of, say, the ageing Tennyson as Isolde Kurz wrote in the 70's of Mörike:

I felt that this large head of a Swabian country parson with its somewhat flabby features and the deep-chiselled, sullen lines was only a droll or protective mask, from behind which the delicate head of a Greek youth or a smiling Ariel might at any moment emerge.

Eduard Mörike was born in 1804 and sprang on both sides from the late eighteenth-century professional classes – doctors and clergymen – in the kingdom of Württemberg. He spent his whole life as a country parson, moving from one Swabian village to another, but within these narrow physical limitations his existence was both complicated and enriched by a number of as it were instinctively chosen handicaps. Chief among these was a form of nervous ill-health or hypochondria revealed in the morbid sensibility of some few of his poems, oddly corrected by the tone of the huge majority. A Lewis Carroll-like strain of infantilism kept him to the end of his life emotionally dependent on a younger sister and found exquisite expression in his instinctive understanding of children and tender domesticity, as well as in nonsense verses and some revealing drawings. But unlike Lewis Carroll, he combined with this a capacity for genuine, if often highly spiritualised, erotic passion which found an outlet in a series of obsessions or engagements, and finally in a marriage which would perhaps have killed any man who had not the neurotic's often characteristic toughness and durability. For at the age of forty-seven this Lutheran pastor married a Catholic wife and set up house with her and his adored sister – assuring both women in a sublimely innocent and tactless letter that he found it difficult in his heart to 'distinguish one from the other'. Though apparently bound to fail and certainly swept with storms of jealousy that reduced the poet to despair, this three-cornered relationship and the two daughters of the marriage brought Mörike an enormous amount of happiness, and it was all the more tragic that at the very end of their lives – after twenty years of marriage – husband and wife felt forced to separate.

Mörike appeared to many of his contemporaries very much like Wordsworth's skylark – 'true to the kindred points of heaven and home' – for it was the tender simplicity of his poems inherited from folk-models, and those imbued with piety or domestic affection, that delighted the wider public of mid-nineteenth century Germany. In fact, however, Mörike's domesticity was very far from complacent sentimentality, as we have seen, and his religious faith, though free from any speck of emotional insincerity, was more an ingredient in his poetical make-up than a fully mature or reasoned attitude to life. To his friend and neighbour David Strauss – author

of the controversial *Life of Christ* translated by George Eliot –
Mörike spoke of his 'permanent inclination to Christianity'; and to
Luise Rau, during their engagement, of the chasm between his
religious emotions and their public, objective expression:

> The gospel (he wrote) offered all its peace and drew me more
> and more deeply into that solitude of spirit, where the angel of
> our childhood meets us again and weeps with us. But what I felt
> belonged only to me myself or to you – I couldn't find a bridge
> from it to my sermon, and what had *there* been pure gold, *here*
> becomes dull lead, as soon as I put pen to paper.

The real trinity of inspiration that lay behind Mörike's poetry
was a different one. It was not the triune God of Christianity but
rather Nature – Love – and Beauty, the trinity that was acknowledged if not proclaimed by the majority of artists in the nineteenth
century, in different degrees and with different emphases. Both the
simple and flexible language and the clear, strong imagery and
atmosphere of Mörike's poems were bound to attract composers
in search of song-texts, but the reaction was oddly long in coming.
Schumann, the contemporary composer with whom he might seem
to have most in common, in fact chose only four of Mörike's poems,
Brahms and Robert Franz even fewer; and it was not until 1888,
thirteen years after the poet's death, that Mörike found his greatest
musical interpreter. Between February and May of that year Hugo
Wolf wrote forty-three of the total fifty-seven settings that he made
of Mörike's poems and in so doing introduced this Swabian parson
– whose fame was inevitably restricted to German-speaking countries – to a universal public. That contradictoriness that Mörike
shared with Goethe, in addition to his lyrical exuberance and purely
linguistic virtuosity, found a strong counterpart in Wolf himself.
Mörike's poetry belongs to both the 'sentimental' and the 'naïve'
of Schiller's categories and he possessed to an astonishing degree
the poet's characteristic chameleon-like ability to identify himself
with personalities, situations and atmospheres of the greatest
diversity.

Not even Eichendorff was more unaffectedly at home in the folk-
poetry world of the *Knaben Wunderhorn*; and Mörike's natural
sympathy with the small, the simple, the humble and the unsophis-

ticated – that quality that so endeared him to his country parishioners – enabled him to write lyrics which could themselves be mistaken for folk poems. Wolf instinctively chose for such poems a simple repeating metrical pattern, such as that which pervades the whole of 'Heimweh', where the open fifths in the bass and the naïve murmuring of the stream in the piano accompaniment, even the very characteristic repeating sequences, add to the song's unsophisticated air, which is only disturbed by the chromatic harmonies that so clearly suggest the puzzled unhappiness of the wanderer from home.

This folk-song simplicity of form is often used by Mörike as a mask to conceal more complex sentiments. 'In der Frühe', for instance, opens with the poet lying restless and awake after a night of anxious insomnia and only comforted by the bells that begin to sound as day breaks. Wolf's setting follows in every detail the simplicity of the poem's *form* and the gradual change from tension to relaxation. The morning-bells when they rise sequentially, prove to be identical with the piano-figure which has dominated the first half of the song – lying low and harmonised chromatically at first, then rising into uninhibited euphony.

At the opposite extreme to the *Knaben Wunderhorn* element in Mörike's poetry lies the impassioned quasi-philosophical lyricism of the love-poems and letters. At the age of twenty the poet underwent a traumatic experience in his passion for Maria Meyer – a beautiful and certainly hysterical adventuress who won publicity by staging fainting-fits in strategically chosen public places, allowing herself to be 'rescued' and then disappearing after breaking a number of hearts, including Mörike's. He used this episode when he came to write his one novel *Maler Nolten*, where Maria Meyer appears as 'Peregrina' and is made the occasion of five lyrics inserted in the text – five of the most intense, immediate and passionately expressed poems in the German language. 'As regards things of the mind', wrote one of his friends, 'Mörike is like a son of Goethe's by some wild, mysterious marriage' – and the 'Peregrina' poems are the best illustration of this. Wolf set two of them, using for the second the full-blown Wagnerian language of chromatic suspensions and dramatically planned sequences that characterised the stricken, agonised erotic atmosphere of *Tristan*.

In complete reaction to the violent sensuality and disorder that Maria Meyer brought into Mörike's life, Luise Rau (to whom he was engaged for four years) was, he said, 'like an airy embodiment of my most sacred thoughts'. The poems which she inspired are in fact interspersed, and even themselves interlarded, with images and expressions of religious devotion. In 'An die Geliebte' the poet finds his 'boldest, his unique desire' fulfilled in a love which unites the sacred with the profane and sets the very stars singing – a sentiment which Wolf echoes by a return to the world of *Tannhäuser*.

With Mörike's directly devotional poems Wolf was not very happy in either his choice or his handling. Both 'Karwoche' and 'Seufzer' belong too patently to the world of *Parsifal* and suffer from rhythmic stiffness and monotony; 'Wo find ich Trost' verges on the rhetorical and 'Neue Liebe' issues in one of Wolf's most banal cadences, while his setting of the exquisite 'Gebet' has been rudely compared to a harmonium voluntary in a village church. The memento mori contained in 'Denk' es, o Seele' on the other hand, plainly stirred the composer. This exquisite poem occurs in Mörike's supremely successful *novelle* – *Mozart auf der Reise nach Prag* – where it is referred to as a 'Bohemian folk-song'. It has a note of eeriness that Wolf has perfectly caught in the hesitant rhythms and suddenly broken phrases of the accompaniment. 'There is a fir tree growing in the forest, a rose blooming in some garden; remember, my soul, they are fated to take root on your grave. Two black horses feeding in the meadow, cantering gaily home. They will go at a funeral pace when they draw your coffin – perhaps even before they cast their shoes I now see gleaming.'

It was of course the duty of nineteenth-century critics to discover in Mörike, as in all poets whom they admired, a 'Hellenic' strain. But in fact there was very little 'classical' about Mörike except the purity and clarity of the language that he uses to describe or suggest even the most transient and mercurially shifting sensations or states of mind. The 'Beauty' which is the conventional third person in his trinity 'proceeded' from the other two, 'Nature' and 'Love' and he was neither intellectually nor aesthetically drawn to that neo-classicism which remains an undercurrent in European art, sometimes disappearing for a generation or more only to emerge in a new form. There was a touch of the Walter Pater or even Oscar Wilde aesthete in one of his stories – *Die Hand der Jezerte* – but the nearest approach to this in his poems is to be found in those inspired by an antique, 'Auf eine Lampe' – or pictures – 'Auf ein altes Bild' or 'Schlafendes Jesukind'. These begin with a kind of Parnassian objectivity, very soon shot through with subjective, personal feeling. 'Auf eine Christblume' begins with the apostrophe of a flower – the Christmas rose – and by miraculously light and natural transitions displays almost the whole gamut of Mörike's intimate emotional world – his feeling for the uniqueness of the flower, its wintry whiteness as a symbol of purity, its purple spotted heart marked with the signs of Christ's Passion. This, as it were, classical vision is suddenly and most characteristically interrupted by Mörike's picture of the elf – an unredeemed and irredeemably Germanic figure – attracted by the radiance of the flower that shines even in the darkness. He stands gazing a moment and then flits uneasily away. There is none of Wolf's Mörike-settings that follows more faithfully or with greater aptness every slightest image and reference, every infinitesimal change of mood and tempo in the poem. From the hymn-like opening the song proceeds like a well-composed picture in which every detail is organic and images are skilfully correlated. The deer cropping the snowy turf by the churchyard wall, for instance, is given the same basic motif as the elf, the one conjured up by gently repeated even quavers and the other by delicate semiquaver triplets.

If the affinity between Mörike and Wolf is at first sight difficult to understand, the truth is that Mörike is a good deal less simple than he at first appears in many familiar poems and Wolf is a good deal simpler. It is certainly true that those of his Mörike-settings that won most admiration for their complexity – those, that is, in which Wagnerian harmony and Wagnerian psychology, as it were, were most remarkable – are no longer among those which we most admire. It is not 'Seufzer' or 'An den Schlaf' that we remember but 'Der Gärtner', 'Fussreise', or the sublime simplicity of 'Schlafendes Jesukind'.

INDEX

Index